THE RAPE OF THE NILE

THE RAPE
OF THE NILE

TOMB ROBBERS, TOURISTS, AND ARCHAEOLOGISTS IN EGYPT

REVISED AND UPDATED

BRIAN FAGAN

Westview
PRESS

A Member of the Perseus Books Group

Copyright © 2004 by Westview Press, A Member of the Perseus Books Group

First Edition published 1975 by Charles Scribner's Sons; Second Edition published 1992 by Moyer-Bell, Ltd.; Third Edition 2004. Printed in the United States of America by Westview Press, 5500 Central Avenue, Boulder, Colorado 80301-2877, and in the United Kingdom by Westview Press, 12 Hid's Copse Road, Cumnor Hill, Oxford OX2 9JJ.

Find us on the world wide web at www.westviewpress.com

Westview Press books are available at special discounts for bulk purchases in the United States by corporations, institutions, and other organizations. For more information, please contact the Special Markets Department at the Perseus Books Group, 11 Cambridge Center, Cambridge, MA 02142, or call (800) 255-1514 or (617) 252-5298, or e-mail special. markets@perseusbooks.com.

Library of Congress Cataloging-in-Publication Data
Fagan, Brian M.
    The rape of the Nile : tomb robbers, tourists, and archaeologists in Egypt / Brian Fagan.— Rev. ed.
        p.   cm.
    Includes bibliographical references and index.
    ISBN 0-8133-4061-6 (paperback : alk. paper)
    1. Egypt—Antiquities.   2. Egyptology—History.   3. Archaeological thefts—Egypt.
I. Title.
    DT60.F24 2004
    932—dc22

                                                                            2004015150

Text design by Brent Wilcox
Set in 11-point Minion by the Perseus Books Group

The paper used in this publication meets the requirements of the American National Standard for Permanence of Paper for Printed Library Materials Z39.48–1984.

10   9   8   7   6   5   4   3   2   1

But every woman shall borrow of her neighbour,

and of her that sojourneth in her house, jewels of

silver, and jewels of gold, and raiment: and ye shall put them upon your sons,

and upon your daughters; and ye shall spoil the Egyptians.

Exodus 3:22

For the Fox and the Vicar
With love and affection, and because of many good times.

Contents

Preface

The Rape of the Nile has a special place in my heart, for it was the first truly general book on archaeology that I ever wrote. It all began with an article commissioned by *Archaeology Magazine* about the theatrical strongman and tomb robber Giovanni Belzoni, one of the great adventurers of early archaeology along the Nile. Patricia Cristol, then an editor at Charles Scribner's Sons, asked me to write a biography of Belzoni. I pointed out that there was already an excellent study in print, and, almost as an aside, offered a history of Egyptian tomb robbing instead. To my astonishment, she sent me a contract for such a book, which put me on the spot, as I knew nothing whatsoever about the subject. For two years, I found myself in a fascinating and long-forgotten world of heroes and villains, of larger-than-life figures whose antics seemed stranger than fiction. Writing *The Rape* (the title was Scribner's Sons' idea) gave me an abiding fascination with ancient Egypt and the archaeologists who worked along the Nile. The book appeared in 1975 to considerable acclaim, and has been translated into eight languages, as well as appearing in a reprint published by Moyer-Bell in 1992. I was nervous when the book appeared, for I assumed that Egyptologists would disapprove of a history written by an outsider. In the event, I have been flattered by their polite words and civilized tolerance of the errors that inevitably crept into the book. A colleague told me some months ago that the book was a "venerable classic" of Egyptology, which is both flattering and slightly alarming.

No question, however, that the original version and the reprint are entering their dotage. A great deal has happened in Egyptology since 1975— new discoveries, fresh insights, and a generation of important conservation work and basic research, combined with ardent specialization. When I wrote the original edition, the literature on the history of Egyptology was scattered in obscure journals and was relatively inaccessible. The past thirty years have seen a flood of biographies and historical studies, which throw new light on early Egyptology, especially during the nineteenth century. I was delighted when Karl Yambert of Westview Press asked me to prepare an updated edition. He gave me a chance to revisit one of the most fascinating projects I have ever undertaken. In the event, the task was a demanding pleasure that involved extensive rewriting and expansion of the original work.

I was pleased to discover that the basic narrative format worked well and that my original story was, on the whole, reasonably accurate. As a result, I decided to maintain the original structure, keeping Giovanni Belzoni's remarkable career as the central part of the book. The major changes have been in the later chapters, where a new generation of research has produced fresh insights into such important figures as Jean-François Champollion, John Gardner Wilkinson, and Howard Carter. As before, I have made no attempt to be comprehensive, focusing on the high points and the major developments rather than describing every important archaeological discovery. I should also stress that this is a narrative of discovery, not of intellectual trends, which are of less interest to a general audience. I have added comprehensive notes to this edition, which provide a guide to further reading for each chapter, as well as references and occasional details on people and sites to provide richer detail to the narrative.

The Rape comprises three parts. Part I, "Tombs and Treasure," begins with the Greeks and the Romans, with that gossipy traveler Herodotus, who wrote the first outsider's account of ancient Egyptian civilization. I describe the thriving tourist trade in Roman Egypt and the activities of Islamic treasure hunters, as well as a long-lasting international trade in mummies, fueled by a belief that pounded-up ancient corpses were powerful medicine and an effective aphrodisiac. European travelers had sailed as far south as the Second Cataract by the late eighteenth century, and most of the major archaeological sites were known. However, Egypt was still difficult to access until General Napoléon Bonaparte and his savants revealed the glories of the ancient Nile to an astounded world in the first years of the nineteenth century.

Part II, "The Great Belzoni," tells the story of a circus strongman who became an adept tomb robber and nascent archaeologist by accident. His flamboyant career along the Nile has all the ingredients of high adventure: diplomats competing for antiquities, loyal followers and ruffians, fisticuffs and gunfire. The tall Italian found the tomb of the New Kingdom pharaoh Seti I, cleared the entrance to the Abu Simbel temple, was the first modern visitor to enter the pyramid of Khafre at Giza, and removed obelisks, statuary, papyri, and small artifacts by the ton, thanks to his expertise with levers, weights, and "hydraulics" perfected in acts of legerdemain on the stage. Belzoni towers over Egyptology as a larger-than-life figure. His adventures, which ended with his lonely death in Benin, West Africa, are the stuff of which archaeological romance is made. At the same time, Belzoni's discoveries inadvertently helped lay the foundations for the scientific Egyptology of today.

Part III, "Birth of a Science," begins with the decipherment of hieroglyphs by the French linguistic genius Jean-François Champollion, and the arrival of a small group of antiquarians and artists in Egypt who were interested not in looting, but in copying and inscriptions. Notable among them was John Gardner Wilkinson, who lived in an ancient tomb at Thebes and wrote a classic, *Manners and Customs of the Ancient Egyptians*, in 1837. His book could be purchased in railroad bookstores and made the pharaohs accessible to all. We trace the stirrings of an archaeological conscience along the Nile, epitomized by the frenetic activities of Auguste Mariette, Egypt's first director of antiquities. Tourism became big business during Mariette's time. We witness the tourist experience through the eyes of novelist Amelia Edwards, who wrote *A Thousand Miles up the Nile* (1877). The scenes of destruction in temple and tomb so moved her that she devoted the remainder of her life to campaigning for the saving of ancient Egypt. Chapters 15 and 16 carry the story from the beginnings of scientific excavation by Flinders Petrie and others in the 1880s to the climactic discovery of the tomb of the pharaoh Tutankhamun in 1922. This discovery changed the landscape of Egyptology, as Egyptians started to play an increasingly aggressive role in research, conservation, and interpretation of the world's longest-lived civilization.

This, then, is an adventure story replete with interesting characters and bold deeds. The stage is set, the players are in the wings. Let the play begin!

Brian Fagan
Santa Barbara, California

Acknowledgments

Patricia Cristol, then of Charles Scribner's Sons, commissioned this book in 1973 and nursed it to gestation, in the process changing my life forever. The debt I owe her is immense. I am grateful to Karl Yambert of Westview Press for commissioning this revised edition and for arranging for the scanning of the original book, which saved me months of work. Many colleagues, too numerous to mention, answered questions, corrected factual errors, and sorted out knotty details for me, notably Donald Reid, Ronald Richey, and Stuart Smith. Steve Brown drew the map and tables with his customary skill.

Acknowledgments for photographic credit are given in the legends. While every effort has been made to locate copyright holders, queries in this matter should be addressed to the author.

Finally, thanks to Lesley and Ana, also the Great Cat of Re, for tolerating my long hours at the computer.

Author's Note

All measurements are given in meters, with equivalents in miles, yards, feet, and inches, as is now common archaeological convention.

Spellings of ancient Egyptian names follow the most common usages in the literature, but you should be aware that there are numerous variations—for example, Rameses or Ramesses, Giza or Gizeh—but in most cases they are obvious. Modern names follow conventions in the *Times Atlas of the World*.

Egyptologists argue continually about the chronology of the pharaohs and of ancient Egyptian civilization. I have followed the most widely accepted time scale, used in most reference books on ancient Egypt, of which there are now too many to list.

As seems obvious, but it is surprising just how many people become confused, spellings and terms quoted from other people's writings conform to those used by the original writers. This includes English spellings, as in "traveller" instead of the American "traveler."

PART ONE

TOMBS AND TREASURE

What of their places?

Their walls have crumbled,

Their places have gone,

As though they had never been!

A HARPER'S LAMENT, C. 2000 B.C.
Miriam Lichtheim, ed., *Ancient Egyptian Literature: A Book of Readings*

1 | Plundering the Pharaohs

Hail to you, Re, perfect each day

Who rises at dawn without failing . . .

When you cross the sky, all see you. . . .

HYMN TO AMUN-RE, THE SUN GOD.
Miriam Lichtheim, ed., *Ancient Egyptian Literature:
A Book of Readings*

"One can imagine the plotting beforehand, the secret rendezvous on the cliff by night, the bribing or drugging of the cemetery guards, and then the desperate burrowing in the dark, the scramble through a small hole into the burial chamber, the hectic search by a glimmering light for treasure that was portable, and the return home at dawn laden with booty." So wrote the British Egyptologist Howard Carter soon after he had discovered the magnificent tomb of the pharaoh Tutankhamun in 1922. "We can imagine these things," he added, "and at the same time we can realize how inevitable it all was."[1]

Howard Carter was writing about the Valley of the Kings, the desolate and rocky valley to the west of the Nile, across from Amun the sun god's city, Waset, known to the Greeks as Thebes and today as Luxor.[2] The arid canyon served as a royal burial place for the Egyptian rulers for at least four hundred years after the sixteenth century BC. The pharaohs of the Eighteenth to Twentieth Dynasties lay in secret rock-cut tombs with meticulously concealed entrances. Their elaborate mortuary temples stood overlooking the Nile floodplain. The dry climate of Thebes has preserved for

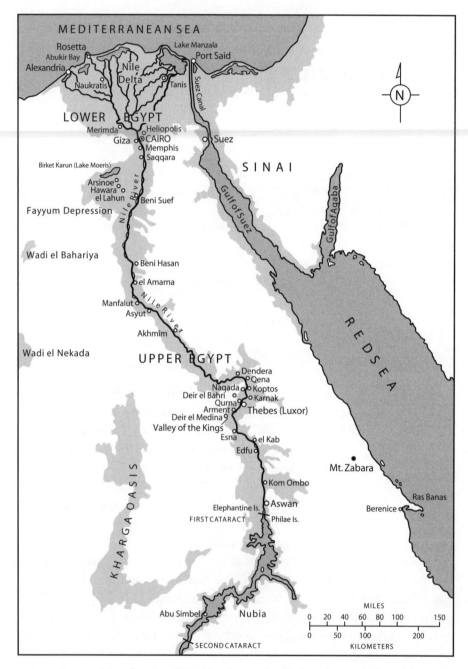

FIGURE 1.1   Map showing the major sites and other locations mentioned in the text. Some minor sites have been omitted for clarity.

us—and generations of tomb robbers—the rich furniture of the royal tombs of the New Kingdom, including inlaid furniture, ceremonial thrones, thousands of funerary statuettes or *shabtis*, magnificent sarcophagi, and fine alabaster vessels. Children's toys, jewelry, regalia of state, even linen shrouds throw a fascinating light on the daily life of the long-dead kings.

The pharaohs lay in distinguished company. Princes and high officials were laid to rest near the Valley of the Kings. Other illustrious personages sought eternity in nearby side valleys and in the adjacent hills. The tombs of the nobles were in the cliffs and hills facing the Theban plain. Their bodies, and those of hundreds of other more privileged Egyptians wealthy or important enough to be buried with the prospect of an afterlife, were buried in rock-cut tombs, caves, or clefts in the rocky hills in brightly painted mummy cases.

An almost hereditary group of necropolis workers labored on royal tombs, living in a special village at Deir el-Medina, close to the desert hills. They were a feisty bunch. There are records of strikes and pay disputes, of absenteeism and family quarrels. Other artisans prepared the tombs of nobles. Their villages are still almost unknown to archaeologists. The royal families, the nobility, and those able to afford it spent lavish sums on their journey to eternity, on the afterlife. By 1070 BC, untold wealth lay below the ground in the Theban necropolis. With so much gold with the dead, looting was inevitable. The rape of the Nile began with the Egyptians themselves.

: :

Tomb robbing was a well-organized pastime in the Theban necropolis in ancient times. Cunning and well-armed grave robbers ransacked the tombs of the pharaohs for their treasures. The thieves often worked in close collaboration with corrupt priests and well-bribed officials. Professional robbers had opened most of the royal tombs in the Valley of the Kings by the end of the Twentieth Dynasty (ca. 1070 BC). Most of the royal treasures vanished forever long before the antiquarians and archaeologists came to Thebes and completed the work of destruction.

The royal burials of the Valley of the Kings remained in comparative peace during the reigns of the great pharaohs of the Eighteenth and Nineteenth Dynasties (1570–1180 BC), kings such as Seti I and Rameses II, who ruled Egypt and a large foreign empire as well. A closely supervised officialdom maintained the royal tombs and prevented much large-scale looting. By

Major subdivisions and developments of ancient Egyptian civilizations		
Years B.C.	Period	Characteristics
30	Roman occupation	Egypt becomes an imperial province of Rome.
332 to 30	Ptolemaic period	The Ptolemies bring Greek influence to Egypt, beginning with the conquest of Egypt by Alexander the Great in 332 B.C.
1070 to 332	Late period	Gradual decline in pharaonic authority, culminating in Persian rule (525 to 404 and 343 to 332 B.C.).
1530 to 1070	New Kingdom	Great imperial period of Egyptian history, with pharaohs buried in the Valley of the Kings; pharaohs include Rameses II, Seti I, and Tutankhamun, as well as Akhenaten, the heretic ruler.
1640 to 1530	Second Intermediate period	Hyksos rulers in the delta.
2040 to 1640	Middle Kingdom	Thebes achieves prominence, also the priesthood of Amun.
2180 to 2040	First Intermediate period	Political chaos and disunity.
2575 to 2180	Old Kingdom	Despotic pharaohs build the pyramids and favor conspicuous funerary monuments; institutions, economic strategies, and artistic traditions of ancient Egypt established.
3100 to 2575	Archaic period	Consolidation of the state (treated as part of the Old Kingdom in this book).
c. 3150	Unification of Egypt under Narmer (Menes)	

FIGURE 1.2   Chronological table of ancient Egyptian civilization.

1000 BC, the pharaohs were much weaker, petty officialdom less thoroughly watched. The custodians of royal tombs and cemeteries were lax in their duties, and a wave of tomb robbing began. During the reign of Rameses IX (1126–1108 BC), a major law case involving tomb robbing was heard in the courts at Thebes, the records of which survive on fragmentary papyri.

The case involved the mayors of the two Thebes. Paser, the mayor of eastern Thebes, was an honest but rather officious local bureaucrat who became concerned at the constant rumors of royal-tomb robberies that floated across the river from Thebes of the Dead on the other bank of the Nile. Perhaps he was anxious to ingratiate himself with higher authority or to discredit his hated rival, Pawero, mayor of the sister community where the royal graves lay. Whatever his motives, Paser started an official investigation into tomb robbing, a subject that officially lay outside his responsibilities. Soon he uncovered all manner of disturbing testimony, including eyewitness accounts of royal-grave robberies. Various witnesses supplied graphic details of surreptitious robbery under torture. They described how they pried open the entrances of royal tombs: "Then we found the august mummy of the king. There were numerous amulets and golden ornaments at his throat, his head had a mask of gold upon it, and the mummy itself was overlaid with gold throughout. . . . We stripped off the gold which we found on the august mummy of the king and the amulets and ornaments, and the coverings in which it rested."[3]

Paser took his damaging testimony to Khaemwese, the local provincial governor, and demanded an official inquiry into the state of the royal tombs. Governor Khaemwese sent an official commission on a tour of inspection. They found that one royal grave, that of Sekhemre Shedtowy, son of Re Sobkemsaf, had been violated as well as some priestesses' tombs. Paser's witnesses were questioned anew. They now protested their innocence and denied their earlier testimony. The result of the inquiry was a disaster for Paser, who had underestimated the extent to which Pawero controlled the thriving robbery business. The governor dropped all charges against the tomb robbers, probably with relief, as it seems certain that he was up to his neck in the racket as well.

Pawero rejoiced at his easy victory over his rival and gloated quietly at home for a while. Then a few months later he collected together "the inspectors, the necropolis administrators, the workmen, the police, and all the laborers of the necropolis" and sent them to the east bank for a noisy celebration. The crowd marched up and down in raucous triumph, paying special attention to Paser's house. The unfortunate mayor ignored the disturbance with a dignity that well became him. Eventually, his impatience got the better of him. He rushed off to complain to the pharaoh's butler, who resided at the temple of Ptah nearby. Paser poured out his troubles, reiterated his charges, and claimed he could prove them. Then he lost his temper and threatened to take his story directly to the king. This was a grave mistake, for his threat involved a gross breach of bureaucratic etiquette that implied that the governor himself was involved in the robberies. The butler carried the story to Khaemwese, who promptly convicted Paser of perjury and told him to stop making a nuisance of himself.

But Paser was not so easily silenced. He continued to bombard the governor with evidence relating to tomb robberies. A year later, even high officialdom could not disguise the violations that had taken place. A new governor, Nebmarenakht, convened a fresh inquiry. Forty-five tomb robbers appeared before the court. Fortunately, the high points of the testimony have survived on a series of famous papyri that were—ironically enough—sold on the illegal antiquities market in Thebes in the late nineteenth century. The witnesses were placed on oath, then beaten to extract true confessions. The evidence was damning. The incense roaster of the temple of the sun god, Amun, recounted how he was approached by a group of robbers at night while asleep:

> "'Come out,' they said, 'We are going to take plunder for bread to eat.' They took me with them. We opened the tomb and brought away a shroud of gold and silver. We broke it up, put it in a basket, brought it down and divided it into six parts." The various accused were beaten on the soles of their feet or tortured with a screw until they either confessed or corroborated each other's testimony.
>
> The scribe of the Necropolis was examined with the stick [until] he said: "Stop! I will tell. This silver is [all] that we brought out. I saw nothing else." He was examined with the birch and the screw. Nesyamenope, the scribe of the Necropolis, said to him: "Then the tomb from which you said the vases of silver were taken is [yet] another tomb. That makes two [tombs] besides the main treasure." He said: "That is false. The vases belong to the main treasure I have already told you about. We opened one tomb and only one." He was examined again with the stick and the birch and the screw [but] he would not confess anything beyond what he had [already] said.[4]

While the (unrecorded) penalties handed out to these particular tomb robbers must have been harsh, any reduction in the tempo of grave robbery can at best have been temporary, for there are scattered records of later trials. Nothing could stop the voracious looters.

Robbers even emptied the tombs of the great Eighteenth Dynasty pharaohs such as Seti I and Rameses II of their riches, despite the opposition of dedicated priests and officials who were determined to protect the dead rulers from destruction. They hustled royal mummies from tomb to tomb, from sarcophagus to sarcophagus, one step ahead of the thieves. Rameses II and Seti I themselves were moved several times. Eventually, the robbers became so daring that the priests obtained a strong, trusted guard and moved every known royal mummy to safe hiding in one of two caches, either in a secret tomb in the Valley of the Kings or in a cleft in the hills overlooking Thebes. This time the kings managed to evade the tomb robbers for 3,000 years, until AD 1881, when a major cache in a remote defile near Deir el-Bahri was discovered by accident by robbers but saved for science.[5]

: :

The wealth and stability of ancient Egypt were proverbial in the Mediterranean world of 4,000 years ago. A rich literature tells of the deeds of the pharaohs.[6] We know their names, have some knowledge of their personalities, and can gaze on their well-preserved treasures. Most people have heard of Rameses II and Tutankhamun. Artistic traditions and works of art have survived in bewildering glory and amazing quantity despite the depredations of ancient and modern treasure hunters. Vivid writings and character sketches give us insights into the daily life of the Egyptians, into the court scandals and causes célèbres of a long-vanished age. Unfortunately, 3,000 years after the apogee of Egyptian civilization, a mere pittance of the riches and glory that made up the world's longest-lasting civilization remains for the archaeologist and tourist to study and admire.

The tombs and great monuments of ancient Egypt have been under siege ever since they were built. The Egyptians themselves used them for building stone. Religious zealots and quarrymen followed the tomb robbers. They eradicated inscriptions and removed great temples stone by stone. Arab treasure hunters tunneled around the pyramids of Giza in search of gold. The inscribed casing stones from all three Giza pyramids formed the walls of Cairo's new citadel. Soldiers used the Sphinx for target practice. Then came the travelers and antiquarians in search of curiosities or commercial gain. Some dynamited the pyramids; others bought mummies and tunneled in the tombs of Saqqara in Lower Egypt. French general Napoléon Bonaparte came to the Nile in 1798 to seize the strategic route to British India. He brought a team of experts with him to study Egypt ancient and modern. His scientists left six years later with Napoléon's defeated army, carrying crates of priceless antiquities. They produced the multivolume *Description of Ancient Egypt* that caused a sensation in Europe. By 1833 the monk Father Géramb was able to remark to the Egyptian pasha Muhammad Ali that "it would be hardly respectable, on one's return from Egypt, to present oneself in Europe without a mummy in one hand and a crocodile in the other."[7]

By Géramb's time, a craze for things Egyptian had taken Europe by storm. Diplomats and tourists, merchants and dukes all vied with one an-

other to assemble spectacular collections of mummies and other antiquities. A craze for things Egyptian affected architecture and fashion. Egyptology became a fashionable subject for the wealthy and the curious. At
the same time as the French genius Jean-François Champollion was deci-
phering Egyptian hieroglyphs, eager travelers were despoiling the very
civilization he sought to understand.

During the past 2,000 years, both Egyptians and a host of foreigners
have effectively gutted our potential knowledge of ancient Egypt. They
have done so for profit, and also, regrettably, in the name of science and
nationalism. The loss to archaeology is incalculable, that to Egyptian history even more staggering. As a result of the looting and pillage of generations of irresponsible visitors, the artifacts and artistic achievements of
the ancient Egyptians are scattered all over the globe, some of the most
beautiful and spectacular of them stored or displayed thousands of miles
from the Nile. Fortunately, something has been saved from the wreckage
by the dedicated work of modern archaeologists and by the efforts of the
Egyptian government during the past hundred years.

We cannot in all conscience blame those who looted ancient Egypt. In
retrospect, they were merely mirroring the moral and intellectual climate of
their times. The Egyptians were motivated by profit, by the need to make a
good living. Dreams of treasure and wealth, incentives of profit, and a driving lust to own the exotic that has been such a pervasive feature of Western
civilization drove many visitors to the Nile. But at least the efforts of the foreigners have made the world aware of the glories of ancient Egypt in a superficial way. The brightly painted mummies of Egyptian pharaohs and their
subjects are commonplace in European and American museums. Everyone
has seen at least a picture of a hieroglyphic inscription or the pyramids. In
these days of swift jet travel and well-organized package tours, many of us
have been lucky enough to gaze on the battered remnants of ancient Egypt
on the banks of the Nile. We are probably stimulated to visit Egypt by a
chance visit to a museum or the reading of a book on the ancient Egyptians.
Yet the artifacts we see in London, New York, or Paris were, many of them,
obtained by people whose interest in antiquity was accompanied by a fatal
curiosity, reinforced with gunpowder, picks, and other destructive instruments. It is one of the tragedies of history that our knowledge of ancient
Egypt is derived in large part from artifacts recovered during centuries of pillage and tomb robbing among the rock-cut tombs and pyramids of the Nile.

2 | The First Tourists

Risen as a god, hear what I tell you,

That you may rule the land, govern the shores,

Increase well-being!

Beware of subjects who are nobodies.

MIRIAM LICHTHEIM, ED.,
Ancient Egyptian Literature: A Book of Readings[1]

"This country is a palimpsest," wrote that remarkable Victorian lady Lucie Duff-Gordon from Luxor more than a century ago, "in which the Bible is written over Herodotus, and the Koran over that."[2] And a palimpsest it is, of conquests and tourists, of dedicated travelers and hardworking archaeologists. The story of the discovery of ancient Egypt owes as much to travelers' tales as it does to the fine words of professional scholars and leisured antiquarians.

The ancient Egyptians themselves knew that that their civilization was the oldest of all civilized institutions. The pharaohs' king lists traced king after king backward through time to the moment of the unification of Upper and Lower Egypts under the pharaoh Horus-Aha, or Menes, in about 3100 BC. Egypt's official history sanctioned by the pharaohs went back even further into a mythic past, to legendary kings known as the "Souls of Nekhen." According to Egyptian belief, at the beginning of time, the god Atum, "the completed one," had emerged from the watery chaos and caused the "first moment," raising a mound of solid earth above the waters. Then the life-giving force of the sun, Re, rose over the land to cause the rest of creation. The Egyptian pharaohs were the personification of *ma'at*, a sense of rightness that defined civilization along the Nile. They ruled by precedent, divine kings presiding over an ever orderly world. Of course, their world was often far from orderly, but the little-changing ideology of Egypt's kings maintained a facade of the triumph of order over chaos, of the pharaoh presiding over the unified Two Lands of Upper and Lower Egypts. The unification was an act of harmony, of reconciliation between warring gods and the forces of chaos and rightness.

Today, the orderly world of ancient Egypt is long gone. The temples are silent. All-powerful gods like the sun deity, Amun of Thebes, have disappeared on the tides of history. Mud-brick walls crumble; temple pylons collapse inexorably into the river alluvium. The chants and invocations, the banners and dances of adoration have long ceased. All that remains are crumbling columns and silent inscriptions massaged by the mocking rays of the sun. But the mystique of Egypt has captivated travelers for centuries.

: :

The Egyptians called their homeland *Kmt*, "the black land," after the fertile dark soil that nurtured their civilization. *Kmt* slashed across the arid wastes of the eastern Sahara like a green arrow, following the course of the Nile. The river is the longest on earth, rising in the East African highlands and flowing more than 10,300 kilometers (4,000 miles) northward to the Mediterranean through some of the world's driest terrain. Fifteen thousand years ago, the Nile flowed through a deep gorge into a much lower ocean. As sea levels rose after the Ice Age, layer upon layer of silt choked the narrow defile and formed the river floodplain of today.

No one knew where the river with its creative forces came from. The pharaohs believed the source lay in a subterranean stream that flowed in the underworld. The Nile's life-giving waters were thought to well to the surface between granite rocks close to the First Cataract, from a cavern under Elephantine Island in the middle of the river more than 1,550 kilometers (600 miles) from the Mediterranean Sea.

Kmt was, in many respects, a paradise on earth. The river fertilized and watered the Egyptians' carefully laid-out fields. Lush marshlands and meadows provided food for domesticated animals and wild beasts, waterfowl abounded along the riverbanks, and fish teemed in its muddy waters. As the Nile rose each summer, the river became a vast shallow lake. Villages and towns became islands. The farmers impounded floodwater in natural drainage basins and behind earthen banks to spread it farther over their fields and irrigation works. But the Egyptians lived at the mercy of a capricious Nile. Everyone dreaded exceptionally high inundations, which swept everything before them—cattle, houses, entire villages. Some years, the river barely flooded at all, the victim of droughts far upstream. The Nile rose slightly, then receded almost at once, meaning that thousands would go hungry and famine stalked the land.

Egypt was a linear kingdom, shaped somewhat like an enormous lotus flower with roots deep in Africa. The stalk and the flower were the Two Lands. *Ta-shema* (Upper Egypt) begins at the First Cataract, where the valley is only 2.4 kilometers (1.5 miles) wide. Upstream lay Nubia, *Ta-Seti*, "the Land of the Bowmen," modern-day Sudan, so named because the Nubians were expert archers. Here the river vanished into a limitless desert and an alien world. Upper Egypt was about 800 kilometers (500 miles) long, often bounded by desert cliffs. In places, the floodplain was as much as 18 kilometers (11 miles) across, but often much narrower. Near the pharaohs' ancient capital at Memphis, the stalk became the flower as the river meandered through a vast silt-choked delta to the sea. *Ta-mehu* (Lower Egypt) encompassed the delta from the Mediterranean upstream to Memphis. Moist and low-lying, with low hills, swamps, and lakes, the 22,000-square-kilometer (8,500-square-mile) delta was the breadbasket and vineyard of Egypt.

The Egyptian state came into being and endured in part because of *Kmt*'s linear geography, a kingdom held together by the Nile. But communication was slow, the Two Lands very different from one another politically and economically. To hold the Two Lands together required vigorous, decisive leadership; great political sensitivity; and outstanding personal charisma. With strong rule and unity came harmony, balance, and order. He who ruled a united land was the living personification of the falcon-headed god Horus, symbol of kings. He embodied a unified Upper and Lower Egypt. King Amenhotep III (1386–1349 BC), perhaps the most magnificent of all pharaohs, erected a stela in about 1360 BC at the temple of the sun god, Re, at Karnak in Upper Egypt that spelled out his job description: "The living Horus: Strong Bull, Arisen in Truth: Two

Ladies: Giver of Laws, Pacifier of the Two Lands, Gold-Horus: Great of Strength, Smiter of Asiatics: the King of Upper and Lower Egypt . . . Beloved of Amen-Re . . . Who rejoices as he rules the Two Lands like Re for ever."[3] The pharaohs *were* Egypt, a kingdom with an ideology of the harmonious, almost mythically unified Two Lands. They thought of their history as an orderly sequence of rulers who passed their kingship from one generation to the next. In fact, Egypt had a turbulent, ever changing political landscape. The kingdom fragmented at least twice, but always managed to restore its greatness at the hands of able pharaohs.

The greatness ended in about 1000 BC, when Egypt ceased to be a major imperial power. Conquerors came and went—Nubian kings, Assyrians, Persians, and Alexander the Great—but the essential fabric of Egyptian civilization and its theology survived into Roman times, when Rameses II (1304–1237 BC) and other great pharaohs were remote memories. By the time Egypt under the Ptolemies became a province of the Roman Empire in 31 BC, the land of the pharaohs was part of a much wider Mediterranean world. The Greco-Egyptian city of Alexandria in the delta had long been a cosmopolitan center where the Mediterranean and Asian worlds met, famous for its fleshpots and its men of learning. Long under Greek rule, the Alexandrians believed that the basic institutions of government and religion associated with civilization had originated with the pharaohs. To the Romans, Egypt was a country full of strange wonders, a place where the learned might acquire arcane knowledge and medical skills unheard of elsewhere.

: :

Long before Anthony and Cleopatra, Egypt's marvels attracted the learned and curious. The Greek historian Herodotus visited the Nile in about 460–455 BC. He wrote one of the first lengthy accounts of the curiosities and antiquities of the Nile, only a few centuries after the decline of the greatest Egyptian pharaohs. In Herodotus's day, Egypt was known territory for a duration of four months' travel upstream deep into Nubia.

Herodotus's writings show clear evidence of a profound, if at times inaccurate, knowledge of the ancient world. His reputation as a historian stood high even in his own time, for he was invited to read his works in public before the Athenians. Fortunately, his *Histories* have come down to us in their entirety. They are a collation of observed facts, folktales, myths, genuine history, and delightful curiosities. Herodotus himself emerges from them as a thoroughly gullible and likable man, with a penchant for accurate observation and an infinite capacity for admiration and wonder. The nine books of the *Histories* do not, of course, measure up to modern historical standards, for their author was much given to exaggeration and was uncritical about his sources. Nevertheless, archaeologists have proven the essential accuracy of his anthropological observations on many occasions. Herodotus took the trouble to describe Egypt at great length, for he seems to have been more enthusiastic about the Egyptians than almost any other people that he met.

In traveling up the Nile, Herodotus merely followed a well-trodden route. Canals and irrigation works dissected the Nile floodplain; any journey on land was at best laborious before the days of roads, railways, and airlines. All governmental business and commercial activity passed up and down the river in barges and sailing vessels, while simple canoes of papyrus reeds served the villagers' needs. Few foreigners ventured into the arid wastes of the deserts that pressed onto the Nile Valley. There was little to see, and the caravan journeys could be arduous in the extreme. So the itineraries of most visitors to the Nile remained basically unchanged right up to modern times—a journey up the river from Alexandria to the First Cataract at Aswan, with stops at the pyramids, Karnak, and Thebes. (Cairo is an Islamic city and did not exist in Roman times.)

Herodotus turned his leisurely journey into one of the most famous passages of the *Histories*, probably the earliest systematic account of the Nile Valley and its wonders. It is difficult to separate the author's personal observations from the hearsay and myth that he collected. For instance, he speculated as to the cause of the annual flood. He reported that some Egyptians believed the floods were caused by rain and melting snow, a theory that was proved correct more than 2,000 years later, although Herodotus disbelieved the tale. "How can it [the Nile] flow from the snow when its course lies from the hottest parts of earth to those that are for the most part cooler?" he asked.[4]

Like so many other classical visitors, Herodotus professed a reverence and enthusiasm for Egyptian institutions. The Egyptians, he observed, were religious to excess, worshiping a large assembly of gods, from whom, he surmised, the Greeks derived at least some of their own divinities. The cat was held in great reverence and buried in special cemeteries, as were other domestic animals. And, like so many visitors after him, Herodotus was fascinated by the burial customs of the ancient Egyptians. He described how the embalmers drew out the brain through the nostrils with an iron hook and then cleaned out and preserved the corpse over a period of seventy days: "Then the relatives take back the corpse and make a hollow wooden coffin, man-shaped. They enclose the corpse therein, and having shut it up, they store it in a coffin chamber, placing it upright against a wall."[5] Modern investigators, who have experimented with Egyptian mummification techniques, have confirmed the essential accuracy of Herodotus's account—clearly based on firsthand observations.

From burial customs he passed to agriculture and fishing, to the hunting of crocodiles and Egyptian boats. No detail large or small escaped the eye of this insatiably curious visitor. He talked to officials and priests, to village headmen and townspeople with an infinite curiosity that is the mark of a gifted traveler. His hunger for information was insatiable. Herodotus recounted the legends of the origins of the Egyptian state, the story of Menes, the first ruler of a unified Egypt. He told how priests showed him lists recording the names of 350 kings. Two centuries later, the Greek priest Manetho published the same lists in his *History of Egypt*, written in about 280 BC, the foundation of modern Egyptologists' dynasties of Egyptian kings.[6] The fragmentary historical narrative in the *Histories* is, at best, little more than hearsay and legend, and the author himself admitted as much. Unfortunately, most of his successors accepted the *Histories* as gospel truth. As so often happens, historical myths became dogmatic fact, slavishly copied by centuries of historians.

Herodotus was in an unusual position. Of all the many travelers and historians who have visited Egypt in the past 3,000 years whose works have come down to us, Herodotus was the nearest to the great pharaohs themselves. He talked to priests and worshipers who were actively carrying on the traditions of millennia of religious devotion. The monuments of the Nile were in a far better state of preservation than they are today, before the disastrous inroads of archaeological plunderers, despoiling Christians, and quarrying Muslims. So his account is a vivid one, perhaps too vivid, of a remarkable and exotic river valley that he and other educated men reasonably accepted as the cradle of their own civilization. The Egyptians of the day come alive in the *Histories*: we read of their drinking bouts, of the story of the theft of the thief's body, and of complex religious ceremonies, with Herodotus at our side occasionally admonishing us that much of what he learned may have been tall tales. His admonitions were timely, but were largely ignored by Herodotus's successors and generations of scholars and historians.

Modern scholars have castigated Herodotus, not least among them the great nineteenth-century French Egyptologist Auguste Mariette. "I detest this traveler," he wrote, complaining that Herodotus visited Egypt when the ancient language was still spoken and thus could have asked all sorts of key historical questions and received accurate answers. Instead, he "tells us gravely that a daughter of Cheops built a pyramid with the fruit of prostitution. Considering the great number of mistakes in Herodotus, would it not have been better for Egyptology had he never existed?"[7] Herodotus was indeed an inaccurate, often gullible observer, with a penchant for the fanciful and marvelous. The tall tales of his informants have haunted Egyptology for centuries. British Egyptologist Sir Alan Gardiner's assessment of Herodotus as the "Father of History" and a "great genius" is probably fairer, for he was experimenting with what at the time was a totally new literary art form.

: :

Numerous Greek travelers followed in Herodotus's footsteps, but only a few of their travelogues survive. The author Diodorus Siculus lived in the Nile Valley from 60 to 57 BC and was one of the first people to write about the huge seated figures of pharaoh Amenhotep III (1386–1349 BC) on the floodplain at Thebes. The Greeks named these 20-meter- (65-foot-) high statues the Colossi of Memnon, after a Homeric hero. Rameses II's nearby mortuary temple, the Ramesseum, became known as the Memnonium. Diodorus admired the temple and its courts with its statues of the king. He found an inscription on one of the figures, which he quoted, attributing the temple correctly to Ozymandias, the Greek equivalent of Userma'a-tre'setepenre', the actual name of Rameses II: "My name is Ozymandias, king of kings; if any would know how great I am and where I lie, let him surpass me in any of my works." Many centuries later, Percy Bysshe Shelley (1792–1822) was inspired by a "traveler from an antique land" who described two "vast and trunkless legs of stone" in the desert. "My name is Ozymandias, king of kings: Look on my works, ye Mighty, and despair!" he wrote in a short poem that is among the classics of the English language.[8]

The Greek geographer Strabo (64 BC–ca. AD 23) was a contemporary of Diodorus Siculus. He accompanied Aelius Gallus, a Roman prefect of

FIGURE 2.1   Obelisk from Luxor in the Place de la Concorde, Paris.

Egypt, on his expedition to Upper Egypt in 25 BC. Strabo's *Geography* is
an enormous compilation of factual information about the Roman
world. Egypt fills much of his seventeenth book. The account is mainly
geographical, a catalog of towns and resources. He treated archaeological
sites like other features of the landscape. At Memphis, he visited the site
of the Serapeum. "One finds also [at Memphis] at the temple of Serapis,
in a spot so sandy that the wind causes the sand to accumulate in heaps,
under which we could see many sphinxes, some of them almost entirely
buried, others only partially covered."[9] Nearly 2,000 years later, French
archaeologist Auguste Mariette used Strabo's account to rediscover the
Serapeum.

Strabo's party paused to admire the statuary at the Ramesseum, across
the Nile from Thebes. Next they examined some inscriptions on obelisks
at the temples of the sun god, Amun, at Luxor and Karnak, one of which
was later given to King Louis XVIII of France by Pasha Mohammad Ali in
the nineteenth century and now stands in the Place de la Concorde in
Paris. "Above the Memnonium," remarked Strabo, "are tombs of kings,
which are stone-hewn, are about forty in number, are marvelously constructed, and are a spectacle worth seeing." This is one of the first references to the Valley of the Kings, for so long the scene of archaeological
rape and pillage. Strabo ended by castigating Herodotus and others for
"talking much nonsense, adding to their account marvelous tales, to give

it, as it were, a kind of tune or rhythm or relish."[10] Strabo was not the first Egyptian traveler to find reality different from history.

: :

When the Romans occupied Egypt in 31 BC, the Nile Valley became a prosperous and stable province of the greatest empire the world had known. Roman interest in Egypt was predominantly political and exploitative. Her fields became one of Rome's granaries, but the old religious ways were tolerated and even revered. The stability of Roman Egypt depended on a political system that was superimposed on the native cultures. In France and Britain, for example, thousands of local people became Romanized, adopting many of the customs and institutions of their conquerors. But the Egyptians remained aloof, worshiping their age-old gods, cultivating their fields as they always had, perpetuating many institutions of earlier times. A distinctive way of life of tremendous antiquity continued to survive comparatively unscathed, surrounded by the lasting monuments of religious and political institutions that extended into the distant past. The security of Roman rule enabled the tourist to move around freely in this strange country. For three and a half centuries the Roman world was at peace. A rich and leisured class enjoyed an easy life of travel and luxury, passing in safety to even the remotest corners of the empire. The centralized administration of the Roman Empire made constant travel between Rome and Alexandria, and between the governor's headquarters and provincial towns, essential. Government delegations, ambassadors, military conscripts, and individual citizens seeking redress all shuttled to and fro from Egypt to Rome. Thousands of tourists also flocked to Egypt and other parts of the Near East in search of education, entertainment, or religious edification.

The Roman tourist took ship at galley ports in southern Italy for a six-day passage to Alexandria, or crossed to Carthage in North Africa and then traveled to the Nile by coast road. Either route was safe and speedy, for the imperial business used the same communication networks. Constant and uninterrupted traffic crisscrossed the Mediterranean. Ships that sometimes reached a length of 53 meters (173 feet) and displaced more than 2,000 tons carried marble, linen, papyrus, glass, and perfumes, as well as passengers. Upon arrival at Alexandria, one could travel by river to the First Cataract and beyond or use the Roman-built post road that now ran alongside the Nile. At Koptos in Upper Egypt, well-maintained mail roads followed the ancient Egyptian route across the desert to the Red Sea ports of Berenice and Myos Hormos, important transshipment points and trading stations for the Arabian and Indian Ocean trade.

Many people traveled to the Nile simply to enlarge their intellectual horizons or out of curiosity. Direct inquiry was the best way of learning about history, geography, and the arts of philosophy, religion, and magic that everyone knew were developed to a high pitch in Egypt. Alexandria had an international reputation for scholarship and medicine. Famous teachers stood ready to accommodate the traveler. The sick could be cured. Then there were the notorious pleasure resorts at Alexandria. Ptolemy I Soter (305–282 BC), a friend and general of Alexander the Great, had founded a temple of the god Serapis at Canopus near Alexandria. By Roman times, this was famous throughout the ancient world for its extravagant and orgiastic rituals. The cult of Serapis was an amalgam of the worship of two Egyptian gods, Osiris and Apis, the latter a sacred bull, important to the Ptolemies as a guarantor of royal power. While the Serapeum complex at Saqqara near Memphis with its ancient bull burials was an important pilgrimage venue, where people flocked seeking cures, the Canopus shrines were a center of ecstatic rituals and feasts.

Tiring of Dionysian pleasures, the tourist could then sail southward up the Nile to another world, where the monuments of antiquity overlooked irrigated fields and centuries-old irrigation systems. We can follow their journeys from the numerous graffiti they left behind them. Although the more serious traveler might examine dozens of ruined temples, most tourists followed an itinerary that took them from Alexandria to Memphis, the pyramids of Giza, then to Thebes and the Valley of the Kings on the west bank opposite the town and the lovely island of Philae with its temple of Isis at the First Cataract, all easily visited by boat or road. Numerous small inns catered to the needs of the weary traveler. Private contractors hired out their boats or pack animals to organized parties of visitors, many of them armed with their Herodotus or Egyptian geographies written by other authors. Like modern guidebooks, these volumes sought to inform and to entertain, to titillate with fantasy and myth, and to embrace all manner of information. Antiquities like the pyramids were only part of a general corpus of information presented to the uncritical reader. Most writers added little to Herodotus, for they plagiarized the great historian's work unmercifully.

The first major stop for the Roman tourist venturing upstream was the pyramids at Giza, still adorned with their magnificent limestone casing stones, later removed by medieval contractors to construct the public buildings of Cairo. Many travelers inscribed their names on the casing stones, a thoroughly human failing that has vandalized ancient monuments throughout history. The Egyptian examples provide, in themselves, a fascinating historical kaleidoscope of pithy observations and reactions to the marvels of antiquity. The earliest recorded Giza inscription dates to about AD 1475, for the older inscriptions were removed with the casing stones, although we know from the travels of Rudolph von Suchem, a German monk who visited the pyramids in 1336, that earlier inscriptions did exist.[11]

Near the pyramids of Giza lay the Sphinx, buried in drifting sand. Pliny the Elder was one of the first Roman authors to describe this most famous of Egyptian monuments.[12] There were other tourist attractions, too: the temple of Apis, the bull god, at the ancient and flourishing town of Memphis, and the famous "Labyrinth" at the Fayyum Depression west of the Nile, a vast palace of Amenemhet III (1842–1797 BC), a Middle Kingdom pharaoh who undertook massive land-reclamation works in the oasis. The Labyrinth was so named on account of its many courtyards and rooms, which caused imaginative Greeks to compare it to the mythical Cretan Labyrinth. "It has twelve courts, all of them roofed," wrote Herodotus; "the passages through the courts, in their extreme complication, caused us countless marvelings as we went through, from the court into the rooms, and from the rooms into the pillared chambers."[13] Herodotus felt that the Labyrinth was even more wonderful than the Giza pyramids. Nearby were the sacred crocodiles of the Fayyum, fed from priestly hands—strictly as a tourist attraction. No traces of the Labyrinth survive today. When Egyptologist Sir Flinders Petrie excavated at the site in 1889, he found only a few columns and architraves, as well as numerous stone chips. For centuries, lime burners had camped among the ruins and slowly reduced them to shredded rubble.

From the Labyrinth, the traveler pressed on upstream to the temples of Amun at Luxor and Karnak at Thebes, where he or she walked through the vast Hypostele hall with its forest of pillars at the temple of Amun at Karnak and ventured across the river into the desolate Valley of the Kings, even then known as the burial place of Egypt's greatest rulers.[14] Visiting the deep burial chambers of the pharaohs quarried into the hills of the

FIGURE 2.2   The temple of Amun at Karnak by the Victorian painter David Roberts (1796–1864). Roberts spent two and a half months in Egypt in 1838, sketching and painting the major monuments and scenes of local life. An expert lithographer, Louis Hague, prepared them for publication over the next eight years. Roberts's colorful and often romanticized works are deservedly popular with collectors. From the author's collection.

valley was an exciting adventure. By the time the Romans came, all the exposed tombs had already been opened and plundered. The tourist tiptoed into the dark chambers and inscribed his name by torchlight on the walls of the desecrated tomb. Generations earlier, Diodorus Siculus had already complained that there was nothing there except the results of pillage and destruction.[15]

The two vast seated statues of the pharaoh Amenhotep III, known to everyone as the Colossi of Memnon, on the floodplain near the Valley of the Kings across from Amun's temples on the west bank were one of the highlights of any visit to the Nile. The Greeks had identified the seated Colossi with the mythical King Memnon of Ethiopia, son of the Dawn, who had assisted the Trojans against Achilles. Like the Labyrinth, the Colossi had received their name from a well-known character of common legend, a familiar historical landmark identified among a landscape of exotic gods and pharaohs. In fact, the two sandstone statues once stood in front of Amenhotep's vast mortuary temple. The pharaoh was enamored of extravagant statements and lavish display. The summer inundation flooded his stupendous mortuary temple each year, leaving only the inner shrine on a small knoll clear of the water. The Nile eventually destroyed the temple; Roman contractors removed the boulders of the collapsed ruins to use in new construction. Eventually, all that remained were the two Colossi.

Both statues had been badly damaged in antiquity, most recently by an earthquake in 27 BC, but this did not prevent the northern statue of the pair from emitting a bell-like sound in the early morning. Tourists flocked to hear the noisy statue at sunrise and to speculate about the strange noises. Some compared the sounds to human voices, others to a twanging harp string. Strabo was more cynical. He suspected that the local priests had installed a mechanism to cause the sound. In fact, the early-morning warmth of the sun caused the stones to expand.

The Colossi attracted both the lowly and the mighty. Many tourists inscribed graffiti on the huge feet. The emperor Hadrian (AD 117–138) visited the site in AD 130. The statue remained silent the first day, but spoke to the emperor and empress on the second, an event that caused an accompanying poetess to inscribe some commemorative verses on the statue in praise of Memnon and, of course, the emperor Hadrian. Memnon's refusal to speak to the Roman general, later emperor, Septimius Severus three-quarters of a century later was fatal. Severus tried to conciliate the god by restoring the head and torso, an act that silenced the statue forever.

We do not know the full extent of the damage wrought by the Romans on the Egyptian past. There are no official records of a widespread trade in antiquities, but some fine pieces certainly left the country. Apparently, Hadrian fancied Egyptian sculpture. In 1771, the Scottish painter Gavin Hamilton acquired a fine Middle Kingdom female sphinx head in Rome, which almost certainly came from the ruins of Hadrian's villa, shipped there to adorn his home. Nor, seemingly, had the apparent medicinal properties of Egyptian mummies been recognized. But the obelisk, a slender pinnacle of granite carved with hieroglyphs, proved of overriding interest to the Romans. Constantine the Great (AD 306–337) was a great looter of obelisks. He caused a granite obelisk erected at Thebes by Thutmose III in the fifteenth century BC to be removed to Alexandria. Bureaucratic inertia delayed the monument at the Egyptian coast until after Constantine's death. Eventually, it found its way to Constantinople, where it was erected in the Hippodrome near the Hagia Sophia Mosque on the orders of Emperor Theodosius I in AD 390. There it still stands. Another was eventually brought to Rome and erected in the great Circus Maximus. In due course it fell down, but was reerected by Pope Sixtus V in 1587.

The slender proportions and exotic hieroglyphic inscriptions on these obelisks seem to have excited the Romans, for they copied the architectural form with their own cruder obelisks. No one was able to comprehend the significance of Egyptian obelisks, although the soldier and naturalist Pliny the Elder suggested they were symbolic representations of the sun's rays. A leisurely inspection of the obelisks in Rome convinced him that the hieroglyphic inscriptions comprised "an account of natural science according to the theories of the Egyptian sages." The same author contemptuously dismissed the pyramids "as a superfluous and foolish display of wealth on the part of the kings."

The emperor Augustus used a looted obelisk in Rome's Campus Martius as a form of calendar to mark the sun's shadow and the lengths of days and nights: "A pavement was laid down for a distance appropriate to the height of the obelisk, so that the shadow cast at noon on the shortest day of the year might exactly coincide with it. Bronze rods let into the pavement were meant to measure the shadow day by day as it gradually became shorter and then lengthened again. But," added Pliny, "the readings thus given here for about thirty years have failed to correspond to the calendar."[16]

The Roman interest in ancient Egypt stemmed from plain intellectual curiosity about a civilization assumed to be the oldest in the world. And, for all their curiosity about the cradle of civilization, many more naive Roman tourists must have aspired to the hopes an Alexandrian visitor inscribed on one of the temples at Philae: "Whoever prays to Isis at Philae becomes happy, rich, and long-lived."[17]

: :

Some fifty years after Constantine the Great had removed the obelisks from Thebes, a nun named Lady Etheria from what is now France visited Egypt as part of a lengthy progression through the holy places of the Near East during the fifth century after Christ. Somewhat bolder than her contemporaries, she visited Alexandria, passed by the pyramids, inspected the dwelling places of hermits, and gazed on the Colossi of Memnon at Thebes. "Nothing else is there now save one great Theban stone in which two great statues are cut out, which they say are the statues of holy men, even Moses and Aaron, erected by the Children of Israel in their honor," she wrote.[18] By Etheria's time, the Bible was the primary literary source in the civilized world, a safe and secure archive of philosophy and information that was capable of explaining the strange ways of the world.

Lady Etheria was traveling in unsettled and changing times, when the great academic centers of the classical world were in decline or turning inward on themselves. Egypt had not escaped the winds of change. The waning of Roman power and the rise of Christianity had brought many changes to traditional economic and religious ways. Christianity itself came to Alexandria in the first century AD, in the hands, so it is said, of Saint Mark. A small group of converts soon mushroomed into a large congregation of Christians who refused to worship the emperor as a god in his own right, a campaign of revolt that led to appalling persecutions and numerous martyrdoms. In AD 313 Constantine the Great recognized Christianity as one of the official religions of the empire. The influence of the Alexandrian Christians grew all-powerful on the Nile. The new religion was at first a faith of townsfolk, of educated Alexandrian Greeks and minor tradesmen. In the fourth century, the Scriptures were translated from Greek into Coptic, the language most commonly spoken by Egyptians. A cult of monasticism, a quest for spiritual perfection through retreat from the secular world, emerged among small communities of monks and hermits who spread the new doctrines to the common people. Christianity among the poverty-stricken Coptic peasants began, perhaps, as a form of anticolonial protest against a sinful world dominated by elitist town dwellers.

The Coptic Christians were far from unified in their beliefs or traditional customs, but were all committed to a new order of religious institutions, which did not tolerate Egypt's ancient beliefs. Whereas the Roman tourist had been curious about ancient Egyptian religion, the native Copts were determined to expunge all traces of older heretical ways. In 397 the fanatical patriarch Cyril and his armies probably destroyed the Serapeum at Memphis, one of the great Roman tourist attractions. Drifting desert sand mantled the ruins, uncovered only in the nineteenth cen-

tury. During the sixth century, the emperor Justinian I actively encouraged Christian zeal. He ordered the temples of Isis on the island of Philae
closed. The temple statues were removed to Constantinople to commemorate his piety in converting the heathen. The ceremonial panoply of ancient Egyptian religion became illegal and the symbols of the ancient religion evil and sinful. Faith-driven chisels and hammers obliterated
inscriptions and faces, heads, hands, and feet from fine friezes on temple
porticoes in the name of God.

3 | "Mummy Is Become Merchandise"

When you set in western lightland,

Earth is in darkness as if in death;

One sleeps in chambers, heads covered. . . .

Earth brightens when you dawn in lightland,

When you shine as Aten of daytime;

As you dispel the dark,

As you cast your rays,

The Two Lands are in festivity.

GREAT HYMN TO THE ATEN,
in the tomb of the vizier and pharaoh Ay (1325–1321 BC),
Tutankhamun's successor

For centuries, the neglected temples of the pharaohs stood empty on the floodplain, occupying valuable agricultural land, or on higher ground that was never flooded by the annual inundation. Villagers quarried them for building stone. Hewn stone blocks were admirable building materials in a country desperately short of wood. There was no need to quarry fresh granite when large numbers of beauti-

FIGURE 3.1   The pylon of the temple of Horus at
Edfu. From *Description de l'Égypte.*

fully cut and squared blocks were available for the taking from the ruins
of a disused temple. Even the ancient Egyptians themselves had recycled
their building stone. Where people did not carry away the stone or deface
temple inscriptions, nature took over. Desert sands drifted over the
Sphinx. Agricultural land was in short supply on the Nile floodplain, so
the people built their villages on patches of higher ground, including the
roof of the great temple of the falcon-headed god Horus at Edfu, deeply
buried under drifting sand.[1] Peasant farmers lived on the roof of the temple for centuries. They knew nothing of the significance of the building
they had commandeered. Lady Etheria and her contemporaries glimpsed
ancient Egypt just as it was entering a long oblivion that lasted for more
than ten centuries.

Islam came to Egypt during the seventh century, unleashing yet more
destructive forces on temple and sepulcher. The soldier-poet Amr Ibn el-
As led the small Muslim army that expelled Cyrus, the Byzantine viceroy of

the Nile. He wrote of Alexandria that he had captured a city "that contains 4,000 palaces, 4,000 baths, 400 theaters, 1,200 greengrocers, and 40,000 Jews."[2] But the city was a shadow of its former learned self. A civil war two and a half centuries before had destroyed the city's famed library. The conquerors founded a new capital upstream at Al-Fustat, a "city of tents," on the east bank of the Nile, for a new body of water was to separate them from the caliph's palace in Medina. Al-Fustat and its nearby successor, Al-Askar, soon became an important link between East and West.

At first, Egypt was little more than a military province of expanding Islamic domains, but the new faith spread slowly southward along the banks of the Nile as more agricultural settlers, bureaucrats, and Islamic scholars settled in Egypt. In 870, a young governor, Ahmad Ibn-Talun, declared Egypt an independent state, free of the Abbasid caliph, who now resided in Baghdad. He founded a new capital, Al-Qatai, in the same general area as its predecessors. After sixty-five turbulent years, a Turkish ruler, Al-Ikhshid, brought Egypt back into the Abbasid fold. There matters remained until 969, when a Tunisian Shiite, Al-Meuz Ledin-Ellah, unleashed his Sicilian general, a former slave named Gawhar, on the Nile Valley. He easily captured the now long-established capital area and founded the Fatimid dynasty, as well as yet another capital, Al-Mansureya, which Al-Muez later named Al-Qahria, Cairo, "the Triumphant." Despite a series of volatile rulers, Cairo flourished, to endure as a great caravan city and center of Islamic learning. The Seljuk leader Salah-el-Din (Saladin) entered Cairo in 1168, threw out the Fatimids, and embarked on an orgy of construction, including a formidable citadel and city walls. He and those who followed him mined the pyramids of their casing stones as building materials. His successors were a dynasty of former slaves, the Mamluks, who ruled over Egypt until 1516, when their domains became a province of the Ottoman Empire based in Constantinople. But the Mamluks still had much control over local affairs, for the Turks were primarily interested in tax collecting.

The few Europeans who visited Cairo found it a bustling, chaotic city with fine mosques and a magnificent university. The local Islamic scholars marveled at the temples and pyramids, but they came from an even more alien culture, which had no appreciation of the history or cultural achievements of its new colony. Without this historical sense, they were at a loss, nor could the Copts, ignorant of hieroglyphs or older religious ways, enlighten their new masters. So the scholars shrugged and ascribed the works of ancient Egypt to giants or magicians long departed from the banks of the eternal river. Some thought of the pyramids as Joseph's granaries used for storing corn in years of plenty, a theory already propounded by the Roman author Julius Honorius before the fifth century. Others believed they were treasure houses of long-dead kings. The great Arab geographer 'al-Masudi (ca. 888–957), famous for his travels from Europe to India, wrote that the Great Pyramid contained "the image of a sheik, made of green stone, sitting on a sofa, and wrapped up in a garment."[3] Unfortunately, the statue could not be moved. Some rather adventurous souls, bolder than 'al-Masudi, entered the pyramids in search of treasure during the Middle Ages. Temples and pyramids became quarries for building stone or were dismembered in a frantic quest for legendary treasure.

For centuries, the Arabs pursued treasure hunting with a frenzied intensity, rivaled only by that displayed by nineteenth-century antiquities collectors. Treasure hunting was so widely practiced in the fifteenth century that it was classified as a taxed industry. People dug everywhere using secret magical incantations and techniques, which, if effective, would be just the thing for a modern archaeologist to use in amplification of his electronic detection methods. Guidebooks to treasure hunting included complicated directions to tomb areas, such as one cemetery complex near Memphis that was visible to a treasure hunter if he performed "fumigations" at a certain point. *The Book of Hidden Pearls and Precious Mysteries* and other such jewels of treasure-hunting lore were regarded as vital parts of the treasure hunter's safari kit. The instructions given in these handbooks would delight any amateur chemist:

> You will uncover some masonry. Break it, perform continuous fumigation, and you will find a sloping way that will lead you to a chamber containing a corpse covered by a cloth of woven gold and wearing golden armour. The incense should be compounded of agalloche, stigmatas of saffron, dung, carob kernels, sycamore figs. Take a *mithqal* of each of these ingredients, grind them fine, moisten them with human blood, roll them into pellets and burn them as incense: the talismans and the hiding places will thus be discovered.[4]

The learned shrugged at such nonsense, among them the wise and sober Arab writer Ibn Khaldun (1332–1395), who mocked the treasure hunters and their magic in the fifteenth century. "Suppose that a man did want to bury all his treasures and to keep them safe by means of some magical process," he wrote. "He would take all possible precautions to keep his secret hidden. How could one believe, then, that he would place unmistakable signs to guide those who sought the treasure, and that he would commit those signs to writing?"[5] Despite Ibn Khaldun's scorn, treasure hunters blasted and probed their way through ancient Egypt well into the nineteenth century, undeterred by murders and thefts, or by repeated failures. As late as 1907, Gaston Maspero, then director of antiquities in Egypt, arranged for the publication of *The Book of Hidden Pearls* at a very low price so that it was freely available as a worthless publication for the most gullible.

: :

The outside world knew little of the Egyptians and even less of their ancient civilization, for the governors of Egypt did little to encourage foreigners to visit the Nile. Christians were far from welcome once Islam took root in the country, as the Catholic monk Bernard the Wise found to his cost in 870. He and two companions had to bribe their ship's captain to put them ashore at Alexandria at all. Then the governor in Cairo cast them into jail until they gave him 300 denarii each. After gazing at "Joseph's granaries" (the pyramids), the pilgrims withdrew hastily to Jerusalem without any further archaeological inquiries. None of the various Christian pilgrims who strayed from the regular stamping grounds of such travelers in the Holy Land could be described as dispassionate observers, for they almost invariably interpreted the pyramids and other monuments in terms of the Hebrews and the biblical story.

A few educated and cultured Muslims contributed far more intelligent and perceptive observations. One such was an Arab doctor from Baghdad, Abdel Latif, who taught medicine in Cairo in about 1200. At that time there were few Europeans in Egypt. The superintendent of buildings in the city was busily quarrying away the smaller pyramids within easy reach of Cairo to construct a defense wall around the citadel. Latif ventured about two-thirds of the way into the upper part of the Great Pyramid, which he found crowded with treasure hunters armed with their pet handbooks and incantations. The much trampled passageways were choked with bat droppings and infested with a noxious stench. Latif fainted away in horror and emerged in a highly fearful state. But he was not too shocked to admire the fine hieroglyphs on the casing stones and the Sphinx. "This figure is very beautiful," he wrote, "and its mouth bears the seal of grace and beauty. It could be remarked that it smiles in a gracious manner." He ventured also to the ancient pharaonic capital at Memphis, where he described the ruins of the huge Roman city. "It requires a half-day's march in any direction to cross the visible ruins," he wrote. Six hundred years later, all that remained were a few mounds of earth and some fragmentary statues.[6]

The educated Europeans of five hundred years ago had access to almost no reliable information on Egypt at all, except for travelers' tales and hearsay brought home by returning Crusaders during the preceding centuries. They could, however, turn to *The Voiage and Travaile of Sir John Maundeville, Knight*, purportedly an accurate guidebook for pilgrims to the Holy Land, illuminated by the personal experiences of its devout author. This entertaining volume, a mine of information compiled from classical sources, fables, folklore, and highly unreliable travelers' tales, was soon regarded as the ultimate authority against which other accounts were checked. In fact, Sir John Maundeville never existed, and the author, Jean d'Outremeuse, a Liège notary, never visited the Nile at all. The whole work was a complete fabrication. This deliberate—and highly successful—literary fraud was widely quoted, especially its description of the pyramids. "And some men say that they be sepulchres of great lords, that were sometime, but that is not true, for all the common rumour and speech is all of the people there, both far and near, that they be the granaries of Joseph," was Maundeville's verdict on the pyramids—perhaps, indeed, a majority view, but not one shared by Brother Felix Fabri of Ulm in what is now Germany, who actually gazed on the pyramids and sensed (correctly) that they were "marvelous sepulchral monuments of the ancient kings of Egypt."[7]

Firsthand accounts of the Nile were still few and far between. Most people turned to the writings of the great Leo Africanus (1485–1554), a Catholic and a scholar whose wanderings over northern Africa in the early sixteenth century are of the greatest interest to African historians. Leo traveled all the way up the Nile to Aswan and the First Cataract, observing the life on its banks and the antiquities, which were not, however, his primary concern. His *History and Description of Africa*, as indispensable to the prospective traveler as Maundeville, makes only cursory mention of the pyramids and describes Memphis as a "citie that seemeth in times past to have beene very large." At Manfalut: "Near unto Nilus stand the ruines of a stately building which seemeth to have beene a temple in times past, among which ruines the citizens finde sometimes coine of silver, sometimes of gold, and sometimes of lead, having on the one side hielygraphick notes, and on the other side the pictures of ancient kings."[8]

: :

Only the most determined of travelers succeeded in reaching Egypt. The sea voyage across the Mediterranean, perhaps in a Venetian or Turkish galley, might take weeks. Brother Felix Fabri complained of drunken passengers who interrupted his Sunday sermons, and the loathsome occupation of all seamen—"the hunting and catching of lice and vermin." He had returned from Egypt on a Venetian spice galley, a vessel engaged in regular trading with the Alexandrians. The spices as well as other commodities came overland from the East and were funneled into Europe through Alexandria. Then in 1517, a few years after the Portuguese had opened up the Cape of Good Hope route to the east and monopolized the spice commerce, the Turks invaded Egypt, which became a province of the Turkish Empire. The new ruler, Selim I, confirmed earlier diplomatic treaties with France and Spain and granted a measure of religious protection to non-Muslims. It was now reasonably safe to travel in Egypt—if one managed to escape the attentions of pirates on the way to the Nile. A trickle of pilgrims, diplomats, and merchants made their way to Alexandria and farther inland in search of holy places, political advantage, or commercial opportunity. Most of these travelers were preoccupied with their commercial or religious objectives and were little concerned with scientific observation. But there were some more ambitious explorers. In 1533 Pierre Belon of France, a botanist, inspected the interior of the pyramid of Khufu at Giza and visited the Sphinx, which by this time had been mutilated—by Sheikh Muhammad in 1300.

: :

Every visitor saw a mummy, readily offered for sale in Cairo's bazaars. The ancient Egyptian dead had become profitable merchandise. The Egyptians themselves broke up wooden mummy cases for firewood and sold the corpses for medicinal purposes. The word *mummy* is derived from the

Persian word *mummia* (Arabic: *mumija*), a term for pitch or bitumen. Pissasphalt from the Near East had long been regarded as a useful cure for cuts and bruises and for the treatment of fractures, nausea, and a host of other ailments. The appearance of pissasphalt closely resembled that of the bituminous materials used by the ancient Egyptians in the mummification process. When supplies of pissasphalt were hard to come by, it became common practice to substitute the materials found inside the bodies of Egyptian mummies for the real thing. From there it was an even shorter step to substitute the dried flesh of the mummy for the hardened bituminous materials found in the body cavities.

"Mummy" had a long and respectable antiquity as a medicinal substance. As early as the tenth century, Arab doctors were describing the properties of a medical specific that had obviously been in use for centuries. The Arab historian and doctor Abdel Latif, whom we have already met admiring the Sphinx's smile, was evidently familiar with mummy: "The mummy found in the hollows of corpses in Egypt, differs but immaterially from the nature of mineral mummy; and where any difficulty arises in procuring, the latter may be substituted in its stead." By the sixteenth century, mummy had become a highly prized drug. A flourishing trade in mummified human flesh came into being. The medicinal substance left Egypt in the form of entire mummies or in fragments packaged in Cairo and Alexandria, whence merchants sent the dried substance all over western Europe. Peasant villagers dug up the tombs and transported mummy to Cairo, "where," recorded Abdel Latif in 1203, "it is sold for a trifle. For half a dirhem I purchased three heads filled with the substance. This mummy is as black as pitch. I observed, when exposed to the strong heat of the sun, that it melts."[9] Another Arab writer recorded in 1424 how

> people who had made a large pile of human corpses were discovered in Cairo. They were brought before the provost, who had them tortured until they confessed that they were removing the corpses from tombs and were boiling the dead bodies in water over a very hot fire until the flesh fell off; that they then collected the oil which rose to the surface of the liquid to sell it to the Franks, who paid twenty-five pieces of gold a hundredweight for it.[10]

Numerous foreign merchants traded in mummy, for the potential profits were enormous. The German traveler Johann Helferich of Leipzig, who visited Egypt in 1565, was so anxious to buy some mummies that he dug the sand out of several tombs in a fruitless search for ancient corpses. But few were as ambitious as John Sanderson, an energetic agent for the Turkey Company who spent a year in Egypt in 1585–1586. Sanderson lived in Alexandria, visited the pyramids and the Sphinx, and studied commercial opportunities in Cairo. But he spent much time at the famous Memphis mummy pits. The enterprising Sanderson was quick to cash in on the ancient Egyptians. He bought more than 270 kilograms (600 pounds) of mummified flesh and a whole body for export to England. Such an enormous shipment of mummy was unusual, but Sanderson simply bribed his way out of Egypt accompanied by his consignment and "divers heads, hands, arms and feet for a sheive." The market value of mummy in Scotland in 1612 was eight shillings a pound, so Sanderson made quite a profit.[11]

A French physician, Guy de la Fonteine of Navarre, investigated the mummy trade of Alexandria in 1564 and found clear evidence of fraud and use of modern corpses to satisfy an apparently insatiable demand for mummy. Many of the merchants who exported the substance cared little about the sources of mummy. Indeed, they marveled that Christians, so particular about their diet, could actually eat the bodies of the dead. Mummy was practically a patent medicine. Even King Francis I of France carried a small package of mummy with him as an emergency precaution. But not everyone was happy about mummy. "This wicked kinde of Drugge, doth nothing helpe the diseased it also inferres many troublesome symptoms, as the paire of the heart or stomacke, vomiting, and strike of the mouth," fumed one writer.[12]

The Egyptian government sought to restrict the wilder excesses of the mummy trade by levying harsh taxes on traders and forbidding the shipment of corpses out of Egypt. Apparently, the ships that carried mummies met violent storms so frequently that the superstitious crews regarded a cargo of mummy as unacceptably dangerous. But the threat of shipwreck and government regulations did not prevent fraud and the export of mummy; indeed, it persisted in medical use until the early nineteenth century.

The Elizabethan philosopher Sir Thomas Browne was very explicit: "Mummy is become merchandise, Mizraim cures wounds, and Pharaoh is sold for balsam." Even in Mark Twain's day, mummy was remembered, if only in a humorous context. On the Egyptian railroad, he recalled in *Innocents Abroad*, "the fuel they use for the locomotive is composed of mummies three thousand years old, purchased by the ton or by the grave-yard for that purpose, and sometimes one hears the profane engineer call out pettishly, 'D–n these plebeians, they don't burn worth a cent—pass out a king.'"[13] Even in the early twenty-first century there is said to be a regular, although very insignificant, demand for mummy among those who deal in magic and the occult. It is rumored that genuine powdered Egyptian mummy can be bought at some New York drugstores for con-siderably more than fifty dollars an ounce.

: :

The European Renaissance had emancipated people's minds from the stultifying fetters of medieval thinking. Culture and learning became fashionable pursuits, the collecting of antiquities a mark of a gentleman. Scholars and librarians dusted off ancient manuscripts, while leisured travelers pursued the Grand Tour to Mediterranean lands and returned home with collections of classical sculpture for their cabinets. The new scholarship triggered a curiosity about human diversity and the history of civilization. Soon, a new generation of dissertations on the state of the world gratified the literary tastes of cultivated gentlemen with specula-tions on the origins of civilization based on Greek and Roman sources.

The Grand Tour had made Italy a familiar stamping ground for even timid travelers. Some bolder souls journeyed as far as Greece, then a Mus-lim country under Turkish rule. Far fewer crossed to Alexandria and the Nile. Ancient Egyptian civilization was still virtually unknown to the out-side world. With the exception of the obelisks in Rome and Constantino-ple, few Egyptian antiquities were to be seen in Europe. Mummy was part of popular pharmacopoeia, so many people were aware of the ancient Egyptians' unusual burial customs. A few casual purchases reached Eu-rope. In 1615 Italian traveler Pietro della Valle brought back the first Mesopotamian cuneiform tablets with their wedge-shaped script from biblical Nineveh on the Tigris River. He also visited Egypt and purchased fine mummies at Saqqara.

Valle's artifacts caused quite a stir, and a rising interest in the mysteries of cuneiform and Egyptian hieroglyphs. They also stirred the acquisitive lusts of European nobility. In 1638, Ambassador du Houssay of France wrote to Cardinal Richelieu from Cairo about the collecting opportuni-ties in the eastern Mediterranean:

Since the most beautiful monuments of antiquity appear to have survived the perils of so many centuries solely to be judged worthy of a place
in your Eminence's libraries and cabinets, may I assure your Eminence
that in order to procure for them so glorious a shelter, that I have already
written throughout the Levant to impose the necessary orders in all
places where there are Consuls of France that they seek with great care all
such things as may be worthy of this honour.[14]

Houssay was merely pandering to the taste of the king and the French nobility for the exotic and curious, for the very finest in antiquities, those
worthy of the honor of gracing aristocratic homes.

The serious business of collecting antiquities had begun in the sixteenth century, when some Italian cardinals and the Medici prince
Cosimo I (1519–1574) had acquired large collections of antiquities, including a few Egyptian pieces. Travelers on the Grand Tour purchased
sculpture and statuary from Greek and Roman temples for their gardens
and cabinets. Early collectors were polymathic in their interests, with little sense of quality or geographic specialization. Coins, mummies, Indian
scalps, baskets, Polynesian axes, and papyri were all part of a cabinet of
curiosities. Large crowds pored over the mélanges of artifacts and exotic
statuary on display, the predecessors of today's museums. Collecting antiquities became a highly acceptable and potentially lucrative activity,
both for collectors and for the dealer who supplied them.

"I never saw a place I liked worse," wrote the Scottish explorer James
Bruce of Cairo in 1768. He added that "it afforded less pleasure and instruction than most places" and possessed antiquities that "less answered
their description."[15] Other travelers who visited the city after the sixteenth
century did not share Bruce's negative views of Cairo, where one could
purchase or experience almost anything. A new breed of visitor now ventured to the Nile in the wake of the merchant and pilgrim—the antiquarian in search of intellectual enlightenment and the antiquities themselves.
A flurry of leisured diplomatic activity had accompanied the Turkish annexation of Egypt. Many diplomatic visitors came to Cairo, some of them
to settle for long periods of time. Both new diplomats and more transient
visitors followed a well-trodden tourist circuit to the pyramids and the
mummy pits of Saqqara. They visited the bazaars in Cairo, where they
were able to examine completely bandaged corpses and marvel at the
blackened limbs and shriveled faces of age-old Egyptians. The curio deal-

ers were only too glad to supply the visitor to Alexandria or Cairo with amulets, scarabs, papyri, or even complete mummies—for a consideration. Even if prices seemed high, one could always sell one's purchases in Europe at an enormous profit.

The French kings and their noblemen were probably the most avid collectors of antiquities during the seventeenth and eighteenth centuries. Special parties of scholars journeyed to Mediterranean lands in search of coins, manuscripts, and all manner of antiquities on their behalf. Their undigested collections provided a catalyst for more detailed inquiry. A more serious objective was part of the specific instructions to Father J. B. Vansleb in 1671, a German in the service of Louis XIV who received orders to seek "the greatest possible number of good manuscripts and ancient coins for His Majesty's library" in Egypt and Ethiopia. Vansleb was to make a description of the peoples of both countries and "of the different manner of burial of divers peoples."[16]

Father Vansleb had an eventful journey, consoled by a "kilderkin of wine" that he guarded jealously from his fellow travelers. He tried to measure the pyramids of Giza with long pieces of string, but was unable to complete the task because of drifting sand. At Saqqara he had himself lowered into the mummy pits, where he acquired some mummified birds in earthenware pots. These he sent back to Paris with some Arab manuscripts, including one that described "the hiding places of all the treasures in Egypt." Disguising himself in Turkish dress, he traveled upstream from Cairo, only to be forced back because of threats on his life. He may well have been in danger, for the Turks knew he was an emissary of Louis XIV, whom they suspected of having designs on Egypt.

Vansleb now abandoned his intention of going to Ethiopia, and wrote to France complaining of the barbarity of the people and the tyranny of the Turkish authorities. In June 1672 he resumed his travels and nearly lost his life while attempting to visit the Coptic monasteries of Saint Macarious in Lower Egypt. His wine cask was the problem. A zealous Turkish magistrate incited some young people to ask Vansleb for a drink, a demand with which he refused to comply, pointing out that Muslims were forbidden wine. The following day, three young ruffians ambushed him and tried to throw his precious barrel into the Nile. Vansleb snatched his kilderkin; his Nubian servant, a man "of stout heart," cast one of the thugs into the Nile, and the incident ended with a fine of ten piastres for drinking alcoholic beverages. He appealed to the local *kachif* (tax collector) for protection and an escort. Instead, the *kachif* said he would accompany him to the monastery himself, and moved Vansleb to his house. Vansleb was now seriously worried, for the *kachif* had a reputation for timely assassinations. Fortunately, one of the *kachif*'s servants, whom Vansleb had tipped well some time before, came secretly and warned him to leave at once. Vansleb "had no further desire for sleep" at this news, stole quickly out of the village, and bribed a boat captain to take him aboard. Moments after they had cast off, the *kachif* and thirty horsemen came galloping along the bank in frustrated wrath. The perils of the king's service were too much for Vansleb, who retired to Constantinople to finish a book on the history of the Church in Alexandria before returning to France in 1676. There he was censured for not persevering with his journey to Ethiopia.

The lust for exotic artifacts turned local diplomats into ardent collectors. Diplomatic duties in Cairo or Alexandria were hardly arduous. The collection of antiquities offered a lucrative sideline, especially through local contacts forged in government service. Benoit de Maillet, one of the first of a new breed of diplomatic antiquarians and collectors, was French consul in Egypt from 1692 to 1708. He visited the interior of the Great Pyramid at Giza more than forty times, corresponded with scholars in France, and developed an outline scheme for the exploration of ancient Egypt that acted as a blueprint for Napoléon's expedition a century later. "We are told," he reported, "that there are still in Upper Egypt temples of which the blue or gilded vaultings are still as beautiful as if they had just been finished; there are idols of a prodigious size; columns without number." His diplomatic reports recommended that an accurate map of Egypt be compiled and that "persons wise, curious, and adroit" be encouraged to make a scientific exploration of the Nile Valley at a slow and deliberate pace. Just over a century later, Napoléon Bonaparte's savants carried out de Maillet's recommendations. Antiquities continued to interest his successors, including Paul Lucas, a goldsmith's son who came to Egypt on his own account to buy gems, coins, and curios. He later became an agent for Louis XIV, ordered in 1716 to "endeavour to open some pyramid in order to find out in a detailed manner all that this kind of edifice contains." But Lucas never opened a pyramid. Instead, he collected mummified birds at Saqqara and took a leisurely voyage upstream through Upper Egypt, where he admired the "vast palaces, magnificent temples, these obelisks, and the prodigious number of thick columns that are still standing," as he drifted slowly past.[17]

FIGURE 3.2
The tourist in Egypt.
A Victorian tourist
climbs a pyramid.

Occasional tourists inspected the pyramids of Giza, and allowed themselves to be pushed and shoved into the burial chambers. Nearly every visitor complained about the heat and stench inside the pyramids. Some fainted away from heat exhaustion; others, too plump for the narrow defiles, became stuck in the passages, to the discomfort of their companions. Local Arabs would help them climb up the outside, assisting them up the huge boulders, a popular excursion for Victorian tourists. To travel farther upstream along the Nile, the tourist struck a bargain with the skipper of a *dahabiyya*, a large sailing vessel that had plied the waters of the Nile as far upstream as the First Cataract and beyond for centuries. The tourist of two hundred years ago merely plugged into the local transportation system and visited the monuments at Thebes, Aswan, and other localities near the Nile. Until the advent of the railroad, motorcar, and airplane, no other logical means of transportation existed for either tourist or local traveler.

Every traveler paused in the bazaars of Cairo, too. Merchandise from all parts of the Arab world was for sale in the city, to say nothing of European trade goods and the products of tropical Africa. Great caravans arrived and departed from Cairo every day. The bazaars were alive with the bustle and never-ceasing ebb and flow of the world's commerce. Antiquities had been for sale in the bazaars of Cairo for centuries—curiosities fashioned into jewelry, as well as gold objects and other artifacts stolen from ancient tombs and offered on the open market. The occasional traveler purchased a shipment of mummy, or even a complete body. Most tourists departed with at least a scarab, statue, or amulet. But the serious collector of antiquities was still a rarity, except for the odd royal emissary or a leisured gentleman making antiquarian inquiries on his own account. A lucrative market in antiquities was already in being, but it was not on the scale that was to develop in later centuries, when the great museums of Europe began to vie with one another in building collections of Egyptian antiquities. But the demand for mummies kept the villagers of Saqqara more than busy with grave robbing. The market for the dead was seemingly insatiable and more profitable than agriculture. Elsewhere, the destruction of temples and pyramids for building stone proceeded apace. Bishop Richard Pococke, a British ecclesiastic who visited Egypt in 1737, was moved to lament: "They are every day destroying these fine morsels of Egyptian Antiquity; and I saw some of the pillars being hewn into millstones."[18]

Ancient Egypt was familiar territory to ardent readers of the Scriptures. Its pharaohs had been the hated oppressors of the Israelites, whose escape from bondage under Moses was familiar to every Bible reader. The biblical associations of the Nile fueled a lively market for travelogues. A gullible public devoured the "itineraries" of antiquarians and other travelers, while Egyptian antiquities became prized possessions of considerable social prestige and market value. Even the most miscellaneous collections excited considerable interest. In 1723, for example, one Thomas Serjeant displayed a "parcel of Egyptian Goods lately come from Grand Cairo" to a meeting of the Society of Antiquaries in London. The members were fascinated by "a brass Osiris, a brass Harpocrates, a Terminus, a naked brass figure distorted of better taste, Isis and bambino, a little Egyptian priest, a cat, a stone beetle, a curious beetle with wings and hieroglyphics in a curious paste of blew colour."[19]

The demand for Egyptian antiquities inevitably outstripped the supply, so prices rose, more people bought antiquities in Cairo and in auction rooms, and a new and lucrative trade came into being. For the first time, there were full-time collectors. European countries were gradually forming their own national museums, repositories for their own cultural heritages as well as those of other nations. One of the first was the British Museum, established by an act of Parliament in 1756. The vast agglomeration of artifacts and curiosities collected by Hans Sloane, an eminent physician and one of the founders of the museum, formed the nucleus of its collection. Some Egyptian lamps, papyri, and other small artifacts formed part of Sloane's collection, acquired, like all early collections, through extensive travel and purchases from dealers.

By this time, it had occurred to some visitors that it would be worth digging for antiquities on their own account. They obtained permits from the Turkish authorities to empty tombs and excavate around temples in search of inscriptions and statuary. The excavations were sometimes richly rewarded with mummies and fine grave ornaments, but were fraught with peril. The Arabs were convinced that Europeans had special magical spells under their command, which enabled them to locate the richest caches of gold and jewels. In at least one instance, reported by English traveler William George Browne, a Moroccan and a Greek were murdered in a temple at Thebes, simply because the Arabs suspected that they had brought spells for treasure hunting with them.[20] When any "treasure" was found, there was fierce rivalry for possession and profit. Collectors, dealers, local authorities, and the government all claimed their stake in any important discovery. When the French vice-consul at Alexandria shipped three statues to Paris in 1751, local envy was so intense that even the indifferent authorities claimed the finds by fiat. Only by the use of tact, maneuver, and money was he able to remove the statues. These types of transactions were to become common as the local people cashed in on temple and tomb with a brazen neglect for historical tradition and a thirst for profit, fueled by a persistent and growing foreign demand.

4 | Napoléon on the Nile

Soldiers, forty centuries of history look down upon you!

NAPOLÉON BONAPARTE,
before the Battle of the Pyramids, quoted in Nicholas Reeves,
Ancient Egypt: The Great Discoveries

By the early eighteenth century, Egypt was better known to travelers. Some of them spent extended periods of time in the Nile Valley wandering from temple to temple admiring the inscriptions and beautiful frescoes that highlighted the dramatic architecture of Egyptian temples. King Christian VI of Denmark was so interested in Egypt that he sent a special expedition out to the Nile. Frederick Lewis Norden (1708–1742), an artist and marine architect, served as leader and traveled deep into Upper Egypt. He tried to reach the Second Cataract, but was forced to turn back at Derr in Nubia. Norden was a thoroughly sober and hardworking observer of the Nile scene who recorded a mass of information on Egyptian monuments. His *Voyage d'Égypte et de Nubie* appeared in 1755 and was widely read by both scholars and the general public. His English translator commented that "the reader seems to accompany the author in his voyage, and to share all his pleasures without undergoing the fatigue and dangers."[1] For the first time, the public at large had access to a corpus of plans and drawings of Egyptian monuments that were both vivid and relatively accurate.

Norden was interested in the details of ancient life, a departure from earlier preoccupations with legend and fantasy. He admired the magnificent frescoes of the Battle of Kadesh executed in the temple at Luxor by order of Rameses II and examined fine tomb paintings that were as fresh as the day they were painted, preserved by the dry atmosphere of the

Egyptian climate. Norden found the Arabs preoccupied with treasure and magic. "Travellers must think themselves happy in being allowed to contemplate the ancient edifices, without daring to stir any thing. I shall never forget what a crowd of people was assembled, while we were mooring at Aswan, in order to see, as they said among themselves, expert sorcerers in the black magic art." His advice to prospective travelers was to the point: "Begin by dressing yourself in the Turkish manner. A pair of mustachios, with a grave and solemn air, will be very proper companions by which you will have a resemblance to the natives." The "sober and continent" antiquarian is advised to steer clear of prostitutes, for they will give him a memento "indelible by time, place, or mercury."[2]

: :

Norden's magnificent descriptions and fine drawings were all very well, but they threw almost no new light on the history of the ancient Egyptians themselves. They remained a shadowy people, known only from their spectacular monuments and the writings of Herodotus and other classical writers. No one knew how old the Egyptians were, nor had anyone been able to decipher their mysterious hieroglyphs. Clearly, the decipherment of ancient Egyptian writing would unleash a cascade of information about what was still considered to be the world's oldest civilization.

The speculations that surrounded hieroglyphs were quite extraordinary. Many people had tried to decipher the script, but their efforts had been in vain, largely because they assumed that Greek writers were correct in assuming that hieroglyphs were picture writing and that the symbols expressed mystical concepts. In 1419, a Greek manuscript titled *Hieroglyphica* written by an author named Horapollo in the fourth or fifth century appeared in Italy. One hundred and eighty-nine sections dealt with individual hieroglyphs. Unfortunately, Horapollo knew only a little about hieroglyphs and indulged his taste for fantasy on them, even inventing some symbols. *Hieroglyphica* appeared in print in 1505 and went through numerous printings. Many intellectuals seized on Horapollo's fantasies with avidity and proclaimed that their symbolic meanings held the secrets of true knowledge. The idea that hieroglyphs had symbolic meanings muddied the decipherment waters for many generations. Theories were legion. One worthy scholar believed that the Egyptians had founded a colony in China and that hieroglyphs were developed from Chinese script. Bishop William Warburton of Gloucester argued more soberly that the Egyptians used their script for day-to-day purposes and not for mystical objectives.[3] He showed how the script had evolved from a form of picture writing into a simpler hand used on a daily basis. But to study ancient Egypt was to become intensely frustrated. The hieroglyphs were apparently unintelligible; most of the principal monuments that were still above ground had been visited and reported upon by more than a few scholars. Large-scale excavation was beyond the resources of any one traveler, and no foreign government had thought to organize such investigations. The serious scholar was baffled, and the treasure hunter still unaware of the tremendous riches that awaited discovery at Thebes, in the Valley of the Kings, and elsewhere.

Only the philosophers flourished, not least among them Constantin-François Chasseboeuf, Comte de Volney (1757–1820), who spent four years in Egypt and Syria studying the history and political and social institutions of both countries. He paused to admire the pyramids and deplored the extravagance of the despots who built these and other massive structures at the expense of the slavery of their fellow countrymen. "While the lover of the arts may wax indignant when he sees the columns of the palace being sawn up to make millstones," he wrote, "the philosopher cannot help smiling at the secret malice of fate that gives back to the people what cost them so much misery, and that assigns to the most humble of their needs the pride of useless luxury."[4] Chasseboeuf was more than a moralist, or even an intellectual revolutionary, for his book was an excellent campaign handbook for generals and a prized possession of one of history's greatest adventurers, Napoléon Bonaparte (1769–1821), who organized the first massive assault on the ramparts of ancient Egypt.

: :

By the late eighteenth century, Europe and the United States were feeling the effects of accelerating technological innovation. The discovery of steam power and the use of coal were transforming industrial production. On the political scene, the American and French Revolutions had excited the imagination of intelligent observers on both sides of the Atlantic. But Egypt remained an obscure and half-forgotten country on the fringes of the Mediterranean. Ruled in name by the Turkish sultan in Constantinople, it was controlled in practice by the Mamluks, aristocratic mercenaries interested in little but the proceeds of harsh taxation. Their country remained an area of negligible political importance—hot, dusty, and entirely alien to European eyes. Yet even in the eighteenth century, Egypt was respected for its original contributions to civilization and for the high antiquity of its institutions. And its geographical position was of key importance, for to control Egypt was to threaten the busy land routes to rich British possessions in India.

Twenty-nine-year-old General Napoléon Bonaparte was the man who pushed Egypt into the center of the world stage. French interest in the Nile had been on the increase since the 1770s, partly because of lobbying by French merchants in Egypt, foreign exiles in a hostile country. Many government officials in Paris also believed that Egypt had tremendous commercial potential and feared a British takeover of the strategically important Nile Valley. They had good reason for apprehension, for the Ottoman Empire was weak and corrupt—so much so that nineteenth-century statesmen called it "the sick man of Europe." Ambitious nations were already chipping away at outlying portions of the sultan's territories. Egypt, under only nominal rule by the sultan, was a natural candidate for annexation by an expanding European power.

The French were slow to contemplate any political initiatives, partly because of domestic upheavals and also for financial reasons. But when Napoléon concluded his bloody conquest of Italy with the Peace of Campo Formio in 1797, his restless mind turned to new projects whose boldness and success would further his political ambitions. He became obsessed with the East, a fascination that was to grip many politicians of the next century, among them Benjamin Disraeli and Napoléon III. General Napoléon's ruthless mind turned toward ideas of worldwide conquest, toward the creation of a great French empire centered on the Orient and ultimately on India, where the British had expelled the French in the mid-eighteenth century.

By April 1798, Napoléon had been authorized to mount an expedition to seize Malta and Egypt and to build a canal at the Isthmus of Suez. The government approved the campaign to get the ambitious Napoléon out of the way. The general was convinced that glory beckoned, that an empire awaited him in the East, as if he were the second Alexander the Great. On May 19, 1798, he sailed from Toulon with a fleet of 328 ships and an expeditionary force of 38,000 soldiers and 10,000 civilians to conquer

Egypt, landing at Abukir Bay near Alexandria on July 1. The special Scientific and Artistic Commission carefully selected by Napoléon accompanied the expedition to provide a cultural and technological background to his ambitious plans for the colonization of the Nile Valley. The commission consisted of 167 scientists and technicians, soon contemptuously nicknamed "the Donkeys" by the military. Napoléon's Scientific and Artistic Commission had been set up on the general's own initiative, although the French foreign minister under the directory, Charles-Maurice de Talleyrand-Périgord (1754–1838), at the time a supporter of Napoléon, had espoused the general idea years before. In the spring of 1798, the young general had attended a meeting of the Institute of France attended by the leading scientists of the Republic. He had harangued them on the importance of Egypt to contemporary scholarship and intellectual life, and pressed for a strong intellectual backing for his new campaign.

The chief recruiter of the savants was Claude-Louis Berthollet, a physician and chemist who succeeded in assembling a remarkable group of talented men around him, with an average age of twenty-five. There were artists, agronomists, botanists, chemists, engineers, even musicians and a master printer. None of the savants were Egyptologists—such a discipline did not exist. But many of them returned as enthusiastic students of ancient Egypt. Jean-Michel de Venture was a distinguished Orientalist, Étienne Geoffroy Saint-Hilaire a zoologist and lifelong friend of the celebrated paleontologist Georges Cuvier. Geoffroy Saint-Hilaire's ideas foreshadowed some of Darwin's evolutionary theories. Gaspard Monge, a mathematician and chemist, was a fervent republican and a steel and gunpowder expert; his most recent appointment had been to a different body, the Government Commission for the Research of Artistic and Scientific Objects in Conquered Countries. This commission had followed in the wake of Bonaparte's armies in Italy and examined art collections, museums, and libraries, deciding which objects were to be ceded to the French Republic under the terms of peace treaties. One has only to tour the Louvre to see how efficient the commission was—the expropriated works include the Mona Lisa. Monge was obviously a highly qualified recruit for the commission.

Then there was fifty-one-year-old Baron Dominique-Vivant Denon, a diplomat and artist extraordinaire. Denon had been the supervisor of a collection of antique gems under King Louis XV and had also, it was rumored, been a favorite of Madame de Pompadour. For a while he filled a

FIGURE 4.1   French savants measure the Sphinx at Giza. From *Description de l'Égypte.*

post at the French Embassy in St. Petersburg, Russia, and was much admired by Catherine the Great. His career as a diplomat gave him a wide experience of the world and a broad knowledge of the arts of eighteenth-century Europe. He was fond of women, a sparkling conversationalist, and a member of the French Academy.

At the time of the French Revolution he was living in Florence, pursuing a leisured life among art treasures and friends whom he enjoyed. Immediately upon hearing the news of political upset, he returned to France only to find that he was on a list of proscribed names and that the revolutionary authorities had confiscated his real estate and financial holdings. Denon was reduced to poverty almost overnight. He vegetated in the Paris slums, eking out a bare existence by selling drawings and the eighteenth-century equivalent of picture postcards. Fortunately, however, he came to the notice of a well-known painter of the French Revolution, Jacques-Louis David, who employed him as a minor functionary in his studio. Through this connection, he won the goodwill of a number of revolutionary leaders. Denon's diplomatic skills soon came again into public view and, indeed, were remembered from an earlier time. The revolutionary government eventually restored Denon's properties at the direct order of the notorious Robespierre. The artist-cum-diplomat soon met Napoléon and the Empress Josephine and was high in the favor of senior French scientists.

Denon's reputation was not only firmly based in scientific circles, however. His *Oeuvre Priapique*, a collection of vivid pornographic etchings, highly explicit even by French standards of the time, was popular reading among the intelligentsia. A major portion of the illustrative responsibility of the commission's work fell to Denon. Fortunately for Egyptology, a rapturous enthusiasm for the antiquities of the Nile and everything Egyptian guided his skills.

The commission's work was the most lasting result of one of Napoléon's most unsuccessful military campaigns. Its members accomplished an immense amount of scientific research in twenty months of work. Fortunately, the members were well prepared for their huge task, bringing with them from France a library of more than five hundred works that contained a copy of practically every book ever published about the Nile, many crates of scientific apparatuses and measuring instruments, as well as printing presses with Arabic, Greek, and other fonts.

The work of the Scientific and Artistic Commission started soon after Napoléon reached Cairo on July 21, 1798. He took immediate steps to set up the Institut de l'Égypte in the capital, housed in an elegant Cairo palace. Napoléon himself took an active interest in its activities and attended many of the institute's regular meetings. His instructions to the savants were simple: study all of Egypt, spread enlightened ideas and habits, and furnish information to the occupying authority.

Months of astonishingly prolific and fruitful scientific activity ensued. Scientists from totally different academic disciplines worked harmoniously together, united by a common fascination with a new and virtually unknown country. They exchanged local knowledge and stimulated one another's creativity by chance conversations and regular seminars. The scientists were deeply involved in the administration of Egypt, too, serving on committees and medical commissions, or answering the myriad practical questions thrown at them by Napoléon and his generals. Yet pure research held pride of place, with important papers read at regular seminars—on the technical processes used by Egyptian craftsmen, on experimental agriculture, and, a topical subject, contributed by mineralogist Deodate Gratet de Dolomicu, on the "selection, conservation, and transportation of ancient monuments" to be shipped to France.

The commission's greatest discovery came not at the hands of one of its members, but from an accidental find made by a soldier named D'Hautpoul, part of a squad erecting coastal defense works just north of the town of Rosetta (el-Rachid) in the Nile Delta. He stumbled across an inscribed granite stela in one of the piles of boulders once used as ballast by ships that had moored in the nearby medieval port that were being recycled into his fortifications.[5] (Experts believe the stone probably originated in the delta town of Sais.) His commander, engineer Lieutenant Pierre François Xavier Bouchard, reported the find to his superiors, who in turn passed the find on to the institute.

On July 19, 1799, a letter from the surgeon Michel-Ange Lancret announced that "citizen Bouchard, officer of engineers, had discovered in the town of Rosetta some inscriptions which may offer much interest."[6] The assembled savants realized at once that the Rosetta stone might provide the key to the decipherment of Egyptian hieroglyphs. There were three versions of a decree, one in formal hieroglyphs; the second in demotic, the freehand version of Egyptian script; and the third in Greek. The inscription itself dated to March 27, 196 BC. The text, promulgated on stone throughout the land by the Egyptian priesthood, honored the anniversary of pharaoh Ptolemy V's succession to the throne. Explicit instructions came from the stone itself: "They shall write the decree on a stela of hard stone in the script of the words of god [formal hieroglyphs], the script of documents [demotic] and the script of the Ionians [Greek] and set it up in the first-rank temples, the second-rank temples and the third-rank temples, in the vicinity of the divine image of the pharaoh living forever."[7]

The Rosetta stone was the most important item in the savants' collections, but there was much more. While Napoléon attempted a draconian overhaul of Egypt's administration, small groups of savants traversed the length and breadth of the country, as far upstream as the First Cataract. They traveled with the army, roughing it under the stars, sometimes fighting alongside the infantry, enduring harsh treks across savage desert terrain. Each of them became field-workers as well as scholars, and served as soldiers and administrators, and, above all, as inventors and archaeologists. They developed new kinds of water pumps, edited a journal for the troops published every ten days, presided over courts, and made pencils from melted-down lead bullets. The 167 scientists were the Enlightenment in action, as interested in traditional medicine and the diversity of the Egyptian population as they were in fish and mammals.

Few scientific expeditions have ever left such a legacy, especially in Egyptology and geography. The cartographers on the commission's staff produced the first detailed map of Egypt, which was of no use to Napoléon, as it was published long after his eclipse. Its artists contributed a stunning visual impression of a hitherto little-known country, especially the omnipresent Denon. When General Desaix de Veygoux marched up the Nile from Cairo in pursuit of Murat Bey in August 1798, Denon, by now a hardened and indefatigable traveler who was able to discover and record with uncanny accuracy the glories of ancient Egyptian architecture and sculpture, joined him.

Denon had spent his early months in Egypt sketching and observing the local scene, attending meetings of the institute, and busily recording his impressions. He was rapturous about the pyramids: "The great distance from which they can be perceived makes them appear diaphanous, tinted with the bluish tone of the sky, and restores to them the perfection and purity of the angles which the centuries have marred." His expectations for the perilous journey with Desaix de Veygoux were boundless, for, as he wrote later: "I was about to tread the soil of a land covered since immemorial times with a veil of mystery from Herodotus to our own times, all the travelers were content to sail up the Nile rapidly, not daring to lose sight of their boats, and leaving them only in order to inspect, hastily and uneasily, the objects closest to shore."[8] The right man had arrived in the Nile Valley at the right moment.

Denon's precise, and perhaps rather stiff, record of the major monuments of the Nile was a remarkable tour de force carried out under incredibly difficult conditions. Desaix de Veygoux's army made forced marches of 40 to 50 kilometers (25 to 30 miles) a day, constantly in danger of raids from marauding warriors. At Hermopolis, the ancient Khemenu, the "Eight Towns," a cult center of the scribe god, Thoth, Denon was given but a few minutes to make a sketch of a New Kingdom temple erected by Seti I and Rameses II in the thirteenth century BC. At Dendera, cult center of the cow goddess, Hathor, south of Abydos, he was more fortunate. The army lingered in admiration at the magnificent temple of Hathor for a day. Denon was enraptured: "Pencil in hand, I passed from object to object, drawn away from one thing by the interest of another. I felt ashamed of the inadequacy of the drawings I made of such sublime

FIGURE 4.2   The interior of the temple of Hathor at Dendera. A
characteristically evocative reconstruction from *Description de l'Égypte*.

things."⁹ The sun set. Denon remained oblivious, wrapped in artistic rapture, until his commanding officer, General Belliard, himself escorted him
home to the distant army at a gallop.

Then, on January 27, 1799, the army rounded a bend of the Nile and
came in sight of the temples of Amun at Luxor and Karnak. The regiments
came to a spontaneous halt and burst into applause. "Without an order
being given, the men formed their ranks and presented arms, to the accompaniment of the drums and the bands," wrote a lieutenant on the expedi-
tion.¹⁰ Denon was already sketching, conscious of a great and emotional moment when an entire army paid a spontaneous tribute to antiquity. Wherever
the army went, Denon went too, riding furiously in search of monuments
and sketching under fire or even when in danger of capture. Denon eventually reached Aswan, where he visited the islands of Elephantine and Philae.

Denon's work aroused tremendous enthusiasm for archaeology, especially among the hydraulic engineers charged with improving Egyptian
agriculture. The engineers were soon neglecting their own dull work and

FIGURE 4.3   French savants sail past the Island of Philae. From *Description de l'Égypte.*

making a beeline for temples and tombs, recording architectural features, hieroglyphic inscriptions, and all the magnificent panoply of ancient Egypt. Pencils ran out, lead bullets were frantically melted down as substitutes, and a vast body of irreplaceable information was recorded for posterity. At the same time, they removed small antiquities by the hundreds from temple and tomb.

::

Napoléon's expedition to Egypt was doomed to military failure from the beginning, largely because of the vulnerability of its seaborne communications. At first, all was success. He captured Alexandria, advanced on Cairo, and defeated the Mamluks at the Battle of the Pyramids, which was actually fought some kilometers away. But disaster stalked downstream. While he occupied Cairo, Admiral Horatio Nelson and his fleet descended on the French armada anchored in Abukir Bay west of Alexandria. On August 1, 1798, Nelson pounced on the trapped transports and warships. By the end of the day, Napoléon was cut off from his supply lines and his army marooned in the Nile Valley. Many of the savants' as yet unloaded books and instruments went to the bottom.

The campaign staggered on for another year. An expeditionary force under General Desaix de Veygoux overran Upper Egypt, his soldiers plagued by misery, hunger, Egyptian eye disease, and many other misfortunes. Finally, on August 19, 1799, Napoléon abandoned his army and fled from Egypt on a fast ship. The army surrendered to British forces in 1801, and the abortive expedition was over. The resulting Treaty of Alexandria guaranteed safe passage for the scientists back to France. By that time, the savants had assembled in Alexandria, where the British inspected their baggage. The French commander, General Abdallas Jacques-François de Menou, surrendered the city to General Hutchinson of the British army. He was one of those persons who cannot conclude an agreement of any sort without recrimination and debate. No sooner had the military agreement been signed than Menou and Hutchinson began to dicker over the savants and their collections. The British claimed all the antiquities under a clause of the capitulation agreement. Menou stated that the Rosetta stone, the prize of the whole collection, was his personal property. But the scientists, led by the zoologist Geoffroy Saint-Hilaire, declared that they would rather follow their collections to England than give them up. Menou was obliged to grant their request and did so with ill grace: "I have just been informed that several among our collectors wish to follow their seeds, minerals, birds, butterflies or reptiles wherever you choose to ship their crates," he wrote pettishly. "I do not know if they wish to have themselves stuffed for the purpose, but I can assure you that if the idea should appeal to them, I shall not prevent them."[11]

The scientists then threatened to burn their specimens if there was a chance they would lose them. Geoffroy Saint-Hilaire was explicit in his discussions with British diplomat Sir William Hamilton:

> Without us this material is a dead language that neither you nor your scientists can understand. Sooner than permit this iniquitous and vandalous spoliation we will destroy our property, we will scatter it amid the Libyan sands or throw it into the sea. We shall burn our riches ourselves. It is celebrity you are aiming for. Very well, you can count on the long memory of history: You also will have burnt a library in Alexandria.

Fortunately, General Hutchinson was a man of some vision and imagination, sufficiently impressed by the savants' eloquence to allow the scientists to keep their collections. But he insisted on retaining the Rosetta stone and some large specimens, including two obelisks and two sarcophagi, as well as a large statue of Rameses II. Menou yielded the stone reluctantly. Even then, the scientists tried to hide the Rosetta stone on a boat, but William Hamilton discovered it and recovered the stela with a military escort. In a concession to science, the French were allowed to keep imprints they had made of the inscriptions before relinquishing the precious artifact.

Everyone already knew that the Rosetta stone was a find of preeminent importance. By order of King George III, it was housed in the British Museum in London. To this day, the Rosetta stone graces the Egyptian galleries of the museum. Only once has it left its adopted home—for a temporary exhibition in the Louvre in 1973. It has never been exhibited in Egypt.

Back in Europe, news of the Scientific and Artistic Commission's work spread rapidly. Denon returned to Paris to an enthusiastic reception. He was made the first director of the Louvre and founded the Egyptian collections of that great institution, continuing to collect works of art for the French national collections throughout the remainder of Napoléon's political career. His *Voyages dans la basse et la haute Égypte* was published in 1801 and soon became a best-seller translated into several languages. The *Voyages* revealed an exotic land virtually unknown in scientific circles. Denon's artistry added spice and color to his adventures, which lost nothing in the telling.

There was far more to come. Napoléon's expedition was an abject military failure, but it was a scientific triumph whose legacy resonates through Egyptology. The 167 savants left a remarkable epitaph behind them, a monument of interdisciplinary research that was the first of its kind. For years, the survivors of the expedition labored on a masterpiece, the twenty-volume *Description de l'Égypte*. The *Description* is a monster work by any standard. Eighteen years in the making, the first volume of twenty appeared in 1809, published "by the orders of His Majesty the Emperor Napoléon the Great." The last volume came out in 1828, largely because of the devotion of the engineer and geographer Edmé Jomard, who lived long enough to see the revival of the Institut de l'Égypte in 1859.[12] A second edition appeared between 1820 and 1830.

The sumptuous and magnificently illustrated folios of the *Description* caused a sensation in European cultural and scholarly circles. They depicted the riches of ancient Egypt with a vivid accuracy that had never been witnessed before. The delicate lines and colors of paintings and inscriptions were brilliantly executed on a large-scale format that made every minor detail spring to the entranced eye. Artifacts, hieroglyphs, temples, and the landscape of Egypt literally spring from the page. It is difficult for us living in a world of instant communication and of easy familiarity with the pyramids and the ancient Egyptians to understand the tremendous impact of the *Description*. The savants revealed a marvelous, flourishing early civilization whose monuments had stood the test of thousands of years of wars and neglect. Temple after temple, pyramid after pyramid, artifact after artifact—Denon and his colleagues laid out before a delighted public a romantic and exciting world of exotic and fascinating antiquity. As many researchers have pointed out, before Napoléon's expedition the monuments of Egypt were quite well known in European antiquarian and scientific circles, where the impact of the *Description* was less marked. The work of the commission added flames to an already general enthusiasm for things Egyptian, reflected, among other things, in the sets for Mozart's opera *The Magic Flute*.

From the museum point of view, the finds of the French expedition were of extraordinary value and rarity. The British Museum, for example, contained but a handful of Egyptian antiquities in 1800, most of them mummies, scarabs, and small ornaments. Now the savants had acquired an enormous new collection of Egyptian antiquities, many of them of great beauty. The new artifacts transformed appreciation of pharaonic art, which was totally different from the familiar classical traditions.

The knowledge obtained from the commission's work was even more significant than its collections. Although the savants did not discover any new sites or spectacular temples, the work of the French was apparently so accurate and was published so beautifully that the general public was able to appreciate the extraordinary range and quality of the antiquities of the Nile. The French expedition and its publications provided a catalyst for further study of ancient Egypt and the decipherment of hieroglyphs when it was later realized that many of the savants' copies were inaccurate.

The *Description* also fueled a frenzied scramble for Egyptian antiquities, triggered, also, by popular enthusiasm for the exotic and by an increasing familiarity with Egypt among soldiers and diplomats.

∷

The British chose to leave Egypt to the Turks rather than annex it in the name of George III. A desultory occupation by the British army under the

earl of Cavan lasted a year, enough time to hand the reins of government
back to the emissaries of the Turkish Empire. The sultan himself had little interest in Egypt, provided his annual taxes were paid on time. Power
ful landlords who harshly exploited the poor for ever higher taxes dominated the Nile Valley. Egypt was desperately in need of leadership and
strong government.

The hour produced the man, a ruler who had a catastrophic effect on
the archaeology of ancient Egypt. Muhammad Ali was an Albanian or-
phan and mercenary who rose to powerful commands in the Turkish
army in Egypt through sheer ability. In 1805 he took the government of
Egypt into his own hands, was named pasha, and, after years of civil war,
broke the power of the Mamluks and became for all intents and purposes
the independent ruler of the Nile Valley. This capable and ruthless man
governed the affairs of Egypt from 1805 to 1849. A well-built and intelli-
gent-looking ruler, Ali provided Egypt with a firmer government than it
had enjoyed in centuries, although his rule was far from benevolent toward his humble subjects, who suffered under high taxes and harsh
corvée-labor drafts. His thirst for power and international influence was
tempered with a desire to bring Western technology to the Nile, to harness
the river for agriculture, and to introduce industrial manufacturing to
Egypt. Competent foreigners with new ideas were welcomed in Cairo.
Many of them were put to work developing factories, encouraging industry, and designing irrigation schemes. Unfortunately, many of Ali's most
ambitious schemes foundered in a sea of bureaucratic inefficiency and the
innate conservatism of the peasants and his ministers.

Muhammad Ali was friendly toward foreigners and did a great deal to
open up the Nile Valley not only to merchants and diplomats but also to
the casual tourist and antiquities dealer. What matter if many of the visitors were interested in antiquities and ransacking ancient tombs? To a
despotic ruler interested in international power and foreign capital, the
monuments of ancient Egypt were of little interest except as a diplomatic
lever or a way of keeping powerful visitors with strange hobbies interested
in Egypt.

Soon, a steady stream of collectors, dealers, diplomats, tourists, and
just plain shady characters descended on Egypt to strip the country of artifacts large and small. Some of them just wanted exotic objects for their
own collections. Most saw a chance for a quick profit from the antiquities
trade.

The British occupation force started the scramble. The earl of Cavan took a fancy to one of the obelisks of Alexandria and obtained a permit from the Turkish authorities to remove it to London as a memorial to the British victories in Egypt. The soldiers themselves were enthusiastic about the scheme, subscribed money for a ship, and volunteered their labor to transport the obelisk. London was unenthusiastic, so the obelisk remained in the squalor of Alexandria until 1877, when it was finally transported to London on the initiative of Erasmus Wilson, a wealthy businessman. The seventy-year delay was entirely due to British government disinterest, despite renewed invitations from both Muhammad Ali and his successor, the khedive Ismail. Only when a Greek landowner threatened to cut up the obelisk for building stone did private initiative save from destruction what is now known as Cleopatra's Needle. The Needle resides incongruously on the London Embankment overlooking the River Thames.

: :

Then came the diplomats. Britain and France, as well as other powers, maintained a diplomatic presence in Cairo and Alexandria during the early nineteenth century. In the early years of Muhammad Ali's rule, the political functions of the consuls were minimal. Diplomats had a great deal of spare time for travel and to fossick in ancient Egyptian ruins.

Bernardino Michele Maria Drovetti (1776–1852), a Piedmontese, was the first French consul general. An ambitious, driven man of magnificently villainous appearance, complete with a curled mustache, Drovetti enjoyed a distinguished military career, acquired French citizenship, and reached the rank of major in Napoléon's Piedmontese regiments, finally giving sterling service as a military judge. In 1802, he was appointed deputy commissioner of commercial relations at the French consulate in Alexandria. He remained at the consulate until 1815, acquiring a reputation as a superlative diplomat, high in Muhammad Ali's favor. He played a major role in stabilizing the pasha's regime. We do not know when Drovetti first became interested in antiquities, but he organized the unwrapping of a mummy in 1812 for some French and English guests, among them that remarkable traveler Lady Hester Lucy Stanhope. "A French surgeon performed the dissecting part, which consisted in dividing a vast number of folds of fine linen or cotton, which bandaged the body tight from head to foot. When these were removed, the right hand was found to hold a papyrus. The features were not in good preservation."[13]

Relieved of his post in 1815, Drovetti was free to devote himself to antiquities and to travel, journeying to the Second Cataract in 1816. He admired the buried facade of the Abu Simbel temple and offered the local headman three hundred piastres to open it, to no avail. These were the years when he collected extensively around Thebes in ferocious competition with Giovanni Belzoni, the strongman turned tomb robber whom we will encounter in Chapter 5. Drovetti also traveled extensively to the oases of the Western Desert before becoming French consul general again in 1821, a post he held until he retired in 1829.

This talented and hardworking man strongly influenced Muhammad Ali in matters of governmental policy. He also enjoyed enormous prestige with the Egyptians themselves. His interest in antiquities appears to have been strictly commercial. He pursued the past with a ruthless intensity that made him considerable sums of money.

Colonel Ernest Missett (?–1820), a well-known and influential diplomat, served Britain's interests as consul from 1802. He retired on grounds of ill health in 1816. Missett was not particularly interested in archaeology, but his successor, Henry Salt (1770–1827), certainly was. Salt's early education was at best desultory until his teens, when he was sent to London to study landscape and portrait painting. He enrolled as a student at the Royal Academy and made a very casual living as a portrait painter, a career that at least brought him in contact with a wide range of people. One of these was Lord Valentia, later to become Lord Mountnorris, a wealthy aristocrat with a penchant for leisured travel to remote parts of the world. In 1802 Lord Valentia planned a journey to India and the East. Salt acquired the post of secretary and draftsman to the expedition. Valentia's journey lasted four and a half years and culminated in a voyage of exploration along the Red Sea coast of Africa on board the warship HMS *Panther*, a side trip that provided Salt with his first taste of exploration.

The young secretary now led a small party sent to the uplands of Ethiopia. At this time Ethiopia was a little-known and mysterious country, almost closed to Europeans. Its diplomatic and commercial potential was still unrealized, although many people were curious about the caliber and ambitions of its rulers. Salt and his party penetrated some distance inland and were hospitably entertained by the *ras* (ruler) of Tigray in northern Ethiopia, who even gave them letters and presents for the king of England purporting to come from the emperor of Ethiopia. This small expedition brought Salt to the attention of the Foreign Office, which sent him out on a second mission to Ethiopia with instructions to obtain details about the state of trade in the country. The new mission failed, for Salt was unable to go farther inland than Tigray, owing to disturbed political conditions in the far interior. Nevertheless, Salt published a book, *A Voyage to Abyssinia* (1814), which brought his name to public notice at an opportune moment when people with experience of Egypt and the Red Sea region were in short supply.

Salt had spent some time in Egypt in 1807 where he had indulged his antiquarian interests, whetted by the discovery of a Greek inscription at the ancient city of Aksum in the Ethiopian highlands.[14] The Nile Valley attracted him enormously, and he was determined to return. In early 1816, he heard that Colonel Missett had resigned. He immediately lobbied for the appointment, getting his influential friends to write to the foreign secretary in his support. Lord Castlereagh confirmed his appointment on very short notice. Henry Salt found himself an influential figure in Egyptian affairs at the age of thirty-five.

The duties of the British and French consuls general were far from arduous. Both enjoyed considerable influence with the pasha, but the political issues were hardly of major importance. Relatively few foreigners resided permanently in Cairo. The British colony was tiny, and a representative in Alexandria handled maritime affairs. It is quite clear, however, that Salt's sponsors had other ideas as to how he might best employ his time. The elderly naturalist Sir Joseph Banks, who had accompanied Captain Cook to Tahiti in 1769 and acquired an international reputation as a scientist as a result, was now a trustee of the British Museum and saw Salt as a potential source of Egyptian antiquities for the national collections. The diplomat Sir William Hamilton, already notorious for his involvement in the Elgin Marbles controversy, was now undersecretary of state at the Foreign Office. He was much more explicit and urged Salt in an official memorandum to collect as many antiquities for "an enlightened nation" as possible.[15]

Salt himself had a firm, and unfounded, belief in his skills as an Egyptologist and developed a deep interest in hieroglyphs. His character was a moody one. He alternated between intense optimism and deep depression, and had a tendency to procrastinate and be irresolute at times when quick decisions were needed, qualities that were dangerous when con-

FIGURE 4.4   Bernardino Drovetti *(left)* and Henry Salt *(right)*. From the author's collection.

fronted with Drovetti's mercurial passion and the pasha's sudden changes of direction and unpredictable moods. Nevertheless, he enjoyed considerable influence with the Egyptian government. Many privileges and concessions were extended to him, a range of opportunities that provoked an intense rivalry between the British and French consuls general—Drovetti with his restless energy and deep bonds of affection with headmen and villages, and Salt, a more remote person, with money to spend and considerable political prestige.

Theoretically, the pasha himself controlled archaeological excavations in the Nile Valley. Any potential excavation required a *firman* (permit) to search for antiquities and to remove them from Egypt. The influential Drovetti and Salt were able to obtain as many *firman*s as they wanted. Their greed and rivalry became so intense that they reached an unspoken gentlemen's agreement, if that is an appropriate description, to carve up the Nile Valley into "spheres of influence." Other acquisitive visitors watched their step. Both Drovetti and Salt were so influential that they could arrange for the denial of *firman*s and ensure that local headmen would warn off potential excavators or refuse them laborers.

The consuls' activities legitimated the antiquities trade by creating an umbrella of casual tolerance for collecting. Some remarkable characters took up residence in Egypt on the alert for a quick killing. The Marseillais sculptor Jean Jacques Rifaud (1786–1852) was one longtime resident who went to Egypt in 1805 with the express intention of excavating and selling portable antiquities. This temperamental man ended up working for Drovetti for some years, accompanying him on his trip to the Second Cataract in 1816. An Armenian merchant named Giovanni Anastasi (1780–1860) was another well-known character. His father had been a major supplier of Napoléon's commissariat and a surveyor who went bankrupt after the French defeat. After great effort, Anastasi became a successful merchant and subsequently Swedish-Norwegian consul general in Egypt, as well as a highly successful dealer in antiquities and especially papyri, bought through agents from tomb robbers at Saqqara. Artists, entrepreneurs, merchants, or just plain adventurers came to Egypt in search of treasure.

No qualifications were needed to become a dealer or excavator, simply a tough constitution to cope with the harsh Nile environment, an ability to use bribery and gunpowder, and the political finesse that enabled successful applications for permits and delicate negotiations with other interested parties. Those were the rough-and-ready days of excavating. An excavator simply appropriated anything to which he took a fancy, from a scarab to an obelisk. They settled their differences with the help of thugs or with guns. One of the main characters of these far-from-heroic years of pillage and destruction was a giant and circus strongman, Giovanni Battista Belzoni, one of the most fascinating personalities ever to become involved in archaeology.

PART TWO

THE GREAT BELZONI

I do not mean to say that fortune has made me rich; I do not consider all rich men fortunate; but she has given me that satisfaction, that extreme pleasure, which wealth cannot purchase; the pleasure of discovering what has long been sought in vain, and of presenting the world with a new and perfect monument of Egyptian antiquity . . . appearing as if just finished on the day we entered it.

GIOVANNI BATTISTA BELZONI,
Narrative of the Operations and Recent Discoveries Within the Pyramids, Temples, Tombs, and Excavations, in Egypt and Nubia, on the discovery of pharaoh Seti I's tomb

5 | The Patagonian Sampson

The principal cause of my going to Egypt was the project of

constructing hydraulic machines, to irrigate the fields.

G I O V A N N I   B E L Z O N I ,
Narrative of the Operations and Recent Discoveries Within the
Pyramids, Temples, Tombs, and Excavations, in Egypt and Nubia

Adventurers and opportunists: the rough-and-tumble tomb robbers who descended on Mohammad Ali's Egypt came in search of fame and, more important, fortune. Ancient Egypt paid a high price for their roistering. A new mania for things Egyptian coincided with the pasha's desire to modernize his country. Napoléon's scientists had copied and measured with reverential care. Now ancient Egyptian masonry vanished wholesale into the walls of new factories. Ali himself used the best sites and finest artifacts as diplomatic lures to further his goal of modernization. After centuries of neglect, the temples and tombs of the Nile crumbled before a ruthless, highly competitive onslaught fueled by Europe's intense curiosity about, and hunger for, all things ancient Egyptian.

Few of the robbers possessed either scruples or even imagination. They labored in obscurity with no ambitions beyond a vague, and usually unfulfilled, desire to acquire quick wealth. Two men dominated this hurlyburly world: the French consul general, Bernardino Drovetti, and one of the most remarkable individuals ever to rob a tomb, Giovanni Battista Belzoni, widely regarded as the greatest, and certainly the most colorful, tomb robber of them all.

Giovanni Battista Belzoni was born in Padua, Italy, on November 5, 1778. He was one of the four children of Giacomo Belzoni, a barber of limited ambition who wanted his son to become a barber's assistant. The young Giovanni never left the narrow world of Padua until he was thirteen years old, but the experience of going elsewhere left him with a life-long wanderlust. In 1794, the strapping sixteen-year-old Belzoni left for Rome on the first of a series of endless wanderings. Padua had given him a sketchy education and some rudimentary understanding of mechanical things, but certainly no ambition to become a barber. For four years the young Paduan tarried in Rome, apparently striving to improve his education. Some biographers talk of his studying for the priesthood and acquiring a basic knowledge of hydraulics, but his education was, at best, sporadic, even by eighteenth-century standards.

Political conditions in Italy were unsettled during Belzoni's youth. Napoléon's armies were in the process of conquering and annexing Italy for the Republic. In 1798 the French armies entered Rome in triumph. Young Belzoni fled northward, perhaps to avoid conscription into Napoléon's regiments, loaded with an itinerant merchant's pack of rosaries, religious images, and relics.

The first trading venture seems to have been successful, for three years later the young Italian set out again, this time with his brother Francesco. They traveled far from home and engaged in petty trading around Amsterdam, Holland, where their imposing physiques and strength must have attracted attention. We do not know whether Belzoni was actually performing on the stage in Amsterdam, for in his later years and in his own biography he drew a complete veil over the early years of his life. The activities of a minor trader and acrobat were hardly a respectable background for a man who considered himself the stuff of which history is made and a public figure in the bargain.

Giovanni and Francesco crossed to London in 1803. Why they sailed over the North Sea, we do not know, but it may have been that stage opportunities were better in Britain. Many Italians are known to have performed there in the early years of the nineteenth century. Whatever restless urge brought Belzoni to England, his stay in London was the first turning point in a remarkably varied life. London in 1803 was a rollicking capital city, full of lively spectacles and bawdy theatrical performances. There were many opportunities for acrobats and gymnasts, for jugglers and strongmen, as well as for straight actors. The London theatrical public demanded diversity on stage and got it. Producers changed their variety shows and individual acts at frequent intervals to cater to lively audiences with fickle tastes. A wide choice of theatrical events flourished in London during the summer months. Handbills and newspapers proclaimed the sensational and spectacular, each theater vying with the others to catch the interest of the volatile Londoner.

Charles Dibdin Jr., owner of Sadler's Wells Theatre, was one of the greatest London impresarios of the early nineteenth century. He had acquired the theater just before Belzoni's arrival and was embarking on a successful entrepreneurial career, combining the offices of author, producer, and stage manager with great panache. In addition to a regular stable of actors, Dibdin bolstered his shows with numerous contract players engaged to play a single act or an entire season.

Dibdin's prompter was an Italian named Morelli, a popular actor and theatrical personality to whom "all the Italian minstrels and gymnastical performers used to apply, on their arrival in England," wrote Dibdin in his memoirs.[1] It was to this well-known agent that Giovanni Belzoni applied for work at Sadler's Wells Theatre. One does not know what qualifications Belzoni brought to his application. One can only assume that he had gained some experience with theatrical work on the Continent. But he must have been an imposing figure, standing more than 1.98 meters (6 feet, 6 inches) high, with a handsome face—well portrayed in the pictures of Belzoni that have come down to us—and immense strength. Charles Dibdin was certainly impressed enough to engage Belzoni as a weight lifter and a player of minor parts.

So in the summer of 1803 the "Patagonian Sampson," a weight lifter of great prowess and skill, treated London theatergoers to a startling act. His act consisted of a series of weight-lifting feats that culminated in a human-pyramid display. The gaily dressed Belzoni would shoulder a massive iron frame weighing 58 kilograms (127 pounds) and fitted with ledges. Twelve members of the Sadler's Wells Theatre company then perched on the frame, and the Patagonian Sampson strode around the stage without any apparent effort, waving two flags in his hands. This tour de force was deservedly popular with the theatrical public, so much so that Dibdin ran it for three months, also using the huge Italian in small plays and charades featured between major acts in the program. Many of these were small dramas, like the saga of Philip Quarll, an imaginative story of "an Englishman who lived a solitary life on an Island inhabited only by Monkies."[2]

FIGURE 5.1
Belzoni's act at Sadler's
Wells Theatre. By
permission of the Trustees
of the British Museum.

In July 1803, Belzoni's three-month contract with Sadler's Wells expired and was not renewed. The reasons are not known, but the nonrenewal is surprising, for Belzoni's act was popular with Londoners and Sadler's Wells had enjoyed its best season in some years. Two months later he was performing in very different surroundings, appearing in a human-pyramid act at Bartholomew's Fair, a popular annual event in the city of London. Bartholomew's Fair, a far cry from Sadler's Wells, was a bawdy and thoroughly hearty carnival with rides, numerous sideshows, stalls displaying everything from hurdy-gurdies to writing baboons, and, at one booth, the "French Hercules."

Fortunately, we have an eyewitness account of Belzoni's act at the fair, from John Thomas Smith, at the time the keeper of drawings and prints at the British Museum and a well-known and garrulous commentator on the London scene. Smith and a friend visited the fair with some trepidation, for there was a real danger of robbery or mugging. The two of them stopped at Belzoni's stall and watched him lift a series of heavy weights. Then the French Hercules asked for volunteers to form a human pyramid on his shoulders. Smith and four others stepped forward and climbed onto chairs to reach Belzoni's massive shoulders. "Sampson performed his task with an ease of step most stately," remarked Smith. Belzoni was carrying quite a weight, for the fourth member of the pyramid was a "heavy dumpling, whose chops, I will answer for it, relished many an inch thick steak from the once far-famed Honey Lane market."[3]

Giovanni Belzoni went on to become a familiar figure in London and the provinces during the next few years, traveling from fair to fair throughout the British Isles, performing acts of strength and doomed, as the *Gentleman's Magazine* put it, "to bear on his colossal frame, not fewer, if we mistake not, than 20 or 22 persons moving across the stage as stately as the elephant with the Persian warriors."[4] He soon expanded his theatrical repertoire to include some trick effects and displays with waterworks and stage hydraulics. He was soon billed as "the Great Belzoni," a title that ensured him bookings all over Britain over the next eight years, a period when his wanderlust was at its most intense and when he acquired a working knowledge of weight lifting, the use of levers and rollers, balancing techniques, and what were known as "hydrauliks," acts onstage involving water, useful skills for any tomb robber.

At about this time, Belzoni met and married his wife, Sarah. We know very little about her, except that she was about twenty years old when she met her future husband. She is variously described as being of English or Irish birth. The marriage was childless and one of perennial wandering in Europe and, later, Egypt. In the twenty-odd years of the Belzonis' marriage, they never had a permanent home or strong family ties. Yet the marriage was apparently a happy one, although Sarah did not hesitate to go off on her own or remain behind if her husband's activities bored her. She endured discomfort, hardship, and long separations with a remarkable equanimity. Her "Trifling Account" in Belzoni's biography is an insight into an observant and basically shrewd woman who had a wry sense of humor and was respected by Turk and Egyptian alike. Sarah outlived Belzoni by almost fifty years, eventually dying in dignified obscurity in the Channel Islands in 1870, long forgotten by the general public.

Accompanied by his new wife, Belzoni became a familiar figure on the circus and fair circuit, performing in Scotland and Ireland as well as London and the provinces at all manner of entertainments. The Belzonis wandered the length and breadth of the British Isles, caged in by

Napoléon's campaigns and severe restrictions on foreign travel. But in 1812 Wellington liberated the southern ports of Spain, including Madrid, and Belzoni ventured abroad. His travel document has survived, showing that he was accompanied by his faithful Irish servant, James Curtin, but not by Sarah.

The pair visited Lisbon—where Belzoni may have performed in the São Carlos Theatre—Gibraltar, and Malaga before returning to England in time for a well-publicized series of performances in Oxford, Belzoni's last recorded show-business appearances in England. The handbill of the first performance, at the Blue Boar Tavern, St. Aldate's, Oxford, on Monday, February 22, 1813, offered an impressive bill of fare. A conjuring turn was followed by a performance on musical glasses. The "French Hercules" demonstrated "several striking Attitudes, from the most admired antique statues uniting Grace and Expression with Muscular strength." A "Grand and Brilliant Display of Optical Illusions entitled the Aggrescopius" completed the performance.[5]

Before leaving England, Belzoni called on Charles Dibdin and told him that he had returned to recruit performers for theaters in Portugal. Whether he took any actors to Lisbon with him we do not know, but in mid-1813 the Belzoni family and James Curtin were in Lisbon and Madrid. After performing at various centers, the Belzonis traveled in Sicily, where we find them in November 1814 exchanging letters with the family in Padua.

Belzoni made no effort to visit his hometown. His wanderlust was turning him in the direction of Constantinople, one of the great centers of popular entertainment in the Western world. The sultan of Turkey was forever laying on vast popular festivals that often lasted for several weeks. Conjurers and wrestlers, acrobats and jugglers were in constant demand. Italians from Bologna, a town close to Belzoni's home community, designed firework displays and illuminations, so he may have had connections at court. He knew, also, that the sultan made considerable use of foreign artists in entertainments and spectacles. Instead of returning home, the Belzonis crossed to Malta on their leisurely way to the Turkish capital. They lodged in Valletta for nearly six months, enjoying a respite from the constant strain of traveling and performing in strange places. It was here that Belzoni had a chance encounter with Captain Ishmail Gibraltar, an agent of Pasha Muhammad Ali, an event that changed his life.

Muhammad Ali's thirty years of rule produced extraordinary changes, many of them far from permanent, for their ultimate success depended on the strong leadership of Ali himself. He himself described Egypt as "utterly barbarous." He advised visitors from Europe not to expect the comforts and stability of home. Much of government was in the hands of Turks, but the reins of official expenditure were tightly controlled by Muhammad Ali. His trusted Armenian minister, Boghos Bey, was ordered to implement a European style of budget mechanism, with detailed accounts and a public audit system, that was successful in keeping Ali's government out of the hands of European moneylenders, even if much corruption still remained.[6] The pasha turned to Europe for expert advice on agricultural improvements, industry, and economic development.

Unfortunately, many of his most ambitious schemes were failures. The French engineer Linant de Bellefonds designed a barrage across the Nile that was supposed to permit complete irrigation of the delta, even in poor flood years.[7] When it was completed, water seeped under the inadequate foundations. The pasha invested vast sums in cotton mills, a tannery, and other commercial ventures. The more elaborate factories failed. Machinery was neglected and never oiled, management sporadic. Peasant farmers were unused to the monotony and regularity of factory work and were soon recruited by force. All the same, Ali transformed many aspects of Egyptian life, with the help of European experts, some of them genuine, others pure renegades or the opportunistic dregs of society.

The pasha recruited most of his experts through chance encounter or with the help of numerous overseas agents. Ishmail Gibraltar, a sea captain, was one such agent, employed to search out engineers and industrial experts who would introduce new products and agricultural methods to replace those that were still in use almost unchanged from the days of the pharaohs.

Captain Gibraltar encountered Belzoni at a time when the strongman was contemplating the commercial value of his various talents in the relative peace of Malta. Belzoni and Gibraltar quickly became fast friends, a friendship that soon had the Italian talking of his idea for a new design of waterwheel that would revolutionize the Egyptian economy. The new water pump would be powered by one ox instead of many, be of simple and robust design, and be cheap to manufacture.

Gibraltar was sufficiently impressed by Belzoni's enthusiasm and apparent expertise to arrange for him to visit Cairo and build a prototype for the pasha. Soon afterward, on May 19, 1815, Belzoni, Sarah, and James Curtin took ship for Alexandria, where they arrived three weeks later, only to be greeted by the news that the plague was raging in the town.[8] Soon the Belzonis made their way ashore, stepping gingerly over the piles of garbage and through narrow streets. They sought lodging in a French house where they were isolated from the rest of the town in a state of quarantine, at that time about the only preventive measure against the plague that seemed to work.

The Belzonis' introduction to Egypt was hardly auspicious. They began by succumbing to a stomach disorder that they carefully concealed from the other lodgers for fear that panic would ensue, for several Europeans had died of the plague in recent days. Giovanni and Sarah suffered under the uninspiring company of their neighbors in the quarantine house. The plague eased by the end of June, and Belzoni was able to get about the town. He called on the British and French consuls, then in Alexandria, who received him with interest. Colonel Ernest Missett, the British representative, was crippled by ill health and about to retire from his post. Apparently, he showed less interest in Belzoni than did the former French vice consul, Bernardino Drovetti, himself of Italian birth, who seems to have taken to the visitor and given him a great deal of assistance.

Drovetti gave Belzoni some letters of introduction to useful people in Cairo and seemed interested in the Italian's hydraulic designs. One suspects that his motives were partly political, for he had already learned that the British planned to give the pasha a steam engine and pumping machine, gifts that had arrived in Alexandria in the company of a mechanic at about the time that Belzoni came on the scene. Belzoni must also have seen some of Drovetti's antiquities and heard firsthand stories of the excitement and profits of archaeological discovery.

Colonel Missett's residence was an important rendezvous for travelers to the Nile, even in times of pestilence and plague. When Belzoni called on the consul, he was introduced to William Turner, a young gentleman-diplomat who was in the middle of a leisurely tour through the Near East.[9] This charming and intelligent young traveler took an immediate liking to the Belzonis and left an engaging description of their journey to Cairo, for they joined company in hiring a boat to carry them up the Nile.

The journey was a fascinating experience for the newcomers, who took five days to make the trip across the Nile bar at the Rosetta mouth and journey through the lush delta country. After the heat and dust of Alexandria, the green oasis of Rosetta and the slow-moving Nile were a revelation, for the travelers were able to observe a way of life along its banks that had not changed for centuries. Then, on the morning of the fifth day, their small sailing boat came to Bulaq, the principal port of Cairo. Turner lodged at a convent, while the Belzonis set up house in a residence provided them by the pasha's minister, Boghos Bey.

: :

Cairo was an imposing sight for the arriving traveler accustomed to the flat monotony of the Nile Delta. The domes and minarets of its many mosques rose above a pall of smoke from innumerable household fires. The city was a bustling, cosmopolitan metropolis, lying a little distance from the right bank of the Nile under the Mukattam Hills. Palm trees and cultivated fields bordered the river. The pyramids of Giza hovered on the skyline in the distance. For more than a thousand years, a city with imposing walls and a citadel had flourished on this spot. William Turner estimated that at least 250,000 people inhabited the streets and bazaars of the busy city, after Constantinople probably the most influential political and economic center in the Near East.

This sprawling commercial center was the terminus of long-distance caravan routes throughout North Africa and the Near East. Timbuktu, the Niger, Damascus, Aleppo, India, and possibly even the Far East could be reached by caravan. No one dreamed of traveling alone through the hostile desert, where drought, marauding raiders, and the crosscurrents of political intrigue could halt a caravan for weeks or even years. Thousands of merchants and their families spent their entire lives wandering over enormous distances, following trading opportunities and bartering all manner of commodities for other merchandise in kind. The bazaars of Cairo thrived on the caravan trade. Cotton, flax, grain, and a thousand and one useful and useless products of Near Eastern craftsmen passed along the caravan routes, in exchange for raw materials and exotic objects from Africa and Asia: slaves, gold, ivory, salt, spices, rhinoceros horn (a well-known aphrodisiac), ostrich shells, fine clothes, and china.

The city was a maze of narrow streets and dilapidated houses. Peddlers and street vendors thronged small alleys boasting of their wares. Small shops housed the many craftsmen for which Cairo was famous; goldsmiths and silversmiths lived in one quarter, while potters and leather workers had their own streets. One could buy, or experience, anything in Cairo—for a price. At night the city was quieter. Wooden doors blocked off many of the streets. The authorities locked the great gates of the central precincts each night. Huge mosques dominated the city's architecture—among them al-Azhar, a major center of Islamic learning for more than a millennium, and the oldest foundation of all, the mosque built by Ibn Tulun in the ninth century.[10]

The anonymous laborers of ancient Egypt had shaped large granite blocks for pyramids and temples. Islamic contractors industriously quarried away at this convenient source of good stone for Cairo's more imposing buildings and mosques. Beyond Ezbekiya Square with its gardens, flooded each August when the Nile rose above its banks, there were few open spaces. Much of Cairo consisted of decaying slums. New shacks and hovels rose on the ruins of old ones. Piles of garbage strewed both streets and courtyards, the home of countless scavenging animals.

Few Europeans lived in Cairo except for some consular representatives, a handful of French merchants who had stayed on after Napoléon's occupation, and a small community of government advisers and travelers. Solid wooden doors isolated the European quarter from the rest of the city, closing off the residences at sunset and in times of plague, riot, or political hostility. A visitor would lodge in the European quarter or, if space was not available, would take up residence at Bulaq, the main port for Cairo to the northwest of the city. The pasha and other wealthy Cairenes built luxurious summer palaces with cool gardens in this quarter of the city. Of the French occupation, little remained. Napoléon's grand plans for great boulevards and impressive buildings had come to nothing. The tiny French community preserved some French interests in the city, which continued to flourish in a decaying, hothouse atmosphere of fast-flowing trade, constant political instability, and intrigue. No one with any taste for the Islamic world could resist the tawdry charm of Cairo.

The Belzoni family disembarked at Bulaq and took up lodgings in a house allocated them by Boghos Bey. His generosity did not extend to palatial lodgings. Their first Cairo residence was hardly inspiring. The windows were boarded up, there was no lock on the front door, and the roof was in danger of collapse. Sarah laid out their sheets and mattresses on the floor of one of the least-ruinous and cleaner rooms. They took their meals sitting on the floor and waited for an audience with the pasha.

Boghos Bey arranged the interview for a week later, but the encounter never took place. Belzoni was riding to the citadel on an ass when a cursing Turkish soldier on horseback, angry at foreigners because he had been ordered to learn European drills, struck him with his sharp stave on the right leg. The blow struck off "a piece of flesh in triangular form two inches deep and pretty broad." The gash on his leg laid him up for several weeks. When the interview eventually did materialize, Belzoni was politely received. He described his invention and undertook to build a prototype "which would raise as much water with one ox, as the machines of the country with four." Muhammad Ali was "much pleased with my proposal," wrote Belzoni, "as it will save the labor and expense of many thousands of oxen in the country."[11]

The building of the prototype took longer than had been anticipated. Turkish soldiers in Cairo mutinied and attempted to storm the citadel. They were rebuffed by the guards and embarked on a rampage of looting and destruction. Belzoni rashly entered the city at the height of the mutiny and was robbed of all his money and his passport when attempting to return to Sarah in Bulaq. The pasha remained inside the citadel for more than a month until the mutiny, over the adoption of European drills in the military, had subsided. But eventually things quieted down, and life returned to normal. The Belzonis moved into a small home near the pasha's palace at Shubra, then an upscale suburb, now one of the most crowded areas of the city. They lived off a small subsistence allowance from the government. The pump was to be erected in the nearby pasha's garden.

Meanwhile, their friend William Turner was busy visiting notables in Cairo and arranging various excursions in and around the city, among them a trip to the pyramids. Belzoni joined the party for the donkey journey out to Giza by moonlight. Soon after sunrise, the travelers stood at the chilly summit of the Great Pyramid of Khufu, admiring the fine view of Cairo and the Nile spread out at their feet. After breakfast, they explored the interior of the pyramid and fired off their pistols in Khufu's burial chamber, a deafening pastime that must have caused them acute discomfort. Belzoni does not seem to have exhibited anything more than the tourist's usual curiosity about the pyramids.

The long delays in obtaining materials and parts for a pump left Belzoni with much time on his hands. The Belzonis had time to go on another excursion with Turner, this time to Saqqara, where more pyramids and the famous mummy pits were to be seen. The Nile was in flood, so they traveled by boat across the flooded fields. After a night in the open, they mounted donkeys for the ride to the famous Step Pyramid built for the pharaoh Djoser (2668–2649 BC), although, of course, the visitors did not know this. They climbed to the top of the pyramid and then breakfasted in its shadow, before deciding not to visit the mummy pits, for the local people told them that ladders and a lamp were necessary. One of the servants was dispatched to fetch a mummy of an ibis. Half an hour later he returned with a narrow jar sealed with a clay stopper, which, he assured them, was a genuine antiquity containing a mummified bird. The Europeans laughed at him, whereupon the furious Arab dashed the pot to the ground and picked up a small bundle of decaying mummy fabric from the broken pot, indeed the remains of a mummified bird. Such jars were commonly empty and sold to gullible tourists as genuine antiquities.

These side trips were but intervals between Belzoni's frantic efforts to build a prototype machine for the pasha. He was delayed on all sides. The pasha's chief engineer was sick, good-quality wood was not available, and permits for construction could not be obtained. Belzoni's plans were quietly opposed by many bureaucrats, strongly resistant to many of the reforms proposed by the pasha, who respected Western ways of doing business.

By mid-1816, Belzoni's pumping machine was complete, "built on the principle of a crane with a walking wheel, in which a single ox, by its own weight alone, could effect as much as four oxen employed in the machines of the country."[12] Belzoni demonstrated his invention before the pasha and "several connaisseurs in hydrauliks." The demonstration took place in the palace gardens, where his prototype machine stood alongside six *saqquias*, the traditional waterwheels used for thousands of years on the banks of the Nile. Belzoni drove an ox into his treadmill drum. Water cascaded down the irrigation channels in the pasha's garden. The owners of the six *saqquias* lashed their oxen into a frenzy, trying to emulate the flood of water pouring from Belzoni's waterwheel.

The pasha was impressed, conferred with his advisers, and pronounced that Belzoni's machine was as good as four *saqquias*. But his advisers, who sensed reduced manpower and profits, were unimpressed at the efficiency of yet another European invention, and the pasha hesitated. He knew he would lose serious face if he was perceived publicly as economizing on either manpower or oxen. To stall for time, he asked what would happen if men replaced the ox in the treadmill. A crowd of excited Arabs jumped

FIGURE 5.2   A *saqquia*, the traditional Nile waterwheel driven by an ox. Photograph by the famed Antarctic photographer Frank Hurley, taken between 1938 and 1945. By permission of the National Library of Australia, Canberra.

into the treadmill wheel. James Curtin, Belzoni's young servant, joined in. The wheel moved merrily and the water flooded, until the Arabs suddenly jumped out, leaving the young boy by himself as a counterweight to the mass of water. He was flung out of the wheel and broke a leg. Belzoni's machine was doomed to failure after that. Ali's Turkish admirers were relieved. No pasha in his right mind would adopt a pumping machine so lethal as this sinister new device. Belzoni's hopes and ambitions as a hydraulic engineer collapsed around him in a few minutes.

6 | The Young Memnon

On the wall of the rock, in the centre of the four statues, is the fig-

ure of the hawk-headed Osiris, surmounted by a globe; beneath

which, I suspect, could the sand be cleared away, a vast temple

would be discovered to the entrance of which the above colossal fig-

ures probably serve as ornaments.

JOHANN LUDWIG BURCKHARDT,
Travels of M. Burckhardt in Egypt and Nubia, on Abu Simbel

Belzoni's demonstration failed just as Henry Salt, the new British consul general, arrived in Cairo. Salt had traveled with Hamilton's fateful Foreign Office memorandum about antiquities in his baggage and was anxious to find a new Rosetta stone as soon as possible. When he arrived at Bulaq, the plague season had enveloped Cairo. He was obliged to lodge in the same dilapidated house that the Belzonis had camped in a year before. There he met Sheik Ibrahim, a tall and prematurely old man who looked and behaved like an Arab, although he was in fact a Swiss native—Johann Ludwig Burckhardt (1784–1817).

Burckhardt was a remarkable scholar, an expert linguist and chemist with a passion for travel. After his family was ruined in the Napoleonic Wars, Burckhardt emigrated to England, where he studied Arabic at Cambridge.

He then met with Sir Joseph Banks, the president of the newly formed African Association, and offered to explore the sources of the Niger

River, at that time a point of some geographic controversy. The association gave him an exiguous allowance and agreed that he could spend two years in Syria perfecting his Arabic before leaving by caravan for Central Africa. Burckhardt promptly steeped himself in Arab life and became so proficient in Arabic and the Koran that Islamic scholars proclaimed him an authority on Islamic law. In 1812 he turned up in Cairo, having adopted the name Sheik Ibrahim ibn Abdullah. His vague objective was to join a caravan journeying across the Sahara to the Fezzan and West Africa. Few caravans were to be found, so he filled in the time by journeying up the Nile as far as Dongola, deep in Nubia, and then making a side trip to the Red Sea. At this point, he was so close to Mecca that it seemed logical to make the pilgrimage and to visit the tomb of the Prophet at Medina. Burckhardt had returned to Cairo at about the same time as Turner and the Belzonis.

This emaciated and weary traveler had an extraordinary amount of knowledge of Islam and the Nile. His surviving letters and notes, which were later converted into splendid books, reveal him as a superlative observer of the trivial and of the important, a man who was totally wrapped up in the world of Islam. He was the first European to visit the magnificent Abu Simbel temples below the Second Cataract in ancient Egypt's Nubia.

Burckhardt had not been impressed by Abu Simbel at first, for he came on the facade from above, looking down from the cliffs above the temple. It was only when he turned upstream a little way that he caught sight of one of the four colossal statues that formed the facade of Rameses II's largest temple. The statues were almost completely buried in sand, so he had to guess what lay underneath. "Could the sand be cleared away, a vast temple would be discovered," he remarked prophetically. And he was vastly impressed by the single exposed head, which had, he wrote, "a most expressive, youthful countenance, approaching nearer to the Grecian model of beauty than that of any ancient Egyptian figure I have seen."[1]

Burckhardt's journeys and observations made him a fascinating and perceptive companion whom Belzoni seems to have been at some pains to cultivate. It was from Burckhardt that he heard of the Abu Simbel temples and the great statues buried in sand. The Swiss wanderer also mentioned another interesting find. While spending a few days near Thebes, Burckhardt had come across a colossal granite head of singular beauty, known to visitors as "the Young Memnon," lying abandoned in the Ramesseum (Rameses II's mortuary temple) on the west bank of the Nile. The head—in fact depicting Rameses II—was well known to antiquarians, for it had been described by diplomat William Hamilton in an authoritative but extraordinarily dull book on Egyptian archaeology as the most beautiful piece of Egyptian sculpture along the Nile. The French had also appreciated its worth and had tried to remove it, without success, despite having all the resources of an army at their backs.

Burckhardt heard of the French efforts from the local people and had even thought vaguely of removing the head himself. Back in Cairo, he suggested that the pasha might give the head to Britain's Prince Regent as a gift, but Muhammad Ali had scoffed at the idea. What monarch, he asked, would want a mere block of stone?

Meanwhile, Belzoni was in a perilous financial position. Then he remembered the Memnon head and went to see Burckhardt. The traveler was sympathetic, but certainly did not have the money to pay for the transportation of the statue all the way to England. But Henry Salt was much more amenable. Belzoni was a godsend to a diplomat thinking of his antiquities-greedy superiors in London. He immediately obtained the necessary *firman* to remove the statue from the pasha and gave Belzoni a letter of instructions, which charged him with the responsibility of bringing the head down the Nile. The consul directed him "to prepare the necessary implements, at Bulaq, for the purpose of carrying the head of the statue of the younger Memnon, and carrying it down the Nile." The letter gave instructions about recruitment of labor and a boat crew, information on expenditures, and specific guidance on how to identify the head. "It must not be mistaken for another, lying in that neighborhood, which is much mutilated," the letter cautioned.[2]

Belzoni threw himself into a fever of preparations, hiring a boat and scouring Bulaq and Cairo for suitable lifting devices. All he was able to obtain were a few poles and some palm-fiber ropes. Evidently, he would have to improvise locally. On June 30, 1816, the Belzonis left by boat for Thebes, accompanied by James Curtin and a Copt interpreter.

This was the first time that Belzoni had been any distance upstream of Cairo, so he paused at intervals to look at places on the way. The party took six days to reach Manfalut, where they met the pasha's son Ibrahim on his way to Cairo. Drovetti was with Ibrahim's party, laden with antiquities he had collected near Thebes. He seems to have welcomed Belzoni warmly, although he had heard that he was on his way upstream to remove the great head. Drovetti warned that the Arabs at Thebes were refusing to work, and—one suspects rather cynically—presented Belzoni with a beautiful granite sarcophagus cover, which was, however, still firmly embedded in a rock-cut tomb near Thebes, all efforts to remove it having failed.

At Asyut a little farther upstream, a town "celebrated for the making of eunuchs," Belzoni called on the local governor and presented his credentials, but he had great difficulty in obtaining boats, materials, and carpenters. Excuses were made—the stone was useless, and permission to obtain workers would not be granted. Then he became more explicit. "He plainly recommended to me not to meddle in this business, for I should meet with many disagreeable things, and have many obstacles to encounter."[3] Obviously, Drovetti had been at work, hoping to secure the head for himself. But he had sadly underestimated Belzoni's determination. With the aid of his interpreter, he hired a Greek carpenter.

On July 18 they were at Dendera and paused to admire the magnificent temple of Hathor so ably described by Dominique-Vivant Denon. They examined the famous round zodiac of the first century AD in the temple ceiling, which showed the sky as it was known to the Egyptians and Greeks. An abandoned village lay on the temple roof. The local people seemed to have little respect for the shrine, except as a place to live above flood level.

Four days later the expedition arrived at Thebes. Transported with wonder, Belzoni wandered among the ruins of the temples of Karnak and Luxor. He waxed lyrical over the temples and statuary: "It appeared to me like entering a city of giants, who, after a long conflict, were all destroyed, leaving the ruins of their former temples as the only proof of their former existence."[4]

Belzoni soon crossed to the west bank to examine the head of the "Young Memnon" in Rameses II's mortuary temple, the Ramesseum, that was the objective of his expedition. "I found it near the remains of its body and chair, with its face upwards, and apparently smiling on me, at the thought of being taken to England," he wrote.[5] Belzoni was impressed by its beauty, but not by its size, which was less than he had been led to expect. Even so, he had a formidable task ahead of him. All he had at his disposal were fourteen poles, four palm ropes, and four rollers. There were no tackles, nor could he obtain more timber in a treeless environment.

The task would have been almost impossible to anyone but a former theatrical strongman. Within hours, the party had a base camp: a small and comfortable stone hut constructed from loose boulders from the temple. While his carpenter made a crude car out of eight of the Cairo poles, Belzoni examined the flood level of the river, which would be lapping at the edge of the temple within a month. Unless the head was dragged to the riverbank before the inundation, it would have to remain in place for another year. Any delay would be fatal, for Belzoni knew well that others were after the trophy.

He set out to recruit eighty workers and soon found that Drovetti's evil influence had been at work. The local Turkish administrator received Belzoni politely, even effusively, but was far from helpful. He claimed that all the local peasants were busy in the fields, which was untrue. Belzoni saw dozens of men idling in the villages. Furthermore, it was Ramadan, and Belzoni should wait until after the flood. In any case, he added, the local people would rather starve than undertake such an arduous task. Belzoni persisted and stood on the instructions in his *firman*. Reluctantly, the headman promised to find men on the morrow, and Belzoni departed well satisfied. But several frustrating days and many bribes were needed before work would actually begin on July 27.

Belzoni wasted no time. He knew the power of levers from his theatrical years and simply worked four long timbers under the edge of the statue, using the combined weight of dozens of men working in unison to heave up the dead weight of the stone. As the levers moved the Memnon higher, Belzoni deftly slipped the wooden car under it. The men were convinced the head would never be moved and gave a great shout when the levers shifted it. "Though it was the effect of their own efforts, it was the devil, they said, that did it; and as they saw me taking notes, they concluded it was done by means of a charm," Belzoni remarked with satisfaction.[6] Next, he used the levers once more to lift the loaded car at both ends, so he could place rollers underneath. By the end of the day, the Memnon had moved some distance toward the Nile. While most of the workers pulled on ropes, others moved rollers from back to front to keep the car moving.

The next day, the head was out of the temple, although Belzoni had to break the bases of two columns to get it out. Despite great suffering from the heat, the men moved the Memnon more than 180 meters (200 yards)

FIGURE 6.1   The triumphal progress of the Young Memnon. From the
watercolor by Giovanni Belzoni.

in the next two days. Then the ground became sandy and the head sank
into the soil, so they had to make a detour of an extra 275 meters (300
yards).

All went well until August 5, when the car reached an area of low-lying
floodplain that would be inundated by the Nile within a few days. There
was no time to be lost. Early in the morning Belzoni arrived to find only
the guards and the carpenter, but no workmen. The headman had forbidden the laborers to work for a Christian dog any longer. Belzoni con-
fronted him angrily in Thebes and received "saucy answers." He attempted patience and kind words, which merely encouraged the official to
more insolence, mistaking Belzoni's forbearance for weakness. As the
Turk drew his sword, Belzoni remembered his experience with angry soldiers in Cairo where decisive behavior had paid off. "There was no time to
be lost; I gave him no leisure to execute his purpose. I instantly seized and
disarmed him, placing my hands on his stomach, and making him sensi-
ble of my superiority, at least in point of strength, by keeping him firm in
a corner of the room."[7] After giving the fellow a good shaking, Belzoni
told him that he would report his behavior to the pasha. Further bribery
was needed before local officialdom was placated with a pistol. The next
morning the head was moving again.

Five days later Belzoni was able to write, "Thank God, the young Memnon arrived on the bank of the Nile." He gave the laborers a bonus payment of sixpence each in addition to their wages, "with which they were
exceedingly pleased."[8]

The next requirement was a boat, but all available river craft were in the service of the pasha. So a letter was sent to Cairo asking Salt to send one to Thebes. In the meantime, two guards were posted at the site and an earthen bank built around the loaded car.

Belzoni now turned his energetic thoughts toward the sarcophagus that Drovetti had given him. It lay inside a burial cave in the hills behind Qurna, one of the sepulchers that were famous for the fine mummies they contained. Accompanied by two Arab guides and interpreters, Belzoni removed most of his clothes, lit candles, and squeezed his way into a narrow cavity in the rock, which extended a fair distance into the hill. The party passed through a labyrinth of burial passages until Belzoni was completely lost. He stumbled upon the sarcophagus, but the guides tried, without avail, to hide the best way to take it out from him.

Belzoni set men to work cleaning the passage to the sarcophagus, only to discover three days later that the local headman had imprisoned his workmen "bound like thieves." Drovetti's agents had arrived from Alexandria and become alarmed at Belzoni's success and determination. The headman informed Belzoni that the lid had been sold to Drovetti and that was the end of the matter. "I feigned to be quite unconcerned about the matter, as well as about the Arabs he had put in prison," he recorded.[9] Playing for time, he promised to write to Cairo about the matter, and turned his attention to other sites.

: :

Having time to kill, Belzoni decided to travel farther upstream, both out of curiosity and also with a view to purchasing more antiquities. His boat could go wherever he wished it to proceed without further cost, and it seemed logical, with the Young Memnon stuck on the bank of the Nile and the matter of the sarcophagus unresolved, to see what lay upstream of well-exploited and highly suspicious Thebes.

The boat trip upstream from Thebes to the First Cataract is normally an uneventful one. The traveler passes through intensively cultivated countryside, with small villages clustered on the higher ground that escapes inundation each August. For the Belzonis, every bend in the river was a new adventure, enlivened by night stops in small towns and villages where they called on the local headmen or entertained them aboard their boat.

Kom Ombo, Aswan, and the island of Elephantine were pleasant inter-
ludes in the monotony of river travel where the travelers visited temples
and Coptic chapels. Belzoni was disappointed in Elephantine, with its
Nilometer and shrines to the creator god, Khnum. He had read the rapturous accounts of it penned by earlier travelers. Perhaps his disappoint-
ment was due to the hazardous ferry crossing. Nine people—one of them
the massive Belzoni—crammed themselves into a matting and palm-fiber
boat only 3 meters long and 1.5 meters wide (10 feet by 5 feet). "It cost,
when new, twelve piasters, or six shillings," he remarked.[10]

The First Cataract breaks the serenity of the river at Aswan. Belzoni
tried to hire a boat to take him upstream to the island of Philae and into
Nubia. The local governor made the mistake of trying to bargain with the
Italian, who argued with such determination that the official eventually
let him have a boat for the local price. The agreed fare for the return trip
to the Second Cataract was $20, a lot less than the governor's original ask-
ing price of $120.

On August 27, 1816, they came to Philae. "Long before the rising of the
sun, I stood at the stern, waiting for the light to unveil that goodly sight,
the beautiful island of Philae," Belzoni recalled. "When I beheld it, it sur-
passed everything that imagination could anticipate." The wind was so favorable that they paused for the briefest of visits, resolving to return for a
more leisurely inspection on the downstream passage. But he did spot "an
obelisk of granite about twenty-two feet in length" close to the water and
quietly noted it for future removal.[11]

Upstream of the Cataract, the Belzonis found themselves in territory
where the pasha's authority counted for little. The day after they left Philae, a group of natives appeared while the crew was ashore. Soon, armed
warriors with spears were swarming around the boat. Only the Belzonis
and their interpreter were on board. They all grabbed pistols, and Belzoni
gestured at the natives to keep away. "I then stepped forward, and with my
right hand prevented the first of them from entering the boat, while I held
the pistol in my left. At last I pointed a pistol at him, making signs, that, if
he did not retire, I would shoot at him."[12] Once again, Belzoni's decisive
behavior had prevented trouble.

They were now in less well-known country, where Belzoni relied on
notes given him by Burckhardt. At Kalabsha, they inspected the large temple near the river.[13] A large crowd of armed locals blocked the entrance as

they turned to leave and demanded money. Belzoni drew himself up to his full and imposing height, told them he would not give them money under duress, stared them in the face, and walked through the crowd unmolested. Later he was able to buy some tombstones with Greek inscriptions.

Leaving Kalabsha, they arrived at Derr, the capital of Lower Nubia, a village of earthen and stone huts in family groups. Here, Hassan Kachif, one of three brothers who ruled this area of Nubia, greeted Belzoni with great suspicion. It was impossible for the travelers to venture farther, he said, for the people upstream were at war with each other. Fortunately, Belzoni had made inquiries in Cairo about Nubian tastes and found out that they valued looking glasses and glass beads above all other possessions. So, in a moment of inspiration, he had taken a stock of mirrors with him just in case.

A handsome looking glass was solemnly presented to Hassan. The gift produced a letter of safe passage addressed to Hassan's brother upstream in record time. "The Kachif was never tired of admiring his bear-like face; and all his attendants behind him strove to get a peep at their own chocolate beauty," exulted Belzoni.[14] Two days later the party reached Abu Simbel, which was the real objective of Belzoni's trip. Ever since he had learned of the huge and beautiful figures that Burckhardt had seen three years before, Belzoni had planned to visit the vast statues and to uncover the great temple that lay behind them.

Having admired the great frieze and the six colossal figures from a distance, Belzoni clambered up the steep, sandy slope to a point where a likeness of the hawk-headed god Horakhty projected out of the sand. This he judged to be above the lintel of the temple doorway. Even Belzoni was daunted by the size of the undertaking. He estimated that the door lay 11 meters (35 feet) below the surface of the soft sand, which poured into his foot imprints as fast as he made them.

After a rapid inspection of the site, the Belzonis landed at the village of Abu Simbel some short distance away, where they found a group of armed men assembled under some trees, among them Daud Kachif, the local headman. Daud was a man of about fifty, clad in a light-blue gown with a white rag on his head as a turban. Somewhat surprised to see a stranger, the villagers greeted Belzoni roughly and inquired as to his business. When he explained that he had come in search of ancient stones and wished to open the buried temple with the help of the villagers, the head-

FIGURE 6.2   Abu Simbel, from a watercolor by Giovanni Belzoni. "Could the sand be cleared away, a vast temple would be discovered."

man laughed scornfully. He had heard that story before. Some months previously, another European had passed by and taken away a lot of gold. Did Belzoni want not the stones but to take gold from them? Patiently, the Italian explained that he was interested in the people who had made the stones, not gold. Besides, asked the headman, what use was money to his people, who never used it? Undaunted, Belzoni gave a piastre to a by-stander and told him to give it to the carefully briefed boat captain, who would give him a measure of corn in exchange. The people were suitably impressed when the man returned with three days' ration of grain.

The headman had met his match in Belzoni, who knew everything there was to know about bargaining. Eventually, the Italian was able to strike a bargain of two piastres a day per man, a bargain that pleased him when he learned that no less a visitor than Bernardino Drovetti had left 300 piastres with the headman as a fee for opening the temple—a fee that was returned, for the people had no use for cash.

Having settled matters at Abu Simbel, Belzoni journeyed on to Askut, a day and a half's sailing upstream, to get permission for the work from

Hussein Kachif, brother of Hassan Kachif. The Belzonis landed on some islands immediately below the Second Cataract inhabited by simple people whose total worldly possessions were a baking stove and a mat to sleep on. There they obtained two pilots who took them right up to the Cataract. The party narrowly escaped shipwreck when the boat was driven against a rock by a strong current. Soon afterward they landed and climbed a high rock that provided a magnificent view of the rapids. "The blackness of the stones, the green of the trees on the islands, intermixed with the white froth of the water, form a fine picture, which can scarcely be described or delineated," wrote Belzoni.[15]

Hussein Kachif, a majestic ruler in his seventies, awaited them at Askut with a fierce bodyguard. He questioned Belzoni minutely, expressed little surprise at his wish to open the temple, a task he clearly considered impossible, and gave permission provided that he received half of all the treasure. Belzoni readily agreed, for he suspected—rightly, as it turned out—that he would find nothing except statuary.

He hastened back to Abu Simbel, only to find that the people had decided they did not want to work. Exasperated, Belzoni pretended to lose interest and leave. The headman saw a useful source of revenue evaporating and called him back. After prolonged arguments, it was agreed that forty men would report for work the next day. No one turned up on the morrow, so Belzoni made the headman send soldiers to round up the men. Eventually, a group of workers began digging in pairs, using long sticks with crosspieces of wood at the ends to drag the sand away from the temple facade. At first the work went quite well, for the men's thoughts were on the treasure they would find. But the pace soon slacked off. The headman was out to extort every piastre he could from visitors. Belzoni got his way only by bribing the tiresome official's brother, who arranged for a bonus of grain to satisfy the workmen's demands.

When the work resumed, Belzoni placed a palisade of palm leaves and saplings upslope of the suspected temple entrance so that new sand did not cascade into the excavation. So many men arrived on the third day of digging that eighty men worked for the wages of forty. At the end of the day the headman's brother took everyone's wages. Belzoni sarcastically observed that his magic for obtaining money seemed to be more effective than his own.

There were other incidents, too. Two of the laborers tried to plunder the boat when only Sarah Belzoni and a young girl were on board. "They were rather impertinent to her," observed Belzoni. "At last she presented a pistol to them, on which they immediately retired, and ran up the hill." It was impossible to identify the culprits, for "they were all like so many lumps of chocolate seated on the sand at work."[16]

By this time the Belzonis' money was running out. Obviously, the clearing of the temple entrance would have to wait for another visit. They had underestimated the dramatic effect that the introduction of money into the local economy would have on the avarice of the local people. The workmen had now uncovered nearly 8 meters (25 feet) of the facade, and one of the two colossal statues in front of the door. If Belzoni's calculations were correct, then there were at least 4.5 meters (15 feet) to go. He marked the spot carefully and extracted a promise from the headman that he would let no one touch the place until he returned in a few months. Not that he had much faith in the man's word, but he gambled on the apparent indolence of the local people.

The Belzonis now made tracks for home and headed downstream. This time they were able to spend more time at Philae and linger among the small but magnificent temples on the island. Again, Giovanni took particular notice of a small obelisk, "which, if brought to England, might serve as a monument in some particular place, or as an embellishment to the Metropolis," he wrote. This delightful monument, 6.7 meters long and 0.7 meters wide (22 feet long and 2 feet wide) at the base, could readily be transported to Cairo in a large boat when the waters of the First Cataract were high. Belzoni sent for the governor of Aswan and made him agree that he was taking possession of the obelisk in the name of his Britannic Majesty's consul general in Cairo.[17]

A small temple at the south end of the island yielded a series of twelve exquisitely carved stone blocks that could be pieced together to show the "god Osiris seated on his chair, with an altar before him, receiving offerings from priests and female figures."[18] The blocks were 76 centimeters (30 inches) thick, far too bulky to be shipped on Belzoni's boat. So he arranged for them to be sawed down for later shipping and moved his headquarters to Aswan, where he sought another boat.

No boats were to be had, for the governor had hidden them all to delay the travelers in the town. As Belzoni was about to hire camels, the same official rented him one of the hidden boats for an exorbitant price. This was one of the rare occasions when Belzoni's tactics did not prevail. He had no option but to press on, for the river was falling rapidly and Young Memnon had to be moved before the flood receded.

There were no boats at Thebes, either, for the pasha had commandeered most river craft. Fortunately, a large boat appeared on October 7 carrying two of Drovetti's agents on their way to Aswan, and Belzoni was able to engage it for the return journey. The agents moored their boat close to the carefully guarded head of Memnon and were moved to observe in their jealousy that the French invaders did not remove it, because they thought it was not worth taking.

The agents went over to Qurna with Belzoni, had the local people assembled, and told them in his presence that if they sold any antiquities to the English, they, the agents, would arrange for them to be flogged by the headman of Arment. Another member of their gang went so far as to warn Belzoni that if he persisted, his throat would be cut by order of his enemies. Undeterred, Belzoni went on with his arrangements, at the same time setting twenty men to work digging for antiquities at a likely spot near Karnak.

The great temples of Karnak were such powerful political and religious institutions that they were richly endowed with magnificent statues and other works of art by generations of wealthy pharaohs.[19] The precincts of the temples were a gold mine for any excavator two centuries ago. We cannot be sure where Belzoni dug, but it was probably somewhere within the precinct of the temple of Mut, the vulture goddess and consort of Amun, well away from where the French had been digging. In the course of a few days he found a cache of black granite statues of the goddess Sekhmet, the lion-headed counterpart of the god Ptah, and other valuable pieces. Only the money at his disposal limited the extent of his finds.

Belzoni's discoveries caused consternation among Drovetti's agents, who could do nothing to stop him. They realized that the hard-driving Italian would return for more digging. Their efforts to prevent his recruiting labor were to no avail, for the people of Karnak, unlike those of Qurna, professional tomb robbers all, were anxious for work. Fortunately, also, Calil Bey, the governor of the province and a relative of the pasha, was in Thebes. Belzoni dined with him on a dish of mutton spiced with green peppercorns, onions, and garlic dropped onto the metal serving dish by careless servants with a noise "like a drumhead." The bey expressed surprise that Europeans would want more stones, when presumably they had plenty of their own. Belzoni gravely assured him that he and his friends had plenty of stones, but thought that Egyptian ones were better. With that more than adequate response, he was given his *firman*.

While waiting for the boat and more funds from Henry Salt in Cairo, Belzoni crossed the Nile to the west bank, the ancient domain of the dead. He admired the temple of Rameses III (ca. 1194–1163 BC) at Medinet Habu, then made his way to the desolate Valley of the Kings behind Qurna.[20] There he examined the open royal tombs, some of which had been visited since Roman times. Belzoni poked into every cranny of the valley with sedulous care. At its western end he came across a heap of stones. Sand and rubbish filled the gaps between the boulders. A stick thrust through the pile met no resistance, so the next day he returned with several laborers. Within two hours, all the stones had been removed and Belzoni was able to enter a palatial tomb, which contained part of a sarcophagus and "several curious and singular painted figures on the walls." This was the tomb of Ay, a priest who briefly annexed the throne of Egypt on the death of Tutankhamun in the fourteenth century BC. Belzoni ascribed this find to luck rather than deliberate search, but it was enough to whet his appetite for another visit later on, a stay that yielded much more important results.

The boat from Aswan now arrived without the stones from Philae and loaded with a cargo of dates. The owners stopped to return the money and break the agreement. "I had much to say to them, as may be imagined in such a case," remarked Belzoni with commendable understatement. Drovetti's agents had succeeded in cowing the captain with stories of shipwreck. Belzoni's situation was desperate. The Nile was falling rapidly, and the Memnon was still on the bank. At this critical moment, fortune played into his hand. A soldier arrived with a gift of anchovies and olives and an invitation to dinner from his old enemy, the headman of Arment, a most unlikely gesture. The messenger provided enlightenment. The French consul had made the mistake of sending him an insulting present, namely, the olives and anchovies now in Belzoni's hands, instead of the sizable gifts he had been expecting. "Strange as it may appear, it will be seen that the effects of a few salted little fish contributed the greatest share towards the removal of the colossus," wrote Belzoni gleefully. Determined to strike while the iron was hot, he hastened to Arment and "set off alertly to my anchovy and olive man."[21] He found the headman in a pliable mood, provided lavish gifts, and the next day obtained a judgment against the boat owners in his favor. They were forced to unload their dates, take on Belzoni's cargo, and hire a boat of the headman to carry their fruit downstream at such an exorbitant rate that there was almost no profit for them.

Belzoni crossed to Qurna at once, for time was running short. He built a large earthen causeway from the top of the bank to the water's edge, for the shrinking Nile was now 30.5 meters (100 feet) from the head and 5.5 meters (18 feet) below it. One hundred and thirty men built the ramp in two days, a straightforward task compared with the loading itself, for the great weight of the head had to be placed right in the middle of the boat to prevent it from tipping over.

The Italian was in top form. He ordered the boat maneuvered to the end of the causeway, then constructed a crude bridge of four large poles from the causeway to the center of the craft, so that the weight of the head bore down fairly amidships. He placed a large sack of sand in the middle of the bridge to stop the Memnon if it rolled away during loading. The boat itself was carefully padded to prevent damage to the head. As his men levered the seven tons of granite toward the boat, others manned thick palm-fiber ropes secured to stout posts and around the colossus to check its descent. The operation was entirely successful, much to the surprise of the boat owners, who were in a frenzy of despair and apprehension. It was not for nothing that Belzoni had been a circus strongman.

On November 21, the Belzonis set off downstream from Thebes. Twenty-four days later, they arrived in Cairo with probably the most spectacular load of antiquities ever to be shipped down the Nile, after an arduous journey of five and a half months.

Henry Salt was away in Alexandria when the Belzonis arrived, but he had left instructions that all the antiquities were to be unloaded at the British consulate, except for the Memnon, which Belzoni was to take on to Alexandria. Belzoni obeyed this unexpected instruction without question, although he was under the impression that everything was to go to the British Museum. Early in the new year, 1817, Belzoni took the Memnon to Rosetta, transshipped it to a larger vessel, this time with proper tackle, and soon reached his destination in Alexandria, where the head was deposited in the pasha's warehouse awaiting a ship to England.

Thus ended a remarkable and exceptionally arduous archaeological expedition. Belzoni had achieved more in a short time than any of his rivals. His unique qualifications derived from circus and theater gave him an advantage in moving large antiquities that even Napoléon's armies had failed to shift. His determination and ruthlessness were matched by a shrewdness in bargaining and political intrigue that enabled him—most of the time—to get his way and outmaneuver his rivals. And rivals they were. From the moment he excavated at Thebes and entered unexplored Nubia, Belzoni had become a marked man whose life was in danger because he dared challenge a comfortable monopoly on antiquities and excited the greed of others for wealth from the Egyptian soil.

7 | "Mummies Were Rather Unpleasant to Swallow"

Then I conveyed King Djeserkare, the justified, when he sailed

south to Kush to enlarge the borders of Egypt. His majesty smote

that Nubian bowman in the midst of his army. They were carried

off in fetters, none missing, the fleeing destroyed as if they had

never been.

A H M O S E , S O N O F A B A N A ,
on the Nubian campaign of pharaoh Amenhotep I,
quoted in Miriam Lichtheim, *Ancient Egyptian Literature:*
A Book of Readings

Henry Salt was delighted with Belzoni's success and hard work. He paid the Italian fifty pounds in addition to the sum of twenty-five pounds against the Memnon that Burckhardt and he had advanced when the expedition was mooted. These payments were intended to cover Belzoni's expenses. Whether they were also wages is unclear. Certainly, Belzoni was unhappy about the arrangement, for he received neither public credit nor financial gain from the sale of the antiquities he had labored so hard on his own initiative to obtain at Thebes and Karnak. Nevertheless, he immediately proposed a second journey to finish the work at Abu Simbel.

Salt had other ideas: he was watching with interest the activities of a Genovese sea captain named Giovanni Battista Caviglia (1770–1845) who was digging in the depths of the Great Pyramid of Khufu at Giza and in tombs near the Sphinx. By great determination, Caviglia succeeded in penetrating to the bottom of the so-called Well in the pyramid, and had made other important discoveries. Salt suggested that Belzoni join the mercurial Caviglia, but the Italian declined, knowing full well that he worked better on his own. He was also worried about the activities of Drovetti's agents at Thebes. Instead, he again pressed for a second journey to Upper Egypt and Nubia, this time to last six months. Salt unwillingly agreed. Belzoni and a small party left Bulaq on February 20, 1817. This time Sarah and the Irish servant, James Curtin, stayed behind. Belzoni was accompanied by a Turkish soldier, a cook, and two employees from the British consulate—Henry William Beechey, Salt's secretary, and an interpreter named Yanni Athanasi, who was soon to become a bitter enemy.[1]

The journey started slowly, thanks to strong head winds. Progress was so leisurely that they were able to witness Arab dances, the last of which "fully compensated for the extraordinary modesty of the first." Belzoni called on the "Admiral of the Nile," Hamet Bey, and presented him with two bottles of rum, a necessary precaution to prevent their boat from being requisitioned by the pasha. Next he visited a Dr. Valsomaky, a druggist and distiller of "aqua vita" (mineral water), who also collected and sold antiquities. Two Copt interpreters in Drovetti's pay were already at his house, so Belzoni shied off rather than interfere with their business.

The next day the party called on Charles Brine, who had set up a sugar factory for the pasha near Ashmunain. Here they learned that Drovetti's Copts were now on their way to Karnak posthaste, presumably to stake out a claim on Belzoni's excavation and to buy up all the antiquities that had been found since the last travelers came through. With characteristic panache, Belzoni sprang into action. Leaving Beechey to come on by river, he hired a horse and a donkey and, accompanied by Athanasi, left in the middle of the night on a forced march of 450 kilometers (280 miles) to Karnak. During the next five and a half days, they had but eleven hours of sleep, stopping at Coptic monasteries or Arab rest houses for only a brief nap or a meal of bread and onions.

The hasty journey was in vain. The governor at Asyut was unsympathetic to Belzoni's activities, on account of a mistake by Salt's secretary, who had failed to reply to letters or send a present. In retaliation, the bey had ordered a Piedmontese doctor named Marucchi to dig in the area where Belzoni had found his lion-headed statues. Officially, the governor was forming his own collection of antiquities, but in practice he had transferred his favor to the French and was selling all the finds to Drovetti's agents. It was some consolation to Belzoni that the excavations yielded only four statues in good condition.

Fortunately, the headman of Arment (he of the anchovies and olives) was still friendly and promised every cooperation. Belzoni immediately set small gangs of workmen to dig on both banks of the Nile and concentrated his efforts on a large seated figure almost 9 meters (30 feet) high, which sat in the forecourt of Amun's Karnak temple. He found a 2-meter (7-foot) seated statue at the foot of the huge seated figure, conveniently divided in two at the waist. So he removed the bust at once and put it under guard, while the chair in which the seated king was ensconced was left in the ground until a boat could be found to transport it.

Drovetti's agents were already hard at work. With the connivance of the governor, they promptly engaged nearly all the available labor, leaving Belzoni with only a few men. So he worked near Qurna on the west bank, where the headmen were more friendly.

While awaiting Beechey and more funds, Belzoni found time to wander alone among the ruins of the vast Karnak temples without the noisy accompaniment of the inevitable touts, who plagued every traveler. Although not a particularly romantic man, he was uplifted by the magnificent architecture: "I was lost in contemplation of so many objects; for a time I was unconscious whether I were on terrestrial ground, or in some other planet." The palimpsest of columns, walls, and friezes transported Belzoni into a state of ecstasy, "as to separate me in imagination from the rest of mortals, exalt me on high over all, and cause me to forget entirely the trifles and follies of life."[2] Belzoni was happy for a whole day, until the gathering darkness caused him to stumble over a stone block and nearly break his nose. The pain brought him abruptly back to earth.

Not that there was much time for reflection. Beechey was so long in arriving that Belzoni took a boat downstream in search of him. A day later, he found his boat at Qena, but it took three days to return to Thebes against the current. Belzoni concentrated his work at Qurna, whose people "were superior to any other Arabs in cunning and deceit, and the most independent of any in Egypt."[3] They boasted of being the last people that the French had been able to subdue, and even then they had forced the invaders to pay for their services. Many hiding places abounded in rocks to the west of Thebes, a place of refuge in times of stress and a rich and apparently inexhaustible source of mummies and papyri, which the villagers sold to consuls, travelers, and antiquities merchants indiscriminately, but always at the highest prices they could extort.

Belzoni seems to have gotten on with these inveterate tomb robbers well enough to embark on a busy search for papyri. He penetrated deep into the tiny burial chambers and caves behind Qurna, where "a vast quantity of dust rises, so fine that it enters into the throat and nostrils, and chokes the nose and mouth to such a degree, that it requires a great power of lungs to resist it and the strong effluvia of the mummies. In some places there is not more than a vacancy of a foot left, which you must contrive to pass through in a creeping posture like a snail, on pointed and keen stones, that cut like glass."[4] One can imagine the problems that the huge Belzoni had in squeezing through such narrow defiles.

After struggling through the passages, some of them up to 275 meters (300 yards) long, the sweating Italian could sometimes find a place to sit down and rest:

> But what a place of rest! surrounded by bodies, by heaps of mummies in all directions; the blackness of the wall, the faint light given by the candles or torches for want of air, the different objects that surrounded me, seeming to converse with each other, and the Arabs with the candles or torches in their hands, naked and covered with dust, themselves resembling living mummies, absolutely formed a scene that cannot be described.[5]

One eventually became inured to the dust and mummies. It helped if, like Belzoni, one had no sense of smell, but even then one "could taste that the mummies were rather unpleasant to swallow." On one occasion, Belzoni

> sought a resting place, found one, and contrived to sit; but when my weight bore on the body of an Egyptian, it crushed like a band-box. I naturally had recourse to my hands to sustain my weight, but they found no better support; so that I sunk altogether among the broken mummies, with a crash of bones, rags, and wooden cases, which raised such a dust as kept me motionless for a quarter of an hour, waiting till it subsided again.

He openly admitted that his purpose "was to rob the Egyptians of their papyri; of which I found a few hidden in their breasts, under their arms, in the space above the knees, or on the legs, and covered by the numerous folds of cloth."[6]

The inhabitants of Qurna lived in the mouths of the burial caves they had despoiled. They neglected their agriculture, finding tomb robbing a more profitable venture than farming. "This is the fault of travellers," wrote Belzoni sententiously, "who are so pleased the moment they are presented with any piece of antiquity, that, without thinking of the injury resulting from the example to their successors, they give a great deal more than the people really expect."[7] The result was high prices, especially for papyri, arising in part from a firm, and probably correct, conviction on the part of the tomb robbers that the antiquities were worth ten times more than they sold them for.

The dwellings of the Qurnese lay in the passages between the tomb entrances, lit by small fat-oil lamps set in niches in the walls. Black soot covered the walls, and the bleating of sheep accompanied the constant murmur of human voices. Belzoni was warmly welcomed. "I was sure of a supper of milk and bread served in a wooden bowl," he recalled, "but whenever they supposed I should stay all night, they always killed a couple of fowls for me, which were baked in a small oven heated with pieces of mummy cases, and sometimes with the bone and rags of the mummies themselves."[8]

At first Belzoni was astonished by the casual way the Qurnese lived among the "hands, feet, or sculls" that littered the floors of their caves. They thought no more of it than if the human remains had been cattle bones. Soon Belzoni himself was indifferent to the constant presence of fragmentary ancient Egyptians. He boasted that he would just as readily sleep in a mummy pit as elsewhere.

The dead were one of Belzoni's primary targets at Qurna, his objective to obtain as many mummies as he could in the shortest possible time. So he paid the village tomb robbers regular wages as well as a bonus for the bodies they found. This made it possible for him to search alongside them. No one was suspicious or out to conceal important discoveries. Finding tombs or burial pits was a matter of luck, for there were few surface indications to go by. Less wealthy people stood stacked in rows in large burial pits, some embedded in a form of cement. Many corpses were wrapped in coarse linen without much ornamentation, their bodies deposited in dense layers right up to the entrance of the burial cave. Such burials were hardly worth the tomb robbers' time, as few ornaments or papyri were to be found in their wrappings.

The robbers eagerly sought the richly adorned burials, for the heavily bandaged and embalmed body often lay in a richly painted sycamore mummy case. Belzoni described some of the cased mummies he found, the garlands of well-preserved flowers still lying on the breasts of the bodies, the carefully wrapped packages of entrails, and the fine colors and varnish of the decorative casings. Such finds were popular with tourists and museums and had commanded a ready market for at least a century.

The burials of the most important people lay in tombs with several painted chambers bearing fine friezes of funeral processions and everyday life. Belzoni was particularly interested in the smaller objects buried with the wealthy—vases containing embalmed viscera, alabaster vessels, clay ornaments, carvings, gold leaf, and scarabs.

By this time Belzoni had accumulated a larger boatload of antiquities than he had acquired the year before, including a magnificent red granite monument bearing the figures of the cow goddess, Hathor, and other gods from the little temple of the falcon god, Montu, at the northeast corner of Karnak. He moved this fine specimen from the temple, hauling it up a slope from a narrow defile to the accompaniment of much ingenuity and clouds of fine dust, under the very noses of Drovetti's Copts. Belzoni's stockpile already contained the fine granite sarcophagus that Drovetti had given Belzoni on his first journey, now safely removed from its apparently impregnable resting place.

Belzoni had been so successful and energetic that his opponents were now seriously concerned. His finds aroused lively jealousy among Bernardino Drovetti's lethargic agents. So they bribed the governor to issue another order forbidding Belzoni to employ laborers or acquire any antiquities. Their pretext was simply that they were unable to purchase anything because Belzoni had such good relations with the people of Qurna that they sold him everything, which was probably true. As was his normal practice, Belzoni promptly called on the bey, who was visiting a village a few miles from Thebes. The official was evasive. Whenever the Italian steered the conversation toward antiquities, the governor talked of other matters. He greeted Belzoni's *firman* from the pasha with indifference, then called for horses and shifted the audience to Qurna, where he summoned the village headman and told him to produce an unopened mummy within an hour as evidence of Belzoni's influence over the locals. When an unopened burial was produced, he flew into a tantrum of rage and ordered his subordinate beaten on the spot.

Belzoni stood silently by, powerless, realizing that a loss of temper would be fatal, while the soldiers inflicted a savage beating on the unfortunate kachif. Eventually, the headman was carried off, practically insensible. Belzoni now calmly stated he would complain to the pasha. The governor realized he had gone too far. The next day an order arrived authorizing Belzoni to employ twenty men for eight days. After some difficulty, for the local people were now afraid even to talk to foreigners, he succeeded in getting enough men to stockpile all his finds on the quay at Thebes and to build a mud wall around them.

Just as the cache was completed, the bey appeared and inspected the collection, apparently in a more pliable mood. Belzoni pressed his case, complaining that his party was being treated unfairly. All he wanted was a chance to buy antiquities on an equal basis with others. The governor apparently relented, leaving orders that he might buy antiquities, as well as issuing a *firman* addressed to the kachif of Aswan, for Belzoni still had his sights on Abu Simbel.

Belzoni quietly prepared to resume work at Qurna, seeking to convince the kachif that it was now safe for him to work in the mummy pits without incurring the governor's displeasure. A public assembly was convened, at which the bey's order was read aloud. To Belzoni's horror, the famous order, which, through some strange oversight, he had never had translated, turned out to be instructions forbidding the locals to sell any antiquities to anyone but Drovetti. It was clearly impracticable to continue, so Belzoni placed a guard on his cached antiquities and took a boat upstream for Nubia in disgust.

He stopped at lovely Philae to await dispatches from Henry Salt. The party spent hours wandering through the magnificent ruins and making a wax impression of the portico of the temple of Isis, a difficult task since the thermometer mercury registered more than 51°C (124°F) in the shade!

Some days before, two young and adventurous English naval officers on half pay, Captains Charles Irby and James Mangles, joined Belzoni's small group.[9] These enterprising and engaging travelers were in the midst of a leisurely journey through Europe and the Near East in search of adventure and excitement that was taking them as far upstream as the Second Cataract. Irby and Mangles were delighted to be traveling in company with an experienced Nubian hand and added considerable strength to the party of seven.

On June 5 Sarah Belzoni turned up, accompanied by the servant, James Curtin. Belzoni gives no reason for her arrival, but he was obliged to leave her behind encamped on the roof of the temple of Isis in solitary splendor, accompanied by Curtin and a brace of firearms. There was not enough room in his single vessel for everyone.

Eleven days later, the travelers left on a boat whose five-man crew was to be a constant headache in the weeks ahead. The chief villain was a blue-shirted gentleman called Hassan, who was promptly nicknamed "the Blue Devil" by the two sea captains. Thirteen days later they arrived at Abu Simbel, only to find that the headman was absent. So they sent complimentary messages and took the opportunity to visit the Second Cataract. At this point the crew decided to mutiny. The local people demanded gifts, and loaded guns were produced. Belzoni remained calm, disinterested, and apparently good-humored. Mangles reasoned with the villagers: admittedly, the foreigners had seen the Cataract without paying, but for their part the locals had seen them, just as novel a sight, without gifts or payment. To their credit, they accepted the argument.

The headman had still not returned to Abu Simbel when the travelers returned on July 5. But two days later a messenger came from Daud Kachif asking if they were the Englishmen to whom Hassan Kachif had made promises. Fortunately, Belzoni had sent turbans from Cairo as gifts, which had not been forgotten. He lavished more presents when the kachif arrived a week later—a gun, a turban, and smaller items.

The digging went slowly at first, for the fifty men spent much of their time singing a Nubian song that proclaimed that they were going to get as much Christian money as they could. A bargain was struck with the kachifs to open the temple for three hundred piastres, a task that Belzoni calculated would take four days. He soon realized that the temple would never be opened by this means. The kachif demanded their money, the men spent a day plundering a caravan, and Ramadan began. Both the headman and the crew bombarded everyone with demands for presents; food was in short supply and could not be purchased.

So Belzoni decided to dig for himself. At three o'clock in the afternoon of July 16 the Europeans quietly slipped up to the temple and stripped to the waist. An hour later some of the crew turned up and were astonished to find the Christians working. They sheepishly joined in. By nightfall the small party had done as much digging as forty locals would have accomplished in an entire day, at the cost of many blisters.

For the next two weeks, the work continued from before dawn until the hot sun became intolerable at nine o'clock. Six hours later, the small group of diggers returned to labor again until sunset. For the most part they made steady progress, sometimes joined by their troublesome boat crew, at others by local people. The headman made repeated efforts to strip them of their firearms and equipment. Two village chiefs from the other side of the Nile came to threaten and offer assistance—for a price. The cook threw a pot of water over a man demanding money, a "truly cook-like mode of assault" that resulted in drawn swords and near bloodshed. Food again ran short, and they were unable to buy more. A foreman tried to cheat them by withholding wage tickets. But persistence was rewarded. On the last day of July, the diggers came on a broken upper corner of a doorway. By dusk they had made a hole large enough to admit a man's body but decided not to enter the temple until the next morning, for they were uncertain how much sand lay inside and the air was probably foul.

Before daybreak on the following day, Belzoni and his companions hastened to the entrance with a good supply of candles. The crew stayed behind, but soon an uproar broke out led by Hassan, the Blue Devil. Belzoni ignored loud complaints about wages and threats to leave at once, whereupon the crew arrived on the site, armed with long sticks, swords, and rusty pistols. The uproar continued amid a litany of farcical and often-repeated complaints until someone noticed that the interpreter, Giovanni Finati, had quietly slipped into the temple during the argument.[10] Immediately, everyone was agog to follow him, and arguments were forgotten.

The diggers quickly built a wall to barricade the door against drifting sand and stones. As the sun rose and shone briefly through the entrance of the temple for the first time in more than a thousand years, Belzoni was able to gaze on one of his most important discoveries. He found himself in a lofty pillared hall where eight huge Osiris-like figures of Rameses II faced one another across a central aisle. The square pillars behind the statues were decorated with brilliantly painted reliefs of the pharaoh in the presence of the gods. A smaller chamber, an antechamber, and a sanctuary opened up beyond the great hall. The rising sun's rays briefly lit up the seated figures of the gods and the pharaoh in the sanctuary—Amun-Re, Horakhty, Ptah, and Rameses himself.

The visitors gazed wonderingly at the large figures and the battle scenes, painted on the walls of the great chamber, in which Rameses conquers the Hittites at the Battle of Kadesh. Belzoni made a thorough search for portable antiquities, but there was little to be found, except for "two lions with hawks' heads, the body as large as life, a small sitting figure, and some copper work belonging to the doors."[11]

The naval men sat down to make a plan of the temple on a scale of 1/25 inch to the foot (0.6 centimeters to 0.3 meters). Meanwhile, Beechey and Belzoni collected portable items and tried to record the essence of the drawings in the temple. Beechey's drawing book was soon spoiled by perspiration, for the air in the temple was like the hottest of steam baths. But they had enough time to write lengthy descriptions of the battle scenes and the executions of prisoners. "The expression of agony and despair in their several features is admirable," recorded Mangles, who was excited and fascinated by the costumes of some of the "perfectly black" prisoners shown in the paintings.[12]

After a last admiring look at the statues, and having further strengthened the barrier at the temple door, the explorers carried their finds down to the boat and loaded them on board despite more vigorous expostulations from Hassan. On August 4, 1817, they set off downstream. It was not until eighteen months later that the interior of the temple was fully recorded for the outside world. English traveler William Bankes, Beechey, and a French draftsman named Louis Linant worked for some weeks at Abu Simbel, recording the inscriptions and paintings and clearing the sand away from the most southerly statue of the facade. Future visitors were then able to appreciate Rameses II's largest temple more fully. The monument became so famous that it was moved to higher ground by international effort in the 1960s when Lake Nasser was rising to flood it forever.

The return trip to Philae was uneventful except for another furious argument with the crew when Hassan tried to stab Belzoni and Irby cut his hand during the fracas. Sarah was waiting patiently at the temple of Isis, but the beautiful stone sculptures that Belzoni had carefully marked down the year before lay in mutilated fragments. Someone had deliberately smashed the carvings and scribbled the scornful words *opération manquée* (operation canceled) in charcoal on the stones. Belzoni was fu-

FIGURE 7.1   William Beechey's painting of Abu Simbel excavations in 1819.
Stapleton Collection/Corbis and the National Trust.

rious and suspected Drovetti's agents. But the damage was done, and he
turned his attention to other projects.

: :

Back in Thebes, Belzoni found himself hampered by Drovetti's agents at
every turn. He found that two of his most hated men had moved in on
Qurna during his absence, were "digging the ground in all directions," and
were finding plenty of mummies. Since one of them, the Piedmontese adventurer Giuseppe Rosignani, had already threatened to cut his throat,
Belzoni decided to concentrate his efforts on the Valley of the Kings,
where he had already obtained promising results a few months before.

The Valley of the Kings, separated from Qurna by a range of stony
hills, had been known as the burial place of pharaohs since classical
times. Belzoni knew of ancient reports that the valley contained at least
eighteen royal tombs. Napoléon's savants had recorded eleven and found
a twelfth, while the Italian himself had discovered the modest tomb of
the vizier and pharaoh Ay in the previous year. There were persistent ru-

mors of more royal tombs—perhaps up to forty—lying within the confines of the valley. By this time Belzoni had developed an instinct for discovery, a "nose" for new sites based on wide field experience and that intangible instinct that leads archaeologists to contemplate an area in detail over a considerable period of time in the knowledge that persistence and experience will yield dividends. He retired by himself into the Valley of the Kings, and after considerable thought chose to work in the western part.

Belzoni set a group of twenty men to work about a hundred yards (91 meters) from the entrance to the tomb of Ay. A few meters below the surface, the men came across several large boulders, apparently the entrance of a rock-cut passage. The next day Belzoni made a crude battering ram from a palm trunk rigged on a cross-pole. "The walls resisted the blows of the Arabs for some time, as they were not Romans, nor had the pole the ram's head of bronze at its end." But a breach was made at last and a staircase revealed. Eight mummies in painted cases covered with a large cloth lay at the bottom of the stairs.[13]

He was not satisfied with this undisturbed find and was even more determined to find a royal burial. On October 6 the laborers were digging in several places at once. Three days later they came across the entrance of a huge but unfurnished tomb, with "painted figures on the wall so perfect, that they are the best adapted of any I ever saw to give a correct and clear idea of the Egyptian taste." We now know that this was the tomb of Prince Montuherkhepeshef, the eldest son of Rameses IX. The same day, October 9, another large but unpainted tomb came to light close to the painted sepulcher. It had been robbed in antiquity and contained two completely naked female corpses with long hair that was "easily separated from the head by pulling it a little."[14]

This unidentified royal tomb had just been discovered when Belzoni had to break off his research to conduct three important English visitors around the temples of Thebes. The visitors were greatly excited by the royal tombs and were lucky enough to witness Belzoni's men discover another sepulcher in the valley, that of Rameses I.[15] The burial chamber still contained a red granite sarcophagus and two mummies, neither of which was that of the pharaoh. A huge wooden figure of the king dominated the chamber, one of a pair of gold foil–covered statues that had guarded the sarcophagus. This tomb lies only 18 meters (60 feet) from that of Tutankhamun, which, fortunately, Belzoni missed.

On October 16, Belzoni was on his own again. He put his men to work at a spot where he had noticed some likely surface indications, where rainwater washed down a bare slope into the floor of the valley. He does not tell us exactly why he chose this spot; indeed, his men, experienced in the ways of ancient tomb builders, thought he was on a wild-goose chase. Just before the end of work the following day, an artificial cut in the rock appeared, and Belzoni's suspicions were confirmed. Five and one-half meters (18 feet) below, the entrance of a tomb came to light, choked with huge stones and rainwater debris from the slope above. With difficulty, the workers dug out a small hole through the rubble. Belzoni wriggled into a half-choked passage beyond, which turned out to be more than 11 meters (36 feet) long. Magnificent paintings adorned the walls and ceiling. A staircase at the end of the passage led to another long and finely decorated corridor. Both passages had sloping floors so that rainwater could drain into a huge pit at their end, 9 meters deep and 4.2 meters wide (30 feet by 14 feet), which blocked further progress. Some fragments of wood and rope, which crumbled to dust at a touch, showed how some earlier visitors had crossed the pit to reach the plastered and decorated wall at the other side of the hole.

The next day Belzoni and Beechey returned with stout beams to bridge the pit and inspected a jagged aperture at the other side. It turned out to have been made by tomb robbers who had not been deceived by the attractive false wall. Belzoni squeezed through the tiny aperture and found himself in a magnificent hall with four beautifully decorated pillars adorned with figures of a pharaoh in the presence of the gods. Three steps led into another chamber decorated with unfinished paintings, another device to convince tomb robbers that the sepulcher was never completed. But they had tapped the walls and exposed a hidden entrance to a lower passage beyond. At the end of this corridor, again beautifully painted with even finer figures and gods, Belzoni came on an even larger hall with six richly painted pillars and a dark-blue ceiling, gleaming with fresh paint.

By the glittering light of candles, the two explorers now gazed on an unbelievable sight, a translucent alabaster sarcophagus covered with hieroglyphs more than 2.74 meters (9 feet) long, but only 5 centimeters (2 inches) thick. They placed a light inside. The magnificently decorated sarcophagus, shaped to accommodate the body and headdress of the pharaoh, glowed softly in the darkness. Hundreds of tiny, delicately inlaid figures adorned the inside. The bare-breasted female goddess Neith lay on

FIGURE 7.2   The alabaster sarcophagus of Seti I on display in Sir John Soane's Museum in London, where it can still be seen.

the bottom of the sarcophagus, waiting to receive the dead king.[16] Unfortunately, the sarcophagus was empty. Ancient tomb robbers had carried off the body and the lid. Belzoni found fragments of the latter, adorned with the recumbent figure of the king, in the debris near the entrance of the tomb.

Five chambers opened off the burial area, the largest of which contained a mummified bull and a large number of *shabti* figures as well as several large wooden statues "with a circular hollow inside, as if to contain a roll of papyrus, which I have no doubt they did."[17] The sarcophagus disguised the entrance of a walled-up subterranean passage, which extended 91 meters (300 feet) under the mountain in the upper part of the valley.

Belzoni had found the magnificent tomb of Seti I (1291–1278 BC), the father of Rameses II.[18] Ancient robbers had gutted the sepulcher; they left few portable items for Belzoni to remove, except for many *shabtis* and, of course, the alabaster sarcophagus, which Belzoni claimed, with reason, merited "the most particular attention" and was unlike anything else ever removed from Egypt to Europe. Fortunately, the paintings and bas-reliefs on the walls of the tomb remained in all their pristine freshness.

In Belzoni's time, no one could read the thousands of hieroglyphs on the walls, but they could admire the scenes of the pharaoh being embraced by the gods, the vultures hovering on the blue ceiling of the tomb, and the figures of the king and the cow goddess, Hathor, dressed in magnificent costumes. Giovanni Belzoni might lust after antiquities, but he was, at heart, a showman, a choreographer of the spectacular and unusual. He realized at once that the richly decorated tomb was his greatest discovery, the one find, with its magnificent decoration, that would bring him fame and success, if properly displayed. Weeks, if not months, of laborious copying lay ahead if he was to exhibit his remarkable find.

Meanwhile, news of Belzoni's spectacular discovery spread rapidly. Firearms crackled in the desert air. A large party of Turks on horseback galloped into the valley. It turned out to be Hamid Aga from Qena, who had heard rumors of great treasure and leaped to his horse to claim his share, completing a two-day journey in a scant thirty-six hours. Belzoni was mildly alarmed at such a display of force, but the governor was all smiles. The *aga* and his soldiers barely glanced at the paintings, but they searched every corner of the chamber and passages "like hounds." They found nothing. At length, the governor turned to Belzoni and asked where he had put the treasure, "a large golden cock, filled with diamonds and pearls." Belzoni, barely concealing his laughter, drew the *aga*'s attention to the glorious paintings on the walls of the empty tomb. The frustrated official just glanced at them and remarked, "this would be a good place for a harem, as the women would have something to look at." With that, he left in a state of what Belzoni called "much vexation."[19]

The three weeks after the discovery were busy ones, for the tomb had to be secured and the extensive operations in the valley shut down. As Belzoni was busy with his preparations, three large and luxurious boats of English visitors arrived at Thebes. Henry Salt himself led the party, accompanied by a Northern Irish peer, the earl of Belmore, his wife and family, and various functionaries, including the earl's private chaplain.[20] Their goal was the Second Cataract. His lordship was out to acquire a private collection of fine antiquities on his travels. Belzoni was soon conducting the distinguished visitors around Thebes and the Valley of the Kings. Belmore, with Belzoni's help and contacts, was able to acquire a large collection of papyri, mummies, and other objects that soon found their way to England. The travelers were entranced with the paintings. Salt was so excited by Seti I's tomb that he abandoned the Belmore party and spent four months digging for a royal sepulcher, but without success.

The French traveler Edouard de Montulé now turned up on his way up the Nile. He had paused at Qurna, where the tomb robbers and their nefarious trade fascinated him. The scenes of destruction surprised de Montulé but did not deter him from acquiring "the mummy of a female, wound around with broad bands of linen, and enclosed in a double case, the paintings of which are pretty well preserved." Soon the Frenchman was wandering through Seti I's tomb, accompanied by the voluble Belzoni. The paintings were entrancing, but de Montulé's conscience seems to have been troubled by the looting and destruction, if not by Belzoni's rather drastic methods. "If any perfect tombs still exist," he subsequently wrote, "I sincerely wish they may escape the research of the curious antiquary; to them the learned are become objects to be dreaded as Cambyses, for the sarcophaguses and mummies which they contained, would inevitably take the road to London or Paris."[21] He bemoaned the lack of an Egyptian national museum to house all the consular loot, a notion that was several decades ahead of its time.

Belzoni was now riding the crest of a wave. He had found no fewer than four new tombs in the Valley of the Kings in twelve days, after years of failure. Seti I's sarcophagus was a symbol of his success, but it was doubtful whether he was getting all the credit—or financial gain—he deserved. The trouble was that his business relationship with the British consul had never been exactly clarified. He had originally undertaken to bring the Memnon to Cairo and to collect other antiquities for Salt, but had received no salary or remuneration for his latest trip beyond funds for food and excavation. Relations were soon strained, despite Salt's promising to pay Belzoni a thousand piastres a month for his services retroactively from the day he left Alexandria ten months before. Belzoni could not understand a relationship that had him doing the work while the credit and antiquities went elsewhere.

But there was work to be done. The ever restless Italian loaded his precious cache of antiquities on his boat and arrived in Cairo with his spectacular cargo on December 21, 1817. The Belmore party fell in with Consul Drovetti on their return visit to Thebes as they journeyed downstream. They showed him Seti I's tomb, where he "completely ran out of the small change of compliment and admiration. He was so lavish of his civilities on entering the tomb, and every thing was so superb, magnifique, superlative and astounding, that when he came to something which really called for epithets of applause and admiration, his magazine of stuff was expended, and he stood in speechless astonishment, to the great entertainment of the beholders."[22]

8 | "Pyramidical Brains"

A great nation like England should not miss the opportunity of

making their own a man of such superior talents. He possesses, to

an astonishing degree, the secret of conciliating the Arabs and

literally makes them do what he chooses.

LIEUTENANT COLONEL CHARLES FITZCLARENCE,
Journal of a Route Across India, Through Egypt to England,
1817–1819, on Belzoni

Always at heart a showman, Giovanni Belzoni fretted at delays in Cairo, when his heart was in the Valley of the Kings and Seti I's tomb. He was short of money, but still managed to engage the services of a young Italian artist named Alessandro Ricci, who was "very clever at drawing" and with practice became an able copier of hieroglyphs. Belzoni sent him upstream with instructions to start copying. Soon he was alone, for Sarah had grown tired of the Nile and wanted to go to the Holy Land, where he planned to join her when the tomb work was completed. A few days after Christmas 1817, she left for Jerusalem dressed in young men's clothes. The faithful James Curtin and the interpreter Giovanni Finati accompanied her, as well as a janissary who was going to Jerusalem to join William John Bankes in Acre.[1]

One piece of tragic news awaited the Belzonis in Cairo. Burckhardt had died of dysentery during their absence, leaving his mission to West Africa uncompleted. At least he had had the satisfaction of knowing that the Young Memnon was on its way to England. Belzoni had lost a valuable and influential friend at a critical moment in his career. Casting around for funds, Belzoni realized that about his only sources of revenue were the few antiquities that Salt had allocated him. Among them were two lion-headed statues of the goddess Sekhmet, which he managed to sell to Count de Forbin, director general of the French Royal Collections, for 7,000 piastres.[2]

By this time, Belzoni was lodging at the British consulate and enter-taining many of the European visitors who were always passing through Cairo. His collection of antiquities—or, rather, Salt's—had become a tourist attraction in Cairo. His discoveries were being discussed, often with considerable heat, in the French and English presses. A letter from Belzoni to a friend at the Louvre was published in a French journal in 1818. His claims and discoveries were promptly castigated by the great Edmé Jomard, the talented editor of the *Description de l'Égypte*. He flatly disbelieved Belzoni's description of Seti I's sarcophagus. But Burckhardt and Salt had warmly praised Belzoni in the *Quarterly Review* and other influential London periodicals, both for his discoveries and for his me-chanical talents, which, to quote Henry Salt, "had enabled him, with sin-gular success, both at Thebes and other places, to discover objects of the rarest value in antiquity, that had long baffled the researches of the learned."[3] Whether the French liked it or not, Belzoni was rapidly acquir-ing a reputation as an archaeologist of genius.

Belzoni happened to show his collections to Major Edward Moore, an army officer with antiquarian interests who was passing through Cairo on his way to England with dispatches from India. Moore was a member of the Society of Antiquaries of London, then, as now, an influential archae-ological society in Britain. His journey to Alexandria was delayed by strong winds, so the courier accompanied Belzoni on a visit to Giza. The two antiquarians speculated idly about the interior of the Second Pyra-mid of Khafre, one of Khufu's sons, which had never been opened, al-though there had been talk among French and British residents of trying.

The Moore visit rekindled Belzoni's interest in Giza. Henry Salt had wanted him to work there before his second journey, but the Italian had refused. A fellow countryman, the volatile sea captain Giovanni Caviglia, was hard at work there and did not fancy working under him. Both Drovetti and Salt were in Upper Egypt, so the field was clear. Belzoni visited Giza a second time with another party of Europeans some days after Moore's visit. While his companion visited the Great Pyramid of

Khufu, Belzoni wandered off by himself and sat down in the shadow of a boulder contemplating "that enormous mass, which for so many ages has baffled the conjectures of ancient and modern writers."[4] He walked around the pyramid, looking for telltale traces of an entrance with an eye honed by months of work in Qurna and the Valley of the Kings. On the north side, he noticed that sand and rubble were piled up at the foot of the pyramid to a greater elevation than the lintel of any door. All his instincts suggested that an inconspicuous doorway lay below the modern ground surface.

The next day, he returned to Cairo without telling anyone of his plans, and with good reason. There had been much talk of starting a public subscription in Europe to open the pyramid, with gunpowder if necessary. Drovetti's name had been mentioned as a possible leader for the enterprise. Influential people might well have blocked Belzoni's plans. Fortunately, Belzoni was able to use backdoor contacts to obtain a *firman* from the pasha's deputy.

Taking a small tent and some food, Belzoni slipped quietly away from Cairo, ostensibly on an expedition to the Mukattam Hills east of the city. He had but two hundred pounds in his pocket and was afraid that his French rivals would try to stop his excavations, or at any rate ridicule them in public. At Giza, he recruited eighty men without trouble and set them to digging in two spots, one on the north side of the pyramid and the other on the east, where the remains of Khafre's mortuary temple, which stood in front of the pyramid, could still be seen.

The digging went slowly at first, for hard deposits of stone and mortar bent the workmen's hoes on the north side. But the temple party was soon digging 12 meters (40 feet) below the surface, where the workers uncovered a stone pavement, which is now known to have run all around the pyramid. After sixteen days of hard digging, uncovering the original surface of the pyramid and removing many large stones, the excavators found a small chink between two boulders. A long palm stick could be inserted into the crack for nearly 2 meters (6 feet) without interference. The next day they removed a loose stone, revealing a small choked-up entrance that led nowhere. After several more fruitless days, Belzoni gave his workers a day off and retreated to brood over the pyramid.

Now Belzoni's incredible "nose" for the past came into full play. He wandered back to the pyramid of Khufu and suddenly noticed that the entrance was offset from the center to the east side of the base. Hastening

FIGURE 8.1   The entrance to the Second Pyramid of Khafre.

back to the unopened pyramid, he measured off the same distance and found a telltale clue—the deposits were apparently less well compacted and there was a slight concavity in the surface of the pyramid where he estimated the entrance might lie. "Hope," he remarked, "returned to cherish my pyramidical brains."[5] He realized that rubbish piled up against the north face was higher than the entrance on the same face of Khufu's pyramid and buried it.

Renewed excavations made slow progress, for the ground was very hard. Soon, three huge boulders came to light, two on each side and one on the top. Both sloped toward the center of the pyramid. Then, on March 2, 1818, Belzoni saw the entrance for the first time. The inclined passageway leading into the pyramid proved to be 1.2 meters (4 feet) high and formed of huge blocks of granite. It took two days to unblock the passage, whereupon Belzoni found the now level defile obstructed by a huge granite boulder fitted in grooves in the walls.

Fortunately, there was a small gap at the base between the stone and a groove in the floor, which enabled Belzoni to measure the thickness of the portcullis stone. He found it was 38 centimeters (15 inches) thick. Careful probings with a barley stalk revealed an empty space ready to receive the stone in the ceiling. Slowly and laboriously, the men raised the stone with levers and propped it up with small boulders. A small Arab slipped in with a candle and reported the passage was clear. It was not long before Belzoni had raised the portcullis high enough to admit his large frame.

A month after starting work, Belzoni penetrated the interior of the burial chamber. He found that the floor dropped away to a low passage that ran back and downward under the first one toward the north face. The walls of the passage were salt encrusted and ended in a huge burial chamber with a gabled ceiling, 14 meters long, 4.8 meters across, and 7 meters high (46 feet long, 16 feet wide, and 23 feet high), carved from solid rock. A large red granite sarcophagus was sunk into the floor. The sarcophagus had been broken into and was half full of rubbish. An Arabic inscription translated by a Copt brought out from Cairo confirmed that others had been there before Belzoni.

Belzoni now cleared the lower descending passage leading from the main access passage that sloped back toward the north face. He found another burial chamber as well as a second portcullis, and established that the actual entrance lay outside the base. In the meantime, a visitor rummaging in the rubbish in the sarcophagus had found a bone fragment. Belzoni excitedly dispatched it to the curator of the Hunterian Museum of Anatomy in Glasgow, who pronounced it to be from a bull. The bovine identification seems to have vexed Belzoni and caused quiet chortling in some quarters. Belzoni described the jokers rather pettily as having "little taste in antiquity."

By this time Henry Salt, who had been digging unsuccessfully for royal burials in the Valley of the Kings, had returned to Cairo. He was closely followed by Lieutenant Colonel Charles Fitzclarence, an aristocratic officer like Edward Moore, carrying dispatches to London from the governor-general of India, Lord Hastings. Fitzclarence had traveled overland to the Nile from the Red Sea and arrived at the consulate, dead tired and after dark, where he was startled by the "extraordinary figures against the walls around me." He imagined he was in the catacombs, "had I not recollected that I was in the *sanctum sanctorum* of an inveterate and most successful antiquarian." Salt was having dinner when the colonel arrived, but their meeting was overshadowed by the appearance of Belzoni, who presented a striking appearance in Turkish costume, "the handsomest man I ever saw."[6]

Two days later, Fitzclarence and Salt accompanied the Italian on an excursion to Khafre's pyramid. Fitzclarence was impressed by Belzoni's achievements and the man himself. "I have had a long conversation with

FIGURE 8.2
Giovanni Belzoni in
Turkish dress.

Belzoni," he wrote. "He professes that his greatest anxiety is to become known to the various antiquarians of Europe. He said he looked upon it as a fortunate circumstance I had passed through Egypt, and trusted I should be able to speak of him in England, so as to bring his merits before a nation to which he declares himself to be most devotedly attached." Soon Fitzclarence was promising to publish an account of the entry of the Second Pyramid written in Belzoni's own hand.

Belzoni's personal relationship with Salt was not so cordial. The consul had immediately offered to pay the full expenses of the pyramid excavations, some 150 pounds. But Belzoni refused and jealously guarded his latest discovery in a fit of deep resentment against the eager antiquarian. By now, the consulate was full of exciting and unique statuary and hundreds of smaller antiquities, many of them of great rarity. Belzoni's only reward had been the money for the Memnon and the price of the two statues he had sold to the French. He was mortified to discover that many of his discoveries had been claimed by others "who had no more to do with them than the governor of Siberia, except as far as related to supplying me with money."[7] He felt that he had gained no personal credit for his remarkable discoveries and that the fame he craved so greatly had eluded him. Only word of mouth from returning travelers revealed the true state of affairs.

A series of long and protracted arguments dragged on. Neither Belzoni nor Salt seemed to be able to communicate with the other. Eventually, they drew up an agreement, under which Belzoni was to receive 500 pounds during the next year, half the price of Seti I's alabaster sarcophagus when it was sold, and assistance in gathering a collection for himself in the Thebes region. For his part, Belzoni undertook to assist the consul to remove some sarcophagi still in Upper Egypt and to help Beechey, now the consul's agent there, in any way possible. The agreement was signed in Cairo on April 20, 1818, and the two men parted on good terms. With that, Belzoni set off for Thebes on his third and final journey up the Nile.

Only pausing to renew his *firman* with the governor, who had given him so much trouble on his earlier journey, Belzoni joined Alessandro Ricci in the Valley of the Kings, where the diligent artist had been busy at work in Seti I's tomb for more than two months. The copying work was well advanced, so Belzoni now began the laborious task of making wax impressions of the major bas-reliefs. Belzoni and Ricci lived in the tomb for most of the summer, a rather cooler base than the searing floor of the valley, but nevertheless a hot and uncomfortable place to copy hieroglyphs and work with soft wax. Wax alone melted too readily and had to be mixed with resin and fine dust to form a workable compound. The hardest task was to make the wax impression without damaging the paint on the walls. Enormous numbers of castings were needed: "The figures as large as life I found to be in all a hundred and eighty two: those of a smaller size, from one to three feet, I did not count, but they cannot be less than eight hundred. The hieroglyphics in this tomb are nearly five hundred."[8] The copying operation was an astonishing feat of patience and skill under very trying conditions.

Seti I's tomb, now protected with a stout wooden door, preoccupied Belzoni for most of the summer of 1818. He had little time for excavation, although his *firman* allowed him full access to both banks of the Nile at Qurna. Unfortunately, Drovetti's agents had staked out both sides of the river. Furthermore, Henry Salt had quietly marked down extensive claims of promising ground before leaving for Cairo. Rather than risk a confrontation, Belzoni had retired to "his tomb," in the extraordinary position of being at Thebes at his own expense for the first time yet unable to dig for himself. "If I pointed out any spot in any place whatsoever, one of the parties, I mean the agents of Mr. Drovetti or those of Mr. Salt, would consider it was valuable ground, and protest that it was taken by them long before. I verily believe, if I had pointed out one of the sandbanks or the solid rocks, they would have said they just intended to have broken into it the next day."[9]

Belzoni's competitors had taken effective steps to see that the most successful archaeologist among them was frozen out. After some abortive excavation at localities that he had already found unproductive and had not been claimed by the others, Belzoni defied Beechey's protests on behalf of Salt and worked over a spot behind the two great Colossi on the Nile floodplain marked out by the British consul. Drovetti had already dug there and found only a few broken statues. But Belzoni had his usual luck. On the second day of excavations, he uncovered a magnificent seated black granite statue of the pharaoh Amenhotep III, in almost perfect condition. With admirable restraint, he ceded the rights of ownership to Henry Salt and merely contented himself with carving his initials on the base. This beautiful statue can be seen in the British Museum.

After this chance discovery, Belzoni abandoned excavation and concentrated on his tomb. But he did manage to accumulate what he modestly called "a little collection of my own, in which I can boast of having a few good articles, particularly in manuscript, &c."[10] His friends among the tomb robbers of Qurna were only too glad to sell him some of their choicest discoveries, for he, of all the excavators of the time, seems to have made a real effort to understand their society and way of life—partly, of course, in strict self-interest.

: :

With Thebes virtually closed to him, Belzoni's interests were shifting. He knew that his time in Egypt was drawing to a close, that rich opportunities as a showman awaited him back in Europe. It was time to cash in on his growing reputation as a tomb robber, so he focused most of his efforts on copying Seti I's tomb and its spectacular burial chamber. Meanwhile, he followed with interest the pasha's sudden interest in the potential of the desert between the Red Sea and the Nile.

Some time before, two Copts had called on the pasha after an arduous desert crossing from the Red Sea to the Nile. They told him that they had seen some old sulfur mines in the mountains near Kosseir, overlooking the ocean. The mildly interested pasha looked around for an experienced European traveler to inspect the mines and, on the recommendation of Consul Drovetti, appointed Frédéric Cailliaud, a young French mineralogist and antiquarian who had arrived in Egypt just before Belzoni and had worked for Drovetti on several occasions, as government mineralogist. Cailliaud had met Drovetti while studying Arabic in Alexandria in 1816. Subsequently, they had traveled widely together, especially in the Western Desert.[11]

Cailliaud was an extremely perceptive geologist by the standards of the day. He confirmed that the sulfur mines were useless, but also visited Gebel Zabara, the famed site of emerald deposits worked by the Ptolemies, described by classical writers, and uninvestigated since then. The young Frenchman returned two months later with glowing reports of the emerald deposits. He was promptly dispatched once again, this time with a party of Syrian miners. Cailliaud came back in a few months with 4.5 kilograms (10 pounds) of rough emeralds and tantalizing stories of a ruined city with eight hundred houses and several temples lying nearby. Although the ruins were at least 18 kilometers (8 miles) from the sea, the armchair antiquarians of Cairo immediately claimed that they were the remains of the ancient city Berenice, the pharaohs' main trading port on the Red Sea and a center of vigorous commerce with Arabia, India, and the Persian Gulf, especially under the Ptolemies. Visions of a new Pompeii rose before the eyes of Cairo's antiquaries, for Cailliaud had written a glowing report of his discoveries.

A few months later, one of the Syrian miners became ill while visiting the Nile to buy provisions. Hearing that a Christian doctor was living in the Valley of the Kings, he called on Belzoni and Ricci and begged for treatment. Belzoni had heard rumors of Cailliaud's discovery and questioned the man closely. The miner soon offered to guide him to the place. Since the work at Seti I's tomb was now almost complete and there seemed to be little going on at Thebes, Belzoni leaped at the chance of a new expedition. Within a few days, on September 16, a small expedition was ready to move. The party of eight included the miner; Belzoni; Ricci, whose artistic talents might prove useful; Beechey; and several servants.

The expedition hired a small boat to take them upstream to Edfu, where they were to cut across the desert toward the Red Sea. On the way, they witnessed a tragedy in the making. It was a year of record flood. The

FIGURE 8.3   *The Nile in flood,* Giovanni Belzoni.

Nile had already risen 1 meter (3.5 feet) above the previous year's flood
level, inundating several villages and drowning several hundred people.
Every available boat carried precious grain to higher ground. One village
they called at was already 1.2 meters (4 feet) below river level. The villagers stood vigil day and night at the surrounding dikes. There were no
boats in the village or palm trees to climb if the earthen barriers broke.
Farther upstream, the situation was even more critical. Whole villages had
washed away. People clustered on patches of higher ground with their
grain and stock. There was danger of starvation, for the flood would not
recede for at least two weeks and there were few watercraft. Some people
had fled to safety on the backs of water buffalo or on bundles of reeds.
Belzoni was unable to do anything to help, for his small boat would have
been swamped by a great press of people. But at Arment, farther upstream, they spent most of a day ferrying people to safety across the river.
The fourth and last trip across the flooded stream brought the women to
safety, "the last and most insignificant of their property, whose loss would
have been less regretted than that of the cattle."[12]

At Esna, they called on Ibrahim Bey, the governor, who received Belzoni very civilly and readily granted them a *firman*, but with strict instructions that they were not to mine for emeralds. As always, the Turks
could not understand why anyone would be interested in ruins or stones
and suspected some more mercenary motives. The chief miner, Muham-

mad Aga, who turned up at Edfu just after Belzoni's arrival, shared the same suspicions. By this time, the local headman had arranged for camels and drivers with Sheik Abeda, the leader of the desert tribe through whose territory the route to the mines passed. Belzoni's bargaining skills ensured camels at a piastre a day and a small wage for the drivers. But the next day he found the sheik less cooperative. Obviously, the chief miner had aired his suspicions, for he had pressed Belzoni to wait on his journey until his own return. Belzoni countered by insisting that the camels depart the same day, before the sheik had time to delay him further. On the afternoon of September 22, 1818, the caravan of sixteen camels, six of them laden with provisions, set out on a well-trodden desert trackway that had been in use for centuries.

Not much was known about Berenice. The city had first come into prominence in the third century BC, when Ptolemy II built the port in a small, sheltered bay protected from the prevailing strong northerly winds. From the sea captain's point of view, off-loading at Berenice cut short the passage up the Red Sea against often blustery head winds, although the port itself was more than 400 kilometers (250 miles) from the Nile. The pharaoh also constructed a road from Berenice to Koptos on the Nile. A southern branch route joined the Nile at Edfu. Both assumed ever greater importance as the volume of Red Sea trade in elephants, precious metals, exotic stones, spices, and such luxuries as "singing boys" increased, especially after the monsoon trade of the Indian Ocean linked Alexandria with Arabia and South Asia in the first century BC.[13]

Belzoni chose the southern route. The first part of the journey passed through level but arid countryside covered with stunted sycamore trees and thickets of camel thorn. Soon the expedition came across traces of an ancient settlement, abandoned caravan stations for early travelers on the road, identified by scattered boulders and filled-up wells. At the end of the second day they camped at the entrance to the Wadi Hiah, near a small rock-cut temple. The remains of a guard station with a camel enclosure and accommodation for travelers lay nearby.

They resumed their journey before daybreak on September 25 and came to more desertic country where little vegetation was to be seen. The same evening Alessandro Ricci was taken violently ill. Belzoni sent him back to the Nile before he got worse. He also split the caravan into two, the heavy baggage going to the east along the main road, while he and

FIGURE 8.4   *Temple on the Road to Berenice,* Giovanni Belzoni.

Beechey took a side trip to look at some ruins described by the local people. They turned out to be another roadside watering place.

The local Ababde people lived in small settlements scattered across the desert. They were independent-minded nomads who owed allegiance to no government. Some made a sketchy living by breeding and trading camels, but most were content to live at a subsistence level. With their dark complexions and black curly hair, they closely resembled the Nubians that Belzoni had met at Abu Simbel. Most Ababde walked around nearly naked, except for elaborate hairstyles, which they covered with small pieces of mutton fat—when they had any. The fat melted in the hot sun, producing "an exquisite odour for those who have a good nose."[14] Belzoni found the Ababde quite friendly and willing to sell a few sheep, although there were few to be obtained owing to a prolonged drought. He marveled at their endurance, for they were able to go for twenty-four hours without water, even in the hottest season.

About two in the afternoon of September 29, after seven days on the road, they saw the blue waters of the Red Sea at a great distance. The following day they reached the miners' encampment at the foot of Gebel Zabara. Conditions in the camp were appalling, with famine a constant reality. Provisions came by camel from the Nile and never arrived on time. The Ababde resented the miners' presence and their rough ways with local women. No emeralds had come to light in the ancient workings, and the work of clearing the old shafts was highly dangerous. Fights were commonplace. At least two miners died in an uprising against their leaders.

Belzoni was anxious to move on. So he stopped for a brief look at the ancient mines, acquired as much (vague) information as he could from the miners, and engaged a local guide for the brief trip to Cailliaud's ancient city.

The journey was a nightmare of thirst and arduous going. Their guide led them through rough, narrow valleys and a steep and craggy pass that exhausted their camels. No sign of Berenice appeared from the summit, although Cailliaud's lyrical descriptions had led Belzoni to expect lofty columns and fine temples.

Clearly, Cailliaud's account was grossly exaggerated. They came across some enclosures and ruined walls close to the ocean, which the guide insisted were the remains of Cailliaud's city. Violent expostulations ensued, for Belzoni was determined to press on to the coast. Finally, he mounted his camel again, much to the annoyance of the animal, which would much rather have stayed where it was. The rest of the caravan followed reluctantly as Belzoni spurred his camel down a south-facing valley. For more than four hours he traversed the valley in all directions looking for the ruins, but without success. The travelers pitched camp under a large rock. They had now run out of water and had but twenty days' supply of biscuits. The nearest water was 24 kilometers (15 miles) away, so the camels were sent off to drink and to fetch water for the human members of the party. Meanwhile, the Europeans dined on biscuits and a three-day-old piece of mutton that made Belzoni thankful he had no sense of smell.

The next morning Belzoni and Beechey made their way over to a hill about 8 kilometers (5 miles) away to survey the landscape. No city, no Red Sea, could be discerned, and Belzoni realized that Cailliaud's report was totally inaccurate. Bitterly disappointed, he compared Cailliaud's ruins to the fantasies of Don Quixote.

The travelers were now practically lost, for they had no maps except Jean-Baptiste Bourguignon d'Anville's famous map of the Red Sea, published in 1766, which was far from accurate and on too small a scale.[16] The trend of the valley drainages seemed to be toward the south, and Belzoni conjectured that the Red Sea lay in that direction. When the weary camels returned, he gave orders to resume the journey by the least-arduous route. Eventually, the caravan set off in a northeasterly direction, which took them down a steep-sided valley to a narrow opening in the mountains known as Khurm el Gemal, translated by Belzoni as "rent of the camels." There they camped at sunset. At noon the following day they sighted the blue waters of the Red Sea and soon were plunging into the ocean "like crocodiles into the Nile."

Belzoni now had but seventeen days' food left and turned southward along the coast in search of the elusive port. The drivers protested. Their protests were in vain in the face of Belzoni's determination, so the camels were watered at a well and the caravan set off along the sandy and rock-strewn coast. They soon encountered some fishermen, who caught a meal for them using a crude dugout canoe to spear large fish some distance offshore. Belzoni also feasted on shellfish taken from the rocks. Unfortunately, these aggravated the travelers' thirst.

The party now split in two. The baggage and most of the camels were sent off to a nearby spring in the mountains, while Beechey and Belzoni, with five men, two boys, and five camels, pressed on to the south with as much water as they could carry. Two days later, the expedition was thirsty, although not hungry, for they had helped themselves to some fish cooking in a deserted fishermen's camp. Beechey scrupulously left money for the meal, for the inhabitants fled at the sight of the strangers and refused to return. On October 7, they reached Ras Banas and camped near the shore with only a little water to satisfy their raging thirst. The following day brought them to the unmistakable signs of a long-abandoned city. "We entered," recalls Belzoni, "and at once we saw the regular situations of the houses; the main streets, their construction, and in the centre, a small Egyptian temple, nearly covered by the sand."[16] The site lay inside an amphitheater of mountains and was sheltered by the mass of Ras Banas to the north. Belzoni measured the town and found it covered an area of more than 609 by 488 meters (2,000 by 1,600 feet). He was convinced—and later archaeological researchers have proved him right—that this was indeed the site of Berenice. But it was far less spectacular than Belzoni had hoped.

Time was running short, for water supplies were dwindling and they had eaten nothing but dry biscuits since the cooked fish of several days before. Their guides were thirsty and restless, so Belzoni had to promise that he would leave at noon the next day. Fortunately, it was full moon and they could survey and sketch at night. One of the Egyptian boys was set to work clearing sand from the temple. For some reason Belzoni had forgotten to bring a spade, so they had to use a large seashell. The boy managed to clear a hole 1.2 meters (4 feet) deep and unearthed a bas-re-lief and part of an inscription engraved on a small tablet of red breccia (naturally cemented rock). They took it away as evidence of their visit. We now know that the temple was dedicated to Serapis, the Apis-Osiris cult so popular through the Nile Valley in Roman times.

While the boy was excavating the temple, Beechey and Belzoni sur-veyed the town. They found that the homes lay close together and were at the most 12 by 6 meters (40 by 20 feet) across. Many were smaller, and Belzoni estimated that there were 4,000 houses at Berenice. But he cut this estimate in half to 2,000, "so that I might not be mistaken for another Cailliaud." Belzoni had just enough time to complete these calculations and to measure the temple—he found it to be 39.6 meters long by 13 me-ters wide (130 by 43 feet). He calculated that a population of about 10,000 people had lived in Berenice at the height of its prosperity.

They were fortunate enough to find water at about midnight on the second day, at a well called Aharatret in the hills behind Berenice. Even better was the sight of a flock of sheep, but the owners promptly "drove the intended repast away." Belzoni sent his drivers in pursuit, and they stopped the two young girls tending the flock as they were slipping into hiding. "We were gallant with them, for the sake of devouring some of their lambs," remarked Belzoni circumspectly, "but the sheep prevailed above all, and took our chief attention."[17] They were soon feasting on half-cooked but tough mutton for the first time in days. Two days later they rejoined the rest of the caravan at the spring of Amusue, where water flowed in abundance, observing traces of the ancient caravan route from Berenice to the Nile on the way.

Belzoni was now certain that he had located Berenice and that all Cail-liaud had seen was a large miners' camp of small houses scattered over an arid and hilly terrain where the sun baked the soil like an oven and life was harsh and lonely. Cailliaud's imagination had been fired by these des-olate ruins. He had wandered in and out of the houses for some time. "With unbounded satisfaction," he wrote, "I greeted and hailed a town, hitherto unknown to all our voyagers, which had not been inhabited, per-haps, for 2,000 years, and almost entirely standing."[18] Belzoni was openly scornful of the place. He counted only eighty-seven houses, as opposed to Cailliaud's estimate of eight hundred.

The homeward journey was wearisome and thirsty. By the time they reached the mountains by the Nile the camels were so tired they could hardly crawl. Four died by the roadside. The travelers were much troubled by bad well water and thirst. By the time they reached the Wadi Hiah temple five days later they were so thirsty that the water in the last well, which had tasted horrible on the way out, "appeared pretty good on our return."

On October 23, after an absence of little more than a month, Belzoni and Beechey reboarded their boat and paid off their weary drivers, taking care to give a present of pocket pistols to the helpful local headman. By this time the Nile flood had receded. "All the lands that were under water before were now not only dried up, but were already sown; the muddy villages carried off by the rapid current were all rebuilt; the fences opened; the Fellahs at work in the fields, and all wore a different aspect."[19]

Belzoni had good reason for satisfaction. He had undertaken an arduous desert journey under difficult conditions and returned without losing a man. He had solved the mystery of Berenice and placed Cailliaud's discovery in a more sober perspective. He could now return to his archaeological researches in the comfortable knowledge that he had established a credible reputation for exciting and unusual discoveries, something that Belzoni prized above all else.

9 | High Jinks at Philae

I must now enter into new contests with evil beings; and in spite of

all the study I made to avoid bringing before the public foul deeds

of malice, I find that I cannot avoid inserting them into this volume.

GIOVANNI BELZONI,
*Narrative of the Operations and Recent Discoveries Within the
Pyramids, Temples, Tombs, and Excavations, in Egypt and Nubia,*
on his enemies

The desert seduced Giovanni Belzoni. For a while, he craved solitary adventure, perhaps as an escape from the internecine rivalries of Thebes. No sooner had he reached the Nile than he began to plan a return to Berenice, or a journey to the great Kharga oasis in the Western Desert, which Cailliaud had also visited. But developments at Qurna intervened.

Henry Salt was now in residence near the village, accompanied by a large party of wealthy travelers. These included baron Albert von Sack, a Prussian nobleman who was a dedicated naturalist with long experience of tropical environments, and William John Bankes, an adventurous young antiquarian with a penchant for travel and sparkling conversation. Bankes had been at university with the poet Lord Byron and shared some of his liberal tastes and values.[1] The party was traveling in high style and proposed a leisurely journey up to the First Cataract, with the general objective of removing the beautiful obelisk that Belzoni had claimed in Salt's name on his first journey.

Salt had now ceded his rights to the obelisk to Bankes, who was evidently delighted when Belzoni accepted a commission to transport it to Cairo. Belzoni joined the party with alacrity, for the luxury was incredible after the privations of recent months. The consul had a large boat, two smaller ones carried Bankes and the baron, while a raucous canoe-load of "sheep, goats, fowls, geese, ducks, pigeons, turkeys, and donkeys" brought up the rear and "accompanied the fleet with a perpetual concert." Belzoni was not long impressed with the luxurious waste. "Even at table," he wrote sarcastically, "we had not ice to cool ourselves after the heavy repast, which was concluded with fruits, and only two sorts of wine. In short our lives were a bother to us from the fatigue and dangerous mode of travelling."[2]

The stay at Qurna gave Belzoni and Salt some time together. Belzoni complained that he had no chance to collect on his own account, so a new, and more satisfactory, agreement was made. He could now dig at Salt's expense on either bank of the Nile in the British claim areas, and one-third of the finds were to be his. It is surprising that Belzoni and Salt did not reach an agreement of this type much earlier, for it was by far the fairest arrangement under the circumstances.

Soon afterward, Bernardino Drovetti arrived in Thebes. He promptly made an offer for Seti I's alabaster sarcophagus, which was immediately rejected. Belzoni and Salt accompanied Drovetti on a tour of the Karnak sites to check the various areas reserved for the British. The meeting was superficially cordial, and any misunderstandings about rival claims were soon worked out. But Drovetti, while amiability itself, persisted in telling stories about a man dressed like Belzoni who was hiding in the ruins and wished to do the Italian harm. So he had warned the local headman about the stranger. Salt laughed at the story, but Belzoni was concerned, for he feared that "if I had happened to go among the ruins, which it was my constant practice to do, and some one had sent a ball at me, they could have said after, that they mistook me for the person who had assumed my appearance in dress and figure."[3] This incident put Belzoni on his guard, which, perhaps, was fortunate.

After the tour Drovetti regaled his guests with sherbet and lemonade in his hut among the ruins. The talk was of Berenice and of antiquities in general, until Belzoni let slip his plan to remove the obelisk at Philae, despite the lateness of the season. Immediately, Drovetti feigned surprise. The rogues at Aswan had deceived him, he said, for they had promised on many occasions to bring the obelisk down for him. Belzoni pointed out that he had taken possession of it on Salt's behalf during his first trip into Nubia and had paid for guards to protect it. He quickly explained that Salt had given the obelisk to Bankes, on whose behalf he, Belzoni, was to remove it to Alexandria. Drovetti then conceded the ownership to Bankes with charming courtesy, rather in the manner that he had given the granite sarcophagus to Belzoni many months before. Presumably, he assumed that the obelisk could never be moved. But he did casually ask when the English party planned to depart.[4]

Two days later, on November 16, the large caravan left for the First Cataract. Six days later they came to the temple of Edfu, where they found Drovetti's agents hard at work.[5] They also heard that one of the agents had just left posthaste for Philae in response to an urgent message from downstream. A little farther upstream they overtook the Piedmontese Antonio Lebolo, one of Drovetti's agents who hated Belzoni, traveling up the Nile at speed in a small boat. He refused to stop in answer to their hails. Belzoni was sufficiently worried to leave the main party at Kom Ombo and charter a special vessel to take him on to Aswan as quickly as possible.

The mischief was done by the time he reached Aswan. Lebolo had started by trying to persuade the local people not to let Belzoni have the obelisk. The governor, who had reason to be grateful to Belzoni, pointed out that the English had taken possession of the obelisk three years before and paid for a guard all this time. The crafty Piedmontese now resorted to bribery. He crossed over to Philae, pretended to read the inscriptions on the obelisk, and told the gullible locals that the hieroglyphs stated that the monument had belonged to Drovetti's ancestors. A bribe and an affidavit in front of the local magistrate completed Lebolo's dirty tricks. He then promptly disappeared.

Belzoni arrived too late to stop Lebolo, but he managed to convince the governor of Aswan of the legitimacy of his own claim. Time was obviously of the essence. The obelisk would have to be removed immediately, or the Nile would be too low for safe transport across the Cataract. So Belzoni decided to ignore Lebolo's phony document of ownership and rely on possession being nine-tenths of the law. Fortunately, he enjoyed much better relations with the local people than did Drovetti's harsh agents. With characteristic effrontery, he gave the governor a handsome present of a watch and presented the boat captain with half his money in advance, as a bribe for moving the obelisk through the Cataract. It's an interesting reflection on Belzoni's powers of persuasion that the same captain had refused to attempt the same task for Drovetti two months earlier on the grounds that the water was already too low.

The strongman wasted no time in bringing his expertise to bear. He assembled a set of hauling tackle and then moored the boat to the riverbank close to the obelisk. His greatest difficulty was finding suitable poles to move the monument the few critical meters to the bank, for wood was in short supply. But enough timber came to hand over the next few days to shift the obelisk by rather similar methods to those used with the Young Memnon. Just as operations were about to begin, the governor himself brought over a letter from Drovetti telling him to allow no one to remove the obelisk except himself. Salt told him to give his compliments to Drovetti and to tell him the English were taking it anyhow.

Meanwhile, the workers had built a rough stone causeway out from the bank, while Belzoni went off to spy out a channel through the Cataract. Then disaster struck. As the obelisk was rolled out along the causeway, the foundation stones sank into the mud. The priceless monument slid slowly into the Nile. Belzoni was transfixed with horror. Only the tip of the obelisk could be seen above the swirling water.

The rest of the party left Belzoni alone with his problems and sailed on upstream into Nubia. A close inspection of the obelisk convinced the Italian that two or three days should see the obelisk in safety. Fortunately, the Philae workmen were both strong and very willing to work. They hauled large numbers of extra stones to the riverbank, then laid them underwater close to the obelisk. Now Belzoni came into his own. He worked large levers under the monument, then gradually lifted it onto dry land, heaping a pavement of stones under it as it was turned toward the shore. In two days the obelisk stood on dry land.

Meanwhile, Drovetti's agent put the whole town of Aswan in an uproar and brought the *aga* to Philae in an attempt to stop operations. But neither the governor nor the local people seemed inclined to stop Belzoni, regarding the quarrel as a matter between the English and the French. Belzoni steadfastly continued the loading operation, using a bridge of palm trunks to move the obelisk aboard the waiting boat.

The next morning, Belzoni brought the boat and its precious cargo to the edge of the steepest part of the Cataract, some 375 meters (300 yards) long. He made careful preparations for the descent. A heavy rope was tied to a large tree upstream of the torrent and the other end passed inboard so that the five men remaining aboard could control the boat as it swept through the rapids. At the same time, Belzoni stationed men on the rocks on either side of the Cataract. They also held ropes attached to the boat, so they could pull or release them to prevent its being staved in against the rocks. Everything depended on the skill of the river men, for the large rope attached to the stern was incapable of stopping the boat on its own. It was merely sufficient to check the breakneck pace of descent through the rapids. The ship's captain was beside himself with anxiety. Tearfully, he begged Belzoni to give him his boat back. Finally, he threw himself on the ground and buried his face in the sand, refusing to witness the imminent destruction of his most valuable possession.

When everything was ready and the men were in position, Belzoni gave the signal to slacken the cable:

> It was one of the greatest sights I have seen. The boat took a course, which may be reckoned at the rate of twelve miles an hour. Accordingly, the men on land slackened the rope; and at the distance of one hundred yards the boat came in contact with an eddy, which, beating against a rock, returned towards the vessel, and that helped much to stop its course. The men on the side pulled the boat out of the direction of that rock, and it continued its course, gradually diminishing its rate, till it reached the bottom of the cataract; and I was not a little pleased to see it out of danger.

Even the workers were thrilled at the safe passage. The captain of the boat "came to me with joy expressed in his countenance, as may easily be imagined."[6]

There were only two or three more dangerous spots to be traversed. These presented few problems, and the precious cargo reached Aswan safely the same day. One of Belzoni's most daring and tricky exploits had ended in brilliant success. Never knowing when he might return, he was careful to pay off the local people and the governor to everyone's satisfaction, setting off downstream to Thebes as quickly as possible. Head winds delayed the passage, so Belzoni went on by land and took up residence again in his old home in Seti I's tomb. There he found Sarah waiting for him.

Sarah had had an adventurous journey to Palestine, one that rivaled Belzoni's own arduous travels in its frustrations and many dangers. Accompanied by James Curtin and Giovanni Finati, she had made her way to Jerusalem in time for Easter, bathed in the Jordan, and visited Nazareth.

Most of the time she was dressed as a Mamluk youth and traveled practically by herself, a dangerous thing to do in the best of times in Palestine in the early nineteenth century. When she realized that her husband would not be joining her, Sarah returned to Alexandria on an evil-smelling packet boat. The cabin she had booked was full of melons and the deck crowded with Albanian soldiers. Soon she came down with a serious stomach fever. "I never suffered on the ocean what I suffered on this insignificant voyage," she wrote some years later. It took her ill-fated packet no less than thirteen calm-plagued days to cross from Jaffa to Egypt.[7]

She engaged a boat to take her to Thebes, accompanied only by a young Mamluk. The journey was uncomfortable, for dense rains soaked her bedding and possessions. The same storm had washed mud into Seti I's tomb, the humidity causing some of the walls to crack. She ordered the mud removed and sat down to wait for her husband. He returned on December 23, and they spent a quiet Christmas together, "in the solitude of these recesses, undisturbed by the folly of mankind."[8] It was a wonderful rest and reunion.

The day after Christmas Belzoni and his Greek interpreter mounted donkeys and, accompanied by two Arab servants, went over to Karnak. The obelisk had arrived safely at Thebes on Christmas Eve. Rather tactlessly, the captain had moored the boat under the noses of Drovetti and his agents at Karnak. "It irritated them," recalls Belzoni, and the irritation led to a violent confrontation, which, according to the Italian, was deliberately engineered by the Frenchman.

As Belzoni made his way toward Karnak, he met an Arab who warned him not to go near the other Europeans. He ignored the warning and soon came upon a party of laborers working on one of Salt's claims. Despite the protests of the interpreter, Belzoni feigned to ignore them, recognizing the provocative stratagem for what it was. So he went on past the great temple of Karnak where the Drovetti party was lodging and inspected some of Salt's claims nearby. He then set off for Thebes, passing again near the great propylaeum of the temple where he met an Arab who cried out that he had been beaten because he worked for the English. Belzoni again ignored this attempt at provocation and passed on his way.

Soon he noticed Drovetti's agent Antonio Lebolo, Giuseppe Rosignani, and about thirty armed Arabs hurrying toward him. In a moment, the angry men had surrounded Belzoni and his interpreter. Loudly, Antonio Lebolo inquired why he had moved Drovetti's obelisk from Philae, for it was not Belzoni's property. With that, he seized the bridle of Belzoni's donkey with one hand and his waistcoat with the other. The Arabs disarmed the Italian's servants and beat them. Rosignani pointed his double-barreled rifle at Belzoni's chest in a rage. It was time, he said, for Belzoni to pay for his deeds. "My situation was not pleasant, surrounded by a band of ruffians like them," remarked Belzoni with almost casual understatement, "and I have no doubt that if I had attempted to dismount, the cowards would have dispatched me on the ground, and said that they did it in defense of their lives as I had been the aggressor." So he decided to stay on his donkey and treat them with contempt. This only inflamed their tempers.

Drovetti and another band of armed Arabs now came on the scene. The consul angrily demanded what Belzoni meant by stopping his men from digging and ordered him to dismount. Belzoni replied that he knew of no such instance and complained of the discourtesy shown him. "At this moment a pistol was fired behind me, but I could not tell by whom. I was determined to bear much, sooner than come to blows with such people, who did not blush to assail me all in a mass; but when I heard the pistol fired behind my back, I thought it was high time to sell my life as dear as I could." So he dismounted in a fury.

At this point, Drovetti evidently realized matters had gone too far and attempted to smooth things over. Among other things, the local Arabs had come to Belzoni's aid and had surrounded Rosignani with menacing threats. The affair ended with Belzoni's "informing Mr. Drovetti that I had resisted many and various sorts of attacks by his agents, but I did not expect they would come to such a pitch, and that it was high time for me to quit the country." He returned to the Valley of the Kings in a state of fear and agitation, where Sarah was having "a violent bilious fever."[9]

It took a month to pack up the valuable wax impressions and records from Seti I's tomb. The fragile alabaster sarcophagus was carefully transported on rollers from its centuries-old home over 4.8 kilometers (3 miles) of uneven terrain to Belzoni's boat. Belzoni even found time to repair some of the damage to the tomb caused by the flood. Then on January 27, 1819, the Belzonis left Thebes for the last time. "I must confess," he wrote, "that I felt no small degree of sorrow to quit a place which was become so familiar to me."[10]

The Belzonis took their valuable cargo all the way to Alexandria with the intention of taking ship for Europe immediately. But a letter from Salt caused Belzoni to delay, for the consul recommended that he institute legal proceedings against the miscreants. Mr. Lee, the British consul in Alexandria, had already taken matters up on his behalf with the legal authorities and the French consul. Drovetti had now returned to Alexandria and intervened on behalf of his agents. So it was agreed to leave matters until Henry Salt returned from Upper Egypt. Belzoni himself was not keen on a legal battle, for he knew only too well how much political influence his opponents wielded. Furthermore, an Italian "stranger," who had helped Belzoni during the fracas, had arrived in Alexandria laden down with antiquities presented to him by Drovetti's agents for resale in Europe. He could hardly be called a potentially reliable witness at this point. While waiting on legal matters, Belzoni had little option but to settle Sarah into a home provided by an English merchant in Alexandria and to cast around for an outlet for his restless energy. He thought of excavating in Lower Egypt, but concluded that it was too close to the "fountain head of our opponents." Instead, he resolved on a side trip into the Western Desert in search of the temple of Jupiter Ammon.

: :

The Siwa Oasis in the Western Desert was famous for its oracle, consulted by none other than Alexander the Great in 331 BC. The priests of the oracle temple there proclaimed Alexander the "son of Amun," giving him divine recognition before his subsequent crowning as pharaoh at Memphis. Two centuries earlier, the Persian king Cambyses sent an army of 50,000 men to destroy the oracle during his depredations along the Nile. They never returned. According to Herodotus, who spoke with the Ammonites of Siwa: "The Persians had reached about half way when, as they were at their midday meal, a wind arose from the south, strong and deadly, bringing with it vast columns of whirling sand, which entirely covered up the troops, and caused them wholly to disappear."[11] Belzoni was looking for a notorious temple.

The English traveler William George Browne had crossed to the Siwa Oasis in 1792 and located extensive ancient ruins and temples there.[12] But he did not attribute the major temple to Jupiter Ammon. No one knew exactly what he had found. Belzoni, certainly unaware of the importance of Browne's discovery, searched at first for the temple in the Fayyum Depression instead. As a result, he never came close to the Siwa Oasis or the temple of Jupiter Ammon, although he had a most enjoyable trip.

Belzoni's last Egyptian journey differed from his earlier travels in being a more solitary expedition. His primary interest seems to have been to discover and examine the great temple rather than to bring home another load of antiquities. We can detect a change in the Italian's interests, brought about both by the pressures at Thebes and by his most recent discoveries in the pyramids, at Berenice, and in the Valley of the Kings. Ever the showman, he now realized that his reputation depended as much on his abilities as an adventurer and explorer as a tomb robber. The temple of Jupiter Ammon might well be the kind of spectacular discovery that would make his name.

The party was a small one—Belzoni, a Sicilian servant, and a pilgrim returning from Mecca who begged passage in the boat and proved "very useful." They left the Nile at Beni Suef, some 130 kilometers (80 miles) upstream of Cairo, on April 29, 1819, and continued their journey into the Fayyum by donkey. The journey to the great depression led them through "a vast plain of cultivated land, along the route of an ancient channel, which brings water into the Faiyum." That night they camped near the brick pyramid of the Middle Kingdom pharaoh Senwosret II after setting a careful watch. Belzoni as usual reclined on his special mattress, "thin enough to serve as a saddle when folded up, but when laid on a mat or on the ground, affording as good a bed as any traveller ought to expect."[13]

The next day, Belzoni climbed the pyramid and gazed over the surrounding countryside, searching for the site of ancient Arsinoe and the fabulous Labyrinth, described by Herodotus as an even greater wonder than the pyramids. He found no trace of the Labyrinth, although he found signs of an ancient town near the pyramid of Hawara. It was not until seventy years later that Englishman Flinders Petrie found the Labyrinth, of which nothing remained except a mass of limestone chips.[14]

The travelers were now in country famous for its rose water, used to keep the stench of Cairo from the delicate nostrils of its inhabitants. Here Belzoni obtained a *firman* and guides. He had avoided doing so in Alexandria or Cairo, for fear that his rivals would disrupt his plans. They passed by the ruins of ancient Arsinoe and left them to be examined on their return, pressing northward to the desolate Birket Qarûn, a brackish lake that lay more than 36.5 meters (120 feet) below sea level. Belzoni had some difficulty in finding a boat to carry the party westward to the far shore of the lake; when one did arrive, he was horrified and fascinated. "It was entirely out of shape," he wrote. "The outer shell or hulk was composed of rough pieces of wood scarcely joined, and fastened by four other pieces, wrapped together by four more across, which formed the deck; no tar, no pitch either inside or out, and the only preventive against the water coming in was a kind of weed moistened, which had settled in the joints of the wood."[15]

Belzoni was still in search of the Labyrinth, which he was convinced lay across the lake. It was a romantic, if crazy, journey. They camped on a deserted shore and dined off fresh fish. "The scene here was beautiful—the silence of the night, the beams of the radiant moon shining on the still water of the lake, the solitude of the place, the sight of our boat, the group of fishermen, put me in mind of the lake Acheron, the boat Baris, and the old ferryman of the Styx."[16] Belzoni later remembered this overnight stay as one of his happiest moments.

At the southwestern corner of the lake they landed to explore a complex of ruins and a temple, now known as Qasr Qarûn. The ruins were nothing spectacular, but Belzoni was startled out of his wits by a hyena, which rushed out at him from a small temple.[17] Fortunately, the animal fled, for Belzoni was unarmed. Still no Labyrinth came to light, despite a two-day search along the northern shores of Birket Qarûn. Belzoni had some accounts of the lake with him, including unreliable maps, which led him to believe that it would be worth venturing into the mountains some distance from the lake. Only 3 kilometers (2 miles) from its shores, they came across another ruined town, consisting of "a great number of houses, and a high wall of sun-burnt bricks, which includes the ruins of a temple."[18] Fortunately, the fishermen had brought their hatchets with them, so they were able to excavate two or three of the houses. Under the collapsed roofs, rubbish choked the dwellings. One contained a fireplace. This was not the Labyrinth either. We now know that Belzoni had stumbled on a Ptolemaic town called Nesos Sokonopaiou.

The travelers now gave up the search for the Labyrinth and crossed to the east side of the lake. Everywhere Belzoni saw fragments of columns and ancient building stone used in the construction of Arab huts. "I have no doubt," he concluded, "that by tracing the source of these materials, the seat of the Labyrinth could be discovered, which must be most magnificent even in its ruined state." This fruitless excursion included an interesting gustatory experience: Belzoni was able to enjoy a meal of pelican meat, which he described as "on the whole very tender, and pleasant to the palate."[19]

The searchers now moved away from the lake, on their way back to Medinet el-Fayyum and the rose-water factories. He passed through Fedmin el-Hanaises, where he heard the legend of the three hundred Coptic churches once said to exist there. The churches were reportedly buried under the town. But, said Belzoni, "the canal cuts through the town and none of the said churches appeared in the progress of the excavation through the town, which must have been the case had it been built on the said three hundred churches."[20]

The following day Belzoni reached Medinet el-Fayyum and immediately set out for nearby Arsinoe, where he admired "sculptures of most magnificent taste" and dug in the filling of an ancient reservoir in the middle of the town. But his real interest was in visiting the oasis to the west of Lake Moeris. He had some difficulty finding a guide, for the area was little known except to the Bedouin. Eventually, his old friend Khalil Bey, formerly of Esna and now stationed at Beni Suef, gave him a *firman* and arranged for a sheik named Grumar to guide him. Belzoni described Grumar as "a tall stout man, six feet three inches high, with a countenance that bespoke a resolute mind, and great eagerness after gain."[21]

On May 19, the caravan of six camels set out from Grumar's camp, where Belzoni had spent several sleepless nights plagued by fleas. They traveled westward along the south side of the Fayyum, passing into the desert and through a formerly populated area that included some large burial mounds, which Belzoni attributed (wrongly) to Cambyses's army. Six days later the caravan reached the Wadi Bahariya, an oasis where they watered their camels and made contact with the inhabitants.[22] The first man they met was a dwarf who threatened Belzoni with a gun. Fortunately, Grumar spoke the local dialect and averted disaster. By using coffee and tobacco, both rare luxuries in the desert, Belzoni was able to persuade the local sheik to show him the ruins near the two villages in the area.

The ruins around the oasis were far from spectacular, but included some mass burials and some terra-cotta sarcophagi whose lids bore modeled heads. Belzoni broke several and took away the heads. At the second village, the father of the headman was a wealthy date merchant who had, it was generally believed, buried his wealth in the ruins near the settlement, so Belzoni could get within only 45 meters (50 yards) of the ruined Roman temple. But he promptly whipped out his pocket telescope and enjoyed a close-up view of the walls. Nearby was a well of hot and cold water, which Belzoni visited several times on the pretext of having a bath. He found that the temperature varied, a phenomenon he attributed to the wide variations in the air temperature relative to water temperature. He confused this spring with the famous Fountain of the Sun at the temple of Jupiter Ammon, alluded to by classical writers. This led him to believe that he had located the temple when in fact it lay in the Siwa Oasis, to the south.

Despite many pleas, the Bedouin Grumar refused to take Belzoni on to Siwa, where he had heard of Browne's and others' discoveries of ruins that might be, and in fact were, the elusive temple. It later transpired that he was well known at Siwa for his prowess as a raider. Reprisals might have resulted if he had visited the area without his people. So Belzoni was forced to visit el-Farafra, an oasis only three days' journey to the southwest. All that was to be seen there was a ruined Coptic church and a few suspicious villagers. At one point, the party was obliged to make a forced march at night to avoid an attack.

Belzoni now turned for home, but was detained at Wadi Bahariya by the headman, who told him that the sheik and his father agreed that Belzoni should turn Muslim and stay with them. They would give him land for new agricultural products and four daughters as his wives. He would be happy there if he gave up constantly looking for old stones. It was with difficulty that Belzoni extracted himself from this situation, by promising to return when he had settled his affairs in Cairo.

The journey home was uneventful, except for a nasty fall from a camel. The animal stumbled on a rock and rolled about 6 meters (20 feet) down a steep slope. Belzoni fell heavily and was badly bruised, perhaps breaking a few ribs. In great pain, he laid up at the home of the sheik of Zabu. His bed was set up in a narrow passage by the house, which was constantly in use by people and animals. Passersby accidentally kicked him in the head. When animals passed, "I had reason to fear the consequence of my being thus situated." A funeral was in progress, and the lamentations and comings and goings disturbed his slumbers. All in all, it was an uncomfortable visit, capped by the widow of the dead man begging Belzoni for two pieces of his "magic paper" for the purposes of obtaining a new husband and protecting him from death. Belzoni tried to persuade her that he was not a magician. "I could not help reflecting, that if I had the art of procuring husbands to widows, I could have obtained employment enough in Europe, without travelling in strange lands for such a purpose."[23]

Three days later Belzoni was well enough to travel, and the camels set off across the desert on what proved to be an arduous journey. They drank some rather salty water, which caused agonies of thirst in the final stages of the crossing, so much so that a crust of salt formed on Belzoni's mouth. The travelers were thankful to reach the Nile on May 14.

A day later Belzoni embarked for Cairo. By this time Henry Salt had returned to base, and the two men met at night to avoid a raging plague epidemic. They settled their accounts and parted on excellent terms. There remained only the matter of the Karnak incident to settle. The legal situation in Alexandria was full of confusion and intrigue. Drovetti had exercised his influence with the French consul, Joseph Roussel. When the consul was recalled to France, the vice-consul took over, but he, again, was under Drovetti's thumb. Belzoni was required to put down a deposit of $1,200 in advance to cover the expenses of the lawyer's travel to Thebes. Just as he got around this requirement, Lebolo and Rosignani turned up in Alexandria and boasted openly of their achievement. In the end, the matter was closed when the vice-consul ruled that the two accused were Piedmontese, not Frenchmen, and could be tried only in Turin.

Belzoni was disgusted and still in pain from his Zabu fall. He was convinced that Drovetti had acted out of jealousy and malice. By mid-September he had had enough and put his affairs in order. Giovanni and Sarah sailed for Europe with considerable thankfulness, "[n]ot because I disliked the country I was in, for, on the contrary, I had reason to be grateful; nor do I complain of the Turks or Arabs in general, but of some Europeans who are in that country, whose conduct and mode of thinking are a disgrace to human nature."[24]

10 | "A Multitude of Collateral Curiosities"

Under the Majesty of Horus: Strong-Bull-arisen-in-Thebes, Who

sustains the Two Lands; Two Ladies: Renewing birth, Mighty of

Sword, Smiter of the Nine Bows in all lands. . . . The King of Upper

and Lower Egypt: Menmare; the Son of Re: Seti, Beloved of Ptah,

given life forever and ever. . . . He speaks before his fathers, all kings

of Upper Egypt, the kings of Lower Egypt, the rulers of people:

Listen to me, ye leaders of Egypt,

And may others listen to you.

PROCLAMATION OF PHARAOH SETI I
in the temple of Wadi Mia in the Eastern Desert,
quoted in Miriam Lichtheim, ed., *Ancient Egyptian Literature:
A Book of Readings*[1]

Giovanni Belzoni left Egypt at a time of feverish interest in ancient Egypt. European antiquaries and gentlemen of leisure were greeting the volumes of the *Description de l'Égypte* with amazement and enthusiasm. Muhammad Ali was favorably disposed to foreigners, and the British and French consuls enjoyed powerful influence with the pasha. It was easier for the wealthy tourist to visit the Nile and sites that hitherto had been accessible only to the adventurous or to official visitors. But few people could emulate the exploits and achievements of the tall Italian. In three short years he had opened up the Pyramid of Khafre at Giza and Abu Simbel, discovered a magnificent pharaoh's tomb, and recovered both the Young Memnon and a host of fine antiquities for the British consul and on his own account.

Belzoni paused only briefly in Italy before going on to London, where he arrived by the end of March 1820. On the last day of that month the mighty London *Times* announced: "The celebrated traveller Mr. Belzoni has arrived in this metropolis after an absence of ten years, five of which he has employed in arduous researches after the curious remains of antiquity in Egypt and Nubia." The newspaper report went on to announce that Belzoni planned an exhibition of his "beautiful tomb" from Thebes as soon as a convenient hall could be found.[2]

The newcomer was a welcome visitor in London. Prominent social hostesses lionized the tall explorer with dark, curly hair and a charmingly broken English accent. His first objective was to publish a book on his travels. The obvious publisher was John Murray of Albemarle Street, probably the most influential English bookman of the nineteenth century, who specialized in travel books written by explorers returning from remote places. (His family later published the works of David Livingstone and other African explorers.) It was an opportune time for a book on Egypt. Belzoni's exploits had been widely publicized in the influential *Quarterly Review*. The Young Memnon was drawing crowds in the British Museum, and interest in Egyptian antiquities was running at a high pitch. Belzoni seems to have written his book with extraordinary rapidity, for it appeared before the end of 1820, in two volumes.

Narrative of the Operations and Recent Discoveries Within the Pyramids, Temples, Tombs, and Excavations, in Egypt and Nubia; and of a Journey to the Coast of the Red Sea, in Search of the Ancient Berenice; and Another to the Oasis of Jupiter Ammon was an immediate and widely read success. Yet it is a verbose and self-serving book, full of contradictions and curious stylistic usages. Belzoni refused all editorial help, basing the book on his extensive journals. "The public will, perhaps, gain in the fidelity of my narration what it loses in elegance," he wrote in the preface.[3] At times the *Narrative* is fiercely polemical, especially against his French rivals. But the story moves along convincingly, as if the reader were at Belzoni's side, sharing in his extraordinary experiences and supplied with the same nervous energy.

FIGURE 10.1   The Egyptian Hall, Piccadilly, London. Hulton Deutsch Collection/Corbis.

The *Narrative* and the expensive—and now rare—folio of plates that went along with it were well received by the reviewers, who admired the author's courage and devotion to the English cause. John Murray sent a copy to the poet Lord Byron, who remarked that "Belzoni is a grand traveller, but his English is very prettily broken." The *Quarterly Review* was especially polite and discussed the book in a thirty-page article. "But though no scholar himself," the *Review* wrote, "he may justly be considered as a pioneer, and a most powerful and useful one, of antiquarian researches; he points out the road and makes it easy for others to travel over."[4] This was a prophetic statement. The *Narrative* was soon translated into French, German, and Italian, and a second English edition was hastily ordered from the printer.

Belzoni staged his exhibit in the Egyptian Hall in Piccadilly, a building that had been designed as an exhibition hall in 1812.[5] By an appropriate coincidence, the facade of the hall was decorated with moldings in the Egyptian style. The exhibition opened on May 1, 1821, and was an immediate success. Nineteen hundred people paid half a crown each to visit the displays on the first day alone. With a superb touch of showmanship, Belzoni asked a crowd of leading doctors to witness the unwrapping of a fine mummy of a young man "perfect in every part" just before the show opened.

Two full-sized models of the two most beautiful rooms in Seti I's tomb dominated the displays—the pillared hall and another showing five human figures. The plaster-of-paris models were taken from Belzoni's wax impressions and colored accurately from Alessandro Ricci's fine paintings. Here the visitor could witness all the splendor of a royal tomb. The magnificent figures of Osiris, Seti I himself, Horus, Anubis, and other gods stood on the walls of the halls, together with vivid depictions of the terrible underworld of the dead. Belzoni also reproduced Abu Simbel in model form. A cross section of the Khafre pyramid revealed the mysteries of one of the greatest monuments of the Nile. Lion-headed statues of the god Sekhmet, mummies, papyri, and what the *Times* called "a multitude of collateral curiosities" accompanied the models.[6]

: :

The exhibition placed Belzoni in the forefront of the travelers of his day, largely because he had the tangible results of his travels to display many thousands of miles from their exotic homeland. So great was the success of the show that Belzoni began to lay plans for displays in Paris and St. Petersburg, Russia, as well. The London exhibition lasted until 1822, when its contents, including the models, were auctioned off to eager buyers. One client paid £490 for the facsimiles of the tomb and some additional models.[7]

Much of Belzoni's time was taken up in frustrating negotiations with the British Museum over the alabaster sarcophagus from Seti I's tomb. Henry Salt had complicated matters, for he was forwarding his magnificent first collection of Egyptian antiquities to the British Museum, in the hope that the trustees would purchase it. He did this in the context of the encouragement he had received from both Sir William Hamilton of the Foreign Office and Sir Joseph Banks, still a trustee of the museum. But he found the museum lukewarm and the trustees outraged at the price he placed on the collection—around £8,000. It was obvious even to the casual bystander that he was out for a handsome profit. Inevitably, Belzoni was tarred with the same brush.

The trustees had just paid £35,000 for the Elgin Marbles from the Parthenon, amid considerable public outcry. They were in no mood to spend more money on foreign antiquities. Negotiations reopened when Seti I's sarcophagus arrived in London on board the frigate HMS *Diana*.

FIGURE 10.2   The Egyptian Room at the British Museum. Bettman/Corbis.

Belzoni now intervened on his own behalf and pointed out that Salt had promised him half of whatever the sarcophagus raised above a base price of 2,000 pounds. The arguments and memoranda flowed desultorily across the trustees' meeting table for many months, much to Belzoni's frustration and Salt's disgust, for the consul was now in need of money to continue his collecting. He was anxious to recover his outlay and make some money to enable him to retire within a reasonable time; "otherwise," he wrote to William Hamilton, "I must be for ever condemned to remain here, which you will allow is no very desirable lot."[8]

Salt ended up spending the rest of his career collecting antiquities and selling them for a profit, practically to the exclusion of his consular duties. In the end, however, he was obliged to sell his first collection to the British Museum for a paltry £2,000. The trustees flatly rejected the offer of the sarcophagus, sensing both legal difficulties and inflated prices, despite protestations by both Salt and Belzoni that they had received higher offers from Drovetti and other buyers. Eventually, the sarcophagus was sold for £2,000 to John Soane, a wealthy London architect and art collector. All the money went to Salt and not a penny to the Belzonis.

Soane placed the sarcophagus on exhibit in the basement of his house, after breaching a wall to install it. "The rank and talent of this country, to an immense number," who viewed the sarcophagus as it glowed softly in the light of a solitary candle placed inside it, attended three open-house evenings. Sarah attended the receptions and received "every attention from the guests."[9] By this time she was a widow; Belzoni had died miserably some time earlier at the outset of his final and most ambitious journey.

: :

The endless restlessness that afflicted Giovanni Belzoni had caused an abrupt shift in his interests and fortunes. Exasperated with the British Museum, tired of city life and of being a celebrity, he hankered for a change. Sometime in early 1822 he decided to leave Europe and search for the sources of the river Niger in West Africa. The Niger problem was still one of the great controversies of African exploration and one of more than passing interest to the British government, owing to the importance of the river as a terminus for the Saharan caravan trade with North Africa. Several enterprising explorers had been robbed or murdered in their search.[10] The government now planned to attach individual travelers to trans-Saharan caravans to improve their chances of survival.

Belzoni ignored the potential dangers. He set off on his own, on the assumption that his Egyptian experience was sufficient to travel independently. He planned to set out across the Sahara from Morocco, but the shifting sands of Arab politics left him deprived of critical *firman*s at the last minute. Eventually, he traveled to West Africa, hitching a ride for the last stage of the journey to the Gold Coast on the warship HMS *Singer*. On October 15, 1823, he arrived on the coast and was at the mouth of the Benin River a month later. The journey to the interior began in the company of a merchant named Houston. The pair soon reached Benin itself, where they were kindly received. But Belzoni came down with a severe attack of dysentery. A week later the intrepid traveler was dead.

Belzoni was quickly buried under a large tree. A wooden notice on his grave recorded the date and circumstances of his death and expressed the wish that the grave be kept cleared and fenced. But forty years later, Victorian traveler Sir Richard Burton could find no trace of the grave, although the local people still remembered the large bearded explorer who had died among them. It was a pathetic ending to a life that packed more experience and energy into it than most men would into twenty lifetimes. An era in Egyptology had ended with a whimper.

Both antiquarians and collectors had admired Belzoni's work in Egypt, but the British and French consuls effectively held a monopoly on all excavations along the Nile. Henry Salt continued to collect antiquities, writing to a friend that he spent most of his consular time "ransacking tombs, poring over old inscriptions, and learning to decypher monograms, in which I assure you I am become very expert." He remained bitter toward Belzoni to the end, feeling that the remarkable Italian had taken all the credit for the discoveries he, Salt, had financed, and that the British Museum had treated him badly over his collection. His extraordinary bitterness was aggravated by the death of his young wife of puerperal fever and by his own poor health. "I have but one wish," he wrote to his London agent, "never to have my name coupled with his."[11] To cap it all, much of Salt's original work on hieroglyphs was anticipated by the work of the French epigrapher Jean-François Champollion.

Salt's later collecting activities were managed by the Greek Yanni Athanasi, who had worked with Belzoni and become deeply embittered against the Italian.[12] Two other major collections found ready buyers in Europe. The first was assembled between 1819 and 1824 and was sold to the king of France for £10,000. It was purchased on the advice of Jean-François Champollion himself, the scholar whom Salt admired yet envied. The last collection was Salt's largest and auctioned at Sotheby's in London eight years after his death, in 1835. A total of 1,083 lots fetched more than £7,000. In eleven years of consular work, Salt had made a collection at a low cost to him from which he had netted more than £20,000. He did not live to enjoy his profits, for he died of an intestinal infection in October 1827, still a lonely consul without the pension and scholarly recognition he had craved all his diplomatic life.

Drovetti lived on for many more years and was reappointed French consul general in Egypt in 1821. He retired for reasons of health in 1829, after twenty-seven years of residence and collecting in the Nile Valley. Over the years, he sold antiquities to numerous travelers and assembled a remarkable collection, which he tried to sell to the French government. Like Salt, he had considerable difficulty disposing of his antiquities. The French government procrastinated, largely because of clerical opposition on fundamentalist grounds. Devout churchmen feared that Drovetti's collection would show that Egyptian civilization was older than 4004 BC, the established date of the Creation, calculated from the Scriptures by Archbishop James Ussher in the seventeenth century and accepted as theological dogma. While the clerics and bureaucrats argued and both the English and the Germans made bids, Drovetti finally sold his finds to the king of Sardinia for £13,000. The French consul also assembled two later collections, the first of which he sold to Charles X of France for one-quarter of a million francs; it now graces the Louvre. Drovetti's last antiquities were bought by the German scholar Karl Richard Lepsius for the Berlin Museum.

Drovetti died in 1852. He was never a great pioneer or expert on Egyptology, his interest being purely commercial. His excavation and collecting methods and those of his agents were quite ruthless. But the fruits of his labors, and those of his diplomatic colleagues, grace the museums of Europe and caused a dramatically heightened interest in ancient Egypt among educated Europeans.

Yet, by a curious twist of fate, the three rival collectors of antiquities—Belzoni, Drovetti, and Salt—whose competition had enlivened the burial grounds and temples of Thebes for so long, enriched the national collections of their rivals' homelands. Belzoni, an Italian, furnished the Egyptian gallery of the British Museum. Drovetti's antiquities formed the basis of the magnificent Turin collection, while Henry Salt's efforts greatly enhanced the galleries of the Louvre. All reaped the rewards of fame, notoriety, or financial gain. The only loser was Egypt.

PART THREE

BIRTH OF A SCIENCE

*In summary, the well-agreed interest of science
demands, not that excavations are interrupted
because science acquires new certainties and
unexpected enlightenment each day through
this work, but that one submits the excavators
to such a control that the preservation of the
tombs discovered today and in the future might
be fully assured and well guaranteed against
the attacks of ignorance or blind greed.*

JEAN-FRANÇOIS CHAMPOLLION
to the pasha of Egypt, 1829, quoted in Lesley Adkins
and Roy Adkins, *The Keys of Egypt*

11 | Decipherment

Into this Egypt already impoverished by Musselman devastators

and European speculators, learned society has now descended like

an invasion of barbarians to carry off what little remains of [its]

admirable monuments.

ÉMILE PRISSE D'AVENNES,
quoted in Elisabeth David, *Mariette Pacha, 1821–1881*

W here Giovanni Belzoni had pioneered, others soon followed. He and his rivals had started a scramble for Egyptian antiquities that soon expanded to a rape of massive proportions.
Hundreds of collectors, amateur antiquarians, and curious tourists descended on the Nile during the twenty years after Belzoni's departure.
Many of them were content to visit and admire. Others were out for loot,
treasure, or simply personal profit. The names of the most active collectors have come down to us through their collections, remnants of which
are scattered in the museums of the world, listed in auction sale catalogs,
and held in private hands. Some of the most acquisitive, and the most
successful nineteenth-century dealers in Egyptian antiquities, are en-
shrined in that admirable publication *Who Was Who in Egyptology*, an exhaustive compilation of the saints and criminals of Egyptology.[1]

One such collector was Anthony Charles Harris (1790–1869), an English merchant who lived in Alexandria. He bought and sold fine antiquities, specializing in papyri. The British Museum acquired his own collection in 1872, one of hundreds of collections, large or small, assembled in

the eighty years between Belzoni's departure and the end of the nine-teenth century. Papyri, mummies, scarabs, even whole temples were re-moved from Egypt by individuals who were anxious for a quick profit or wanted to gratify a collector's desire to acquire a tangible relic of the Egyptian past, a type of disease described by one French scholar, Henri Codet, in 1922 as "a passion so violent that it is inferior to love or ambi-tion only in the pettiness of its aims."[2]

The trouble was that collecting was so easy. Muhammad Ali had no cause to legislate against the removal of antiquities, for Egypt had no national museum to keep them in. The Turkish rulers of Egypt had no interest in, or identity with, the ancient past. To them the antiquities of the Nile were a significant political tool, useful for gratifying eccentric but powerful visitors or diplomats with curious collecting habits. The tangible monuments of ancient Egypt were merely a source of building stone, or perhaps the site for a modern village elevated above the annual floodwaters.

The museums of Europe were now so eager to obtain Egyptian antiq-uities that they were quite prepared to ship entire rooms, friezes, or tombs. Forty-five years after Belzoni's excavations, the French philoso-pher Joseph-Ernest Renan wrote:

> Purveyors to museums have gone through the country like vandals; to se-cure a fragment of a head, a piece of inscription, precious antiquities were reduced to fragments. Nearly always provided with a consular in-strument, these avid destroyers treated Egypt as their own property. The worst enemy, however, of Egyptian antiquities is still the English or American traveler. The names of these idiots will go down to posterity, since they were careful to inscribe themselves on famous monuments across the most delicate drawings.[3]

By the 1840s, the secrets of ancient Egypt had been at least partially unlocked by the decipherment of hieroglyphs, and some people had begun to realize the full extent of the awful damage that had been done. But it was too late. Firm government leadership and legislative action had been urgently needed and were sadly lacking, even as the *Description* was published.

: :

FIGURE 11.1   The zodiac of Dendera, as illustrated by Napoléon's savants. From *Description de l'Égypte*.

The 1820s to 1840s were a time of intense academic debate over the chronology of ancient Egypt and over the age of humanity, which revolved around astronomy and zodiacs that displayed the heavens. A French antiquarian and collector, Sébastien Louis Saulnier, heard about the zodiac in the temple of Dendera.[4] He hired an agent, Jean-Baptiste Lelorrain, to remove it from the ceiling of the temple and ship it to France. The circular zodiac dates from the end of the Ptolemaic period or even later. It represents celestial Egypt, which the Egyptians thought of as a duplication of terrestrial Egypt with the same districts and features.

Saulnier and Lelorrain decided that the zodiac, which had been located by General Desaix de Veygoux during the French expedition, had "in a way become a national monument," and should therefore be moved from Dendera to Paris. Lelorrain arrived in Alexandria in October 1820 prepared to export the zodiac by any means possible. Carefully concealing his real intentions, he announced that he planned to try some digging at Thebes. Even so, he had to eject an "observer" from his boat, a spy planted by Henry Salt to keep a watch on his activities.

Some English visitors were sketching at Dendera when Lelorrain took his first look at the zodiac. So he went on upstream to Thebes, where he bought a few mummies and other antiquities to cover his tracks. When the French returned to Dendera the artists had left, so Lelorrain was free to begin his operations. The zodiac lay in the ceiling of the center room of three in a small building near the magnificent temple that Napoléon's soldiers had so greatly admired.[5] The task of removal was a formidable one, for the zodiac was carved on two huge blocks 0.9 meters (3 feet) thick. Lelorrain had only chisels and saws with him, so he resorted to gunpowder to blow holes in the temple roof. Fortunately, his carefully controlled blasts did not bring the ceiling down. He set a large workforce laboring day and night to saw through the limestone.

Twenty-two days later, in a scene reminiscent of Belzoni at the Ramesseum, Lelorrain dragged the zodiac down the slope of earth that still filled the building and levered it onto special wooden rollers for the journey to the waiting boat more than 6.4 kilometers (4 miles) away. The rollers soon wore out. Lelorrain had to revert to levers and brute strength to move a heavy sledge carrying the blocks to the Nile. The Frenchman did not possess Belzoni's artistry at moving large objects. He tried to lever the sledge aboard the riverboat on sloping planks, but it slipped and the zodiac plopped into the soft mud by the river's edge. Fortunately for Lelorrain, he was paying his workers exceptionally well, so they were as keen as he was to see the boat safely loaded. By prodigious labor they managed to rescue the slabs and load them safely into the boat that was now leaking disastrously. Frantic caulking of the spurting seams saved the day.

Then the captain refused to cast off. A passing American had seen Lelorrain at work and told Henry Salt, who had arranged for a timely bribe. Lelorrain paid the captain a 1,000-piastre gratuity and started downstream. Halfway to Cairo, one of Salt's European agents presented the Frenchman with an order from the pasha's grand vizier forbidding Lelorrain to remove the zodiac. Lelorrain ran up the French colors and boldly challenged the English to board his vessel. His bold stratagem worked, and the agent sailed away in ineffectual rage. Salt, who had been on the point of removing the zodiac for himself and William Bankes of obelisk fame, was furious. He pursued Lelorrain to Alexandria and interceded with the pasha, claiming he had dug at Dendera before the Frenchman had even heard of the place and therefore owned the zodiac, but to no avail.

Eventually, the zodiac arrived in Paris amid scenes of great enthusiasm. Saulnier and Lelorrain made a handsome profit. They sold the zodiac to King Louis XVIII for 150,000 francs. It can now be seen in the Louvre. The visitor to Dendera must be content with a plaster replica.

The impudent tricks of Lelorrain and Salt were but typical of the antiquarian morality of the times, for people like Saulnier, Drovetti, and Athanasi were motivated partly by curiosity, but mainly by greed. No one had any understanding of what they were seeing or removing, because no one was able to read hieroglyphs.

: :

Egyptian hieroglyphs had fascinated scholars for centuries before the discovery of the Rosetta stone in 1799. The fascination began during the Renaissance, with the revival in classical learning and the assumption that much wisdom came from the ancient Egyptians. Between 1582 and 1589, six Egyptian obelisks were either resited or reerected in Rome, each covered with elaborate hieroglyphic script. A Venetian scholar, Pierius Valerianus, was the first to write a book on hieroglyphs. His attempts to decipher hieroglyphic symbols were, at best, fantasy.

In 1666, the German Jesuit Athanasius Kircher (1601–1680) was entrusted with the publication of a hieroglyphic inscription on an obelisk in Rome's Piazza della Minerva, erected by the order of Pope Alexander VII. He produced an elaborate reading of an inscription that merely recites the name of the pharaoh Psammeticus spelled phonetically! Kircher was a brilliant scholar, with a flamboyant, imaginative mind, like his contemporaries convinced that hieroglyphs were picture writing. When Jesuit missionaries in China wrote saying there was no resemblance between Chinese script and hieroglyphs, the mystery deepened. In the 1790s, a Danish scholar named Jörgen Zoega hypothesized that the script might, in fact, be phonetic, an important step toward decipherment.[6]

The discovery of the Rosetta stone in 1799 changed the playing field dramatically. Napoléon's savants knew from the outset that this prosaic

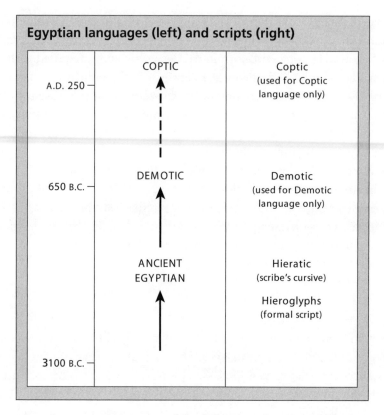

FIGURE 11.2   A summary of the different ancient Egyptian scripts.

inscription in three scripts would serve as the key to hieroglyphs. Wax copies of the stone circulated widely in Europe amid general confidence that the secrets of ancient Egyptian writing would soon become apparent. But the experts could make no sense of "picture symbols" of the formal hieroglyphic script. They were trying to translate them as individual ideas rather than sounds, which was entirely the wrong approach. At the same time, they hypothesized correctly that the demotic inscription was an alphabetic form of the formal script.

If this theory was correct, then the obvious attack was through demotic. Eminent scholars such as Sylvestre de Sacy, a well-known French Orientalist, and Johan Åkerblad, a Swede, tried to work out the demotic alphabet, with mixed results. Everyone was feeling discouraged when Thomas Young, an English doctor with broad research talents in medicine, natural philosophy, mathematics, and languages, became interested in a papyrus shown him by a friend. He obtained a copy of the Rosetta inscription in 1814 and began a comparison of the demotic and Greek scripts. He also noted the striking resemblance between some demotic symbols and corresponding hieroglyphs. Young concluded that demotic script was a mixture of alphabetic signs and hieroglyphic symbols. Napoléon's savants had suggested that royal names lay within ovals in Egyptian scripts. The Rosetta inscription had six such cartouches, which contained the name Ptolemy, a name he assumed was spelled alphabetically—a foreign name.[7] By matching the hieroglyphs to the letters of the Greek spelling of Ptolemy, Young assigned sound values to various symbols. Many of them were correct. Then he made a false assumption—that the remaining hieroglyphs used to write Egyptian language were nonphonetic. As a result, he never achieved full decipherment.

Young's principal rival was a Frenchman, a linguistic genius of impatient personality. Jean-François Champollion was born on December 23, 1790, in Figeac, France, the son of an impoverished bookseller. His formal education did not begin until he was eight years old, but he soon displayed a precocious ability in languages and drawing. His brother Jacques-Joseph supervised his formal education in Grenoble, where he acquired a passionate interest in Egypt. This brought him, at the age of eleven, to the attention of the mathematician Jean-Baptiste-Joseph Fourier, who had been one of Napoléon's Egyptian savants and was writing the historical introduction to the *Description de l'Égypte*.[8] Fourier and his collections inspired the young Champollion with the desire to break the secrets of hieroglyphs. From this time on, they exercised a strong influence on one another. Formal schooling bored Champollion, who became increasingly obsessed with Egypt and by a conviction that antiquity was best studied through languages. By the time he was seventeen, Champollion had learned Hebrew, Arabic, Sanskrit, Persian, and other Eastern languages, as well as English, German, and Italian. He also added Coptic to his repertoire, in the belief that the language of Christian Egypt might have retained something of ancient Egyptian speech.

In 1807 Champollion and his brother went to Paris, at the time the leading cultural center in Europe, filled with loot from Napoléon's conquests. While living in great poverty, Jean-François studied under the Orientalist de Sacy, worked for the commission compiling the *Description*, and took language courses. The young linguist acquired priceless contacts with the leading scholars of Oriental languages and culture. Despite ill health and poverty, he immersed himself in all the Coptic scripts he could find, assuming that Coptic alphabetical letters matched those of ancient Egyptian. Later, he realized that he was wrong. Coptic was a late development of ancient Egyptian, and hieroglyphs were not a simple alphabet. He also turned his attention to the Rosetta stone.

Within a few months, Champollion had used his knowledge of Coptic and the Greek inscription to tease out the value of a number of the demotic letters. His findings agreed with those of the Swedish scholar Johan Åkerblad, published some years earlier. He also pored over papyri with their hieratic writings, but was unaware that demotic and hieratic were different scripts.

He studied the Rosetta stone for months, apparently without result. Seven years later he published two volumes on the geographical place-names of ancient Egypt in which he proclaimed rather brashly that he could read the demotic inscription on the stone. He was nearly right, for he believed that Coptic was the closest surviving relative of ancient Egyptian. The research was demanding, frustrating, and full of dead ends. Champollion responded by immersing himself in Coptic, amusing himself by translating his thoughts into the language. By this time, he had convinced himself that the decipherment of hieroglyphs was his destiny.

After two years of fruitless study, Champollion returned to Grenoble, where he was appointed to a teaching position at the new university there. He continued to work on hieroglyphs, discarding theory after theory in his search for decipherment and working on Egyptian place-names along the way. His *L'Égypte sous les pharaons* appeared in 1811. Jealous rivals promptly accused him of plagiarism.

Political upheavals and the restoration of the monarchy cost Champollion his teaching job and brought research to an end until 1818, when he received much better copies of the Rosetta stone from London. Even then, distractions such as teaching got in the way of his work.

In 1819 the *Encyclopaedia Britannica* published a long article by Thomas Young on ancient Egypt, in which he summarized his own attempts to read hieroglyphs. He concluded that there were three consecutive Egyptian scripts and ended his article with what he called the "Rudiments of a Hieroglyphical Vocabulary," some information on sounds and phrases, and a list of monuments.[9] The vocabulary showed how Ptolemy's name occurred six times in the demotic inscription. Young also believed that he had deciphered other royal names at Karnak and Philae. He thought he had worked out fourteen letters of a hieroglyphic alphabet; in fact, only five letters were correct.

At the time, Young had achieved far more than Champollion and seemed to be far ahead in the race for decipherment. He also believed that little more progress could be made until more bilingual inscriptions became available. The Frenchman was much distracted by political events in Grenoble, which caused him to lose his job as a librarian. He was threatened with a treason trial, but the charges were dismissed. Some time passed before he read Young's article, and disagreed with it, by which time he had returned to Paris and settled with his brother in a rented house a few yards from the Academy of Inscriptions and Literature. He was soon accepted into leading academic circles, but was left alone to study demotic, which he compared to Coptic. His academic colleagues were preoccupied with Egyptian zodiacs, and especially with the newly arrived Dendera example, as a means of dating Egyptian civilization and the age of the world, a controversial subject in ecclesiastical circles.[10]

Champollion rejected Young's view that hieroglyphs were an alphabetic script. On December 23, 1821, he decided to carry out a numerical analysis of the Rosetta-stone texts. He found that 1,419 hieroglyphic signs paralleled 486 words of the Greek text. He could not establish a numerical relationship between the Greek and hieroglyphic texts, which made him realize that the hieroglyphs were at least partly phonetic and far more complex than previously realized. He tried transliterating the later demotic texts into the earlier hieratic, and then into hieroglyphs, despite being unable to read them. The transliterations gave him a first understanding of how the scripts worked and how they related to one another. Instead of using the Young approach of relying on bilingual texts, he looked at all aspects of Egyptian writing, something he could do because of his remarkably broad knowledge of related languages.

A series of fortunate discoveries came along. Some Greek papyri from Abydos enabled him to identify a Ptolemy cartouche and possibly that of Cleopatra. Champollion converted the latter into a hypothetical hieroglyphic version, but it was not until a colleague passed along a lithograph of the Philae obelisk with its Cleopatra cartouches that he saw that the real thing was a close match. He now worked with heightened excitement, for he was able to work out the possible meanings of ancient Egyptian words that were similar to Coptic ones.

On September 14, 1822, Champollion received copies of the hieroglyphs on the Abu Simbel temple duplicated precisely by architect Jean-
Nicholas Huyot. He pored over the cartouches, where he soon identified
the name Rameses, then another pharaoh's name, Tuthmosis. The cartouches gave him the underlying principle of hieroglyphs. Carefully, he
rechecked his results, then dashed out of his attic room into the street to
tell his brother at the nearby Institute of France. Panting with excitement,
he burst in on Jacques-Joseph, shouting, "Je tiens l'affair" (I've got it) and
fell to the floor in a dead faint. He had discovered the complex phonetic
principles of hieroglyphs, "a script at times figurative, symbolic and phonetic, in the same text, phrase, I would almost say the same word."[11]

Within days he was hard at work again on his famous *Lettre à M.
Dacier, secrétaire perpétuel de l'Académie royale des Inscriptions et Belles-
Lettres, relative à l'alphabet des hiéroglyphes phonétiques* (Letter to M.
Dacier, Secretary-General of the Royal Academy of Inscriptions and Literature, concerning the alphabet of phonetic hieroglyphs), published in late
October 1822, in which he announced his discovery. He had read the
paper at a meeting of the Academy of Inscriptions and Literature on September 27. By chance, Thomas Young was in the audience and was generous in his praise. The discovery was considered so important that the king
himself was informed.

Champollion now tried to acquire as many hieroglyphic texts as he
could, for most of the available material was going to England and was
accessible to Young rather than himself. He even went so far as to copy
hieroglyphic texts before their sale in Paris auction rooms. Decipherment came easier and easier, using a method where he transliterated the
text into Coptic, then into French, not a perfect system, but one that
worked well enough at the time. In 1824, he published his *Précis du sys-
tème hiéroglyphique des anciens Égyptiens* (A summary of the hieroglyphic system of the ancient Egyptians), in which he went into far
greater detail than he had in his *Lettre*. There were explanations of hieroglyphic signs, discussions of points of agreement and disagreement with
Thomas Young, and discourses on the names of kings, on royal titles, and
the different types of Egyptian writing. The *Précis* was an astounding
tour de force, received with acclaim by Champollion's supporters and
with disdain by his enemies, most of them on the other side of the Channel. Decipherment soon became a nationalistic issue, to the French a
striking demonstration of national pride. In May of the same year, the

young Frenchman was able to visit London and see the Rosetta stone for the first time. But, as he well knew, the stone, the very symbol of decipherment, had been of limited use. The hieroglyphic inscription was too damaged to be of much use.

Jean-François Champollion was now a man obsessed with decipherment and with teaching others how to translate hieroglyphs. He traveled to Italy to catalog the Drovetti collection in Turin, where he worked on papyri and identified the Turin Royal Canon with its list of Egyptian kings. His reputation had preceded him. Pope Leo XII received him in audience and offered to make him a cardinal. The stunned Champollion declined, because he had a wife and daughter. Instead, the pope persuaded the king of France to appoint him a knight of the Legion of Honor. Meanwhile, opposition to his decipherment surfaced on many sides, accentuated by Champollion's low tolerance of any form of criticism. He was gratified when Henry Salt, once a fervent supporter of Young's approach, declared that he was wrong and that the Frenchman was correct. By this time, Champollion was curator of the Egyptian section at the Louvre, where he arranged the Drovetti and Salt collections that had transformed the Louvre into one of the finest museums in Europe. He used his knowledge of hieroglyphs to arrange the material in the correct order.

The man who had unlocked the secrets of ancient Egypt had never visited the Nile. In 1828, his influential supporters at court persuaded the king to support a joint French and Tuscan expedition under Champollion's leadership, with the patronage both of the monarch and of the grand duke of Tuscany. Thirty years after Napoléon's savants sailed for the Nile, Champollion, the Italian Egyptologist Ippolito Rosellini, and twelve others, including artists, draftsmen, and architects, disembarked at Alexandria.[12] They were delayed for several weeks waiting for permits, probably because Drovetti was concerned at the prospect of excavations outside his control. Champollion warned him that the expedition had the full backing of the king of France and that he had the ear of the court. The permits arrived a few days later. Meanwhile, the expedition acquired comfortable Turkish clothing for their journey.

Champollion's expedition was a triumphal journey. It was an electrifying experience both for the master and for the other members of the party. For the first time they were able to read the inscriptions on the great temples and understand the significance of some of the oldest monuments in the world. Champollion's ideas and the many startlingly revo-

FIGURE 11.3   Jean-François Champollion and his companions of the Egyptian expedition in a romantic pose. Ippolito Rosellini stands to the seated Champollion's left. The expedition made few discoveries, but concentrated on recording what had been found and survived. Scala/Art Resource, New York.

lutionary hypotheses about the significance and context of Egyptian monuments that had welled up in his mind were confirmed again and again by his field observations.

The expedition traveled upstream in two boats named *Isis* and *Hathor*, sailing fast to the First Cataract and then into Nubia as far as the Second Cataract. Having assessed different locations, the travelers would take their time coming downstream for more detailed studies. On their way south, they visited Memphis and Saqqara, the pyramids of Giza, and the tombs of Beni Hasan. Earlier travelers had reported wrongly that they contained little of significance, but a few moments with a wet sponge revealed spectacular wall paintings.[13] But it was Dendera that was the most overwhelming experience, the very Dendera that Napoléon's soldiers had saluted in 1799.

Unable to restrain themselves, the members of the expedition rushed ashore from their boats on a brightly moonlit night and stormed the temple in a state of wild excitement. "The moonlight was magnificent. . . .

[A]lone and without our guides, but armed to the teeth, we set off across the fields. . . . We walked like this, singing the most recent opera marches." They were lost when a villager appeared and promptly bolted at the sight of them. Champollion caught him and persuaded him to serve as a guide. "I will not try to describe the impression which the great propylon and especially the portico of the great temple made on us. . . . It is grace and majesty brought together in the highest degree."[14] For two glorious hours the travelers wandered through the moonlit temple, drunk with enthusiasm and rapture, before returning to their boat at three in the morning. The next day, they inspected the temple in daylight. Champollion could read enough hieroglyphs to establish that Dendera was a Ptolemaic temple dedicated to the goddess Hathor.

From Dendera, they traveled to Karnak and Thebes, where Champollion raced from "marvel to marvel," carving his name high on a column at Karnak. Eventually, they sailed as far as Wadi Halfa, just below the Second Cataract—any further progress southward would have meant a journey on land through desert terrain where a famine was raging. They had paused at Abu Simbel on the way upstream, clearing sand from the entrance. Champollion slipped through the narrow defile in the door on his stomach into the cavernous interior, where his mind reeled at the sight of the beautiful reliefs. On the return journey, the artists and draftsmen drew everything in temperatures like those of a "heated Turkish bath." Champollion and Rosellini concentrated on the hieroglyphs, double-checking everything before entrusting their copies to a draftsman. The work of copying took thirteen days.

After six days at Philae, they settled into the first three chambers of the empty tomb of pharaoh Rameses IV in the Valley of the Kings, a favorite camping spot for visitors.[15] The expedition recorded the paintings and inscriptions of the sixteen accessible royal tombs, contributing to the destruction by removing areas of plaster with friezes from the tomb of Seti I. After more than four months of seemingly endless copying, everyone was exhausted, but the work continued around Qurna and in the temple at Medinet Habu. Here Champollion finally proved that ancient Egyptian art developed without any influence from classical Greece, that it "only owes to itself," as he put it in a letter to his brother. After brief stays at Thebes and Karnak, the boats rode the inundation down to Cairo and Alexandria. In January 1830, the thirty-nine-year-old Champollion returned to Paris, where ill health dogged him. He died of a stroke on

March 4, 1832. His devoted brother published his dictionary of hieroglyphs between 1841 and 1844.

: :

The seventeen months that Champollion spent in the Nile Valley were the
climax of a remarkable and intensely productive career. It was not given
to Champollion to excavate sites and recover ancient Egypt from the
ground. Rather, he was content to observe the remains themselves and put
them into a true chronological perspective. Jean-François Champollion
had, in one stroke, extended the frontiers of written history by thousands
of years into unknown epochs where the origins of Egyptian civilization
were to be found.

The prospects for scientific investigation were stupendous, yet all that
Champollion saw was destruction and looting. Not that he was above recommending that an obelisk from Thebes be removed to Paris as a memorial to Napoléon's troops. Muhammad Ali eventually agreed to the request, although he had originally given the Theban obelisks to the British.
At colossal expense, one of the two obelisks in front of the temple at
Thebes was transported to Paris in 1830—on a special barge named
Dromedaire. On October 25, 1836, it was erected in the Place de la Concorde in the presence of the king of France and 200,000 spectators.

Meanwhile, the destruction continued. The antiquarian Sébastien
Louis Saulnier of zodiac fame found Egypt divided between Bernardino
Drovetti and Henry Salt. The situation was more complicated on the
ground, complete with demarcation lines drawn through the middle of
temples. The consuls' agents patrolled their respective banks, ever watch-
ful for intruders on their cherished monopolies. Both had the ear of the
pasha. Both were obsessed with collecting and regarded ancient Egypt as
their exclusive property. Saulnier likened them to competing monarchs:
"They concluded a peace treaty. Like kings who, in accommodating their
differences, want to preclude all causes that could renew them, they took
a river for the border of the respective possessions that they granted
themselves in Egypt. For two or three years now, it is the flow of the Nile
that has separated them."[16]

There was still room for smaller operators, among them the Trieste-
born adventurer Giuseppe Passalacqua, who came to Egypt to set up business as a horse dealer and turned to tomb robbing instead. In 1832, he

stumbled over the tomb of a queen named Mentuhotep at Dra Abu'l Naga near Qurna on the west bank opposite Thebes. He arrived at the tomb soon after it was partially looted, but recovered the queen's mummy and a painted canopic box that had once belonged to her husband.[17] Passalacqua left the queen's heavy wooden coffin in the tomb. A decade or so later, Englishman John Gardner Wilkinson recorded the ten columns of inscriptions—the earliest record of the Book of the Dead recorded for science. The former horse trader made other spectacular discoveries, including a passageway cut some 46 meters (150 feet) into a cliff, crammed with mummies, some of them buried with the tools of their trade, such as a scribe's palette and a hunter's weapons.

By 1820, years of indiscriminate collecting had ravaged Egypt's temples and tombs. The Theban necropolis remained a battlefield for looters and treasure hunters. Thousands of artifacts lay in museums and private collections, with no record as to where they were found or under what circumstances. Only a few could be placed within a general area, or within a specific cemetery. Ancient Egypt was nothing more than a moneymaking enterprise, a way of providing artifacts to collectors, museums, and scholars at a profit.

12 | Artists and Archaeologists

Of all possible locations at Thebes, Wilkinson had chosen the most

thrilling. Straight down, he looked upon the tawny desert, filled

with the tumble rubbish of ancient tombs. Just below him was the

Ramesseum, from which Belzoni had snatched the colossal head.

Over to the right were the twin statues which Westerners call the

Colossi of Memnon, as well as the great sprawling temple of

Medinet Habu. . . . Then the ever-changing, ever interesting Nile

cut its pulsing course across the land. On the far side of the river

were to be seen the columns of the Luxor temple and the soaring

obelisks of mighty Karnak.

EGYPTOLOGIST JOHN A. WILSON,
Signs and Wonders upon Pharaoh: A History of American
Archaeology, on the view from John Gardner Wilkinson's
tomb-residence at Thebes

Jean-François Champollion considered himself the sole deci-
pherer of hieroglyphs, as the man who unlocked the secrets of
ancient Egypt. Like all decipherments, no one epigrapher made all the advances, secured all the clues. Champollion drew on the work of others, on
copies made by Napoléon's savants and other visitors. Without question,

however, it was his decisive advances that were in considerable part responsible for a new era in the study of the ancient Egyptians, a time when artists and antiquarians devoted months, even years, to copying and recording rather than destructive excavation and looting. The treasure hunting still continued, but a few voices now deplored the ravaging of temple and tomb.

Champollion himself wrote to the pasha deploring the widespread destruction of archaeological sites and the trade in antiquities. He pointed out how many tourists were now visiting the Nile simply to see the monuments and admire the marvels of the past. Tourists meant money, and in the long run a greater profit than that obtained from demolition and looting. He recommended that excavation be controlled, that quarrying stone from temples be forbidden, and that the exportation of antiquities be strictly regulated.

Champollion's strongly worded pleas had an effect on Muhammad Ali's thinking and led to a landmark government ordinance published on August 15, 1835. The preamble of the ordinance noted that museums and collectors were so hungry for antiquities that there was a danger that all traces of ancient monuments would vanish from Egyptian soil to enrich foreign countries. The ordinance forbade all exportation of antiquities, authorized the construction of a museum in Cairo to house antiquities owned by the government or found in excavations conducted by it, made it illegal to destroy monuments, and endorsed efforts at conservation. At the same time, Muhammad Ali appointed an inspector of museums to travel through Upper Egypt and inspect key sites. The ordinance was, of course, unenforceable. But it was a step in the right direction, even if the pasha's museum got off to a shaky start and most of the antiquities in it were sold or given to foreign dignitaries by Ali and his successors.

Fortunately, a few visitors to the Nile now came in search of knowledge rather than artifacts, out of a profound curiosity and enthusiasm for the world's earliest civilization. By 1821, the handful of antiquarians with a serious interest in Egypt sensed that decipherment was imminent, among them the classical archaeologist and traveler Sir William Gell, who corresponded with Thomas Young and mentored a promising young scholar—John Gardner Wilkinson (1797–1875), destined to become one of Egyptology's seminal figures.[1]

: :

FIGURE 12.1
Sir John Gardner Wilkinson
in Turkish costume. Courtesy:
The National Trust.

Wilkinson's parents died at an early age, leaving him with modest private means. He planned an army career, but while awaiting a commission embarked on an old-style Grand Tour through Mediterranean lands. His itinerary included Egypt, which had fascinated him from an early age. In Rome he met Sir William Gell, who promised to brief him thoroughly on ancient Egypt. At the time, Gell probably knew more about ancient Egypt than anyone. He had read virtually all the published work on the subject and corresponded regularly with Salt, Young, and others. Gell himself had planned to go to the Nile, but his gout and other commitments prevented him.

The young Wilkinson arrived in Alexandria in late 1821 with a smattering of Arabic and boundless enthusiasm. Gell had steeped him in Thomas Young's approach to hieroglyphs and supervised him while sketching Egyptian artifacts, to the point that he was better prepared than any traveler before him. Henry Salt welcomed him in Cairo and took him to the pyramids at Giza. The consul's dragoman, Osman Efendi, a former Scottish drummer boy named Donald Thomson, lived as a Turk and a Muslim. Osman dressed Wilkinson in Turkish clothes, a wise precaution in a country where Europeans were still rare and moved around at their peril.

After a trip as far upstream as the Second Cataract, Wilkinson threw himself into Egyptology. He had no interest in excavation, except to clear an inscription, and acquired relatively few artifacts for himself, and certainly not for personal gain. He was a copyist of inscriptions, monuments, and tombs whose sketches were freehand, but surprisingly accurate. His copies of hieroglyphs were said by experts to be superior to those in the *Description*, at the time the major source of information. During the next twelve years, Wilkinson traveled widely in Egypt and the surrounding deserts, sometimes alone, at others in the company of a small number of like-minded antiquarians and artists. He and his friend James Burton adopted a Turkish lifestyle right down to costume, passing themselves off as Muslims to their servants and acquaintances.[2] In so doing, they became part of the local aristocracy, maintaining a suitable distance from the native Egyptians. They recoiled with horror at first against the pervasive slavery, but later acquired slaves of their own as mistresses.

By 1824, Wilkinson's antiquarian interests sharpened. Salt obtained a *firman* from the pasha for him, which gave him permission to visit sites, to excavate, and to intervene to protect them from destruction. At the time, no one knew anything of ancient Egyptian history or chronology. The knowledge he and his colleagues had to draw on was rudimentary at best, and usually wrong. His wide travels took him to el-Amarna on the east bank, about 480 kilometers (300 miles) downstream of Thebes. Many years later, in 1887, another Englishman, Flinders Petrie, unearthed the Amarna diplomatic tablets and identified the abandoned city as Akhetaten, the capital of the New Kingdom pharaoh Akhenaten (1350–1334 BC). As far as we know, Wilkinson was the first antiquarian to visit the extensive site and the burial caves behind it. He puzzled over the exotic and often naturalistic frescoes in the sepulchers, where "the sun is represented with rays terminating in hands," something he had seen nowhere else.[3] When he sent Sir William Gell a copy of the now-famous mural of Akhenaten and Queen Nefertiti raising their arms to the sun disk, his mentor pronounced it a depiction of two pregnant women offering sacrifice.

Wilkinson, who worked almost single-handedly, deciphered dozens of inscriptions and recognized many royal cartouches correctly for the first time. We owe to Wilkinson the first attempts to put the royal dynasties and kings of Egypt into proper order. He made exact drawings of the tomb paintings at Beni Hasan before Champollion and Ippolito Rosellini worked there, identified the long-lost site of the Labyrinth at Hawara, and covered the pages of many notebooks with minute and exact records far in advance of those of his contemporaries. Unlike Champollion, Wilkinson worked without government support and achieved miracles with minimal resources.

Wilkinson was continually on the move, copying, visiting, and puzzling over hieroglyphs. He achieved some insignificant results with Young's approach, but lacked the knowledge of Coptic essential for real progress. Sir William Gell sent him Champollion's *Lettre à M. Dacier* in 1823, but it was not until he received the *Précis* with its lists and more detailed analysis that Wilkinson began to comprehend the extent of the Frenchman's understanding of hieroglyphs. In tomb and temple, he copied inscriptions and accumulated a hieroglyphic vocabulary by comparing Coptic and ancient Egyptian words. Soon he began to make discoveries on his own account, developing a chronology for different monuments and for Egyptian history as a whole. He found himself correcting Champollion's "terrible mistakes." He was upset by Champollion's disregard for Young and put off by the Frenchman's arbitrary and often high-handed ways. This may be why he did not meet Champollion during his 1828 expedition, preferring to work discreetly in the background. He wrote to Gell: "Ch may read a wall of hierogs, so can I or anyone else when no Egyptians are present, but I like better proofs. . . . Besides he has an unfair way of changing without informing his reader of former errors."[4] There's a common perception that Champollion deciphered hieroglyphs, which is an overstatement. His research provided vital impetus to a process that continued for decades. Fifteen years passed before the controversies died down and there was some consensus that he was correct. No one could translate a running hieroglyphic text until the 1840s.

Wilkinson was the first person to work in Egypt with at least some philological background. He could have made substantial contributions to hieroglyphic studies, but, restless as ever, chose to move on to other interests once he had acquired a working knowledge of the subject. But his research and copies were of immense value for the future.

From 1827 onward, Wilkinson spent most of his time on the west bank at Thebes. He appropriated the T-shaped and long-looted tomb of the New Kingdom vizier 'Amechu as his residence. He installed partitions to make rooms, threw down carpets, and installed his library and Egyptian furniture, while enjoying a magnificent view over the Nile Valley, with the temples of Luxor and Karnak in the distance. Here he held court, entertaining friends and burning wooden mummy cases in the fireplace, as everyone did. The wood gave off a horrible odor. His visitors would tie up their boats nearby and stay for days in a home filled with laughter and good times. Wrote one casual visitor: "the odour of the mummies had long since been dispelled by the more congenial perfume of savory viands."[5] They were astonished at Wilkinson's leisurely routine, which began with breakfast at 10:30 AM. Nevertheless, he completed an astounding quantity of work, including the first topographical map of western Thebes. He surveyed and numbered the tombs of the Valley of the Kings, a numerical system still used today. His main interest was the paintings in nobles' tombs, for he realized that they provided rich insights into the daily life of the ancient Egyptians. Wilkinson considered the naturalistic friezes the "epitome of life" and a chance to journey back into the society that created them, as if one were a spectator of the events on the walls. Many of the tombs recorded by Wilkinson and his colleagues were damaged or destroyed soon afterward by vandals or local people using the tombs as their homes.

The future of ancient Egypt lay in the hands of John Gardner Wilkinson and a small group of mainly British artists and travelers in the 1820s and 1830s. They worked together and independently, exchanging information, visiting one another, and thoroughly enjoying themselves. Unfortunately, almost none of them published their work. Robert Hay (1799–1863) came from Scottish landed gentry, entered the Royal Navy, and then inherited the family estate. A naval cruise in the eastern Mediterranean had given him a lasting interest in Egypt, so he decided to go on a Grand Tour that included Egypt. Hay traveled in the style of his eighteenth-century predecessors, complete with a retinue of artists and architects, among them a talented artist, Joseph Bonomi. He also recruited another Scotsman, Frederick Catherwood, who was to achieve international fame some years later for his drawings of Maya cities.[6] Hay's team produced as accurate copies as they could, often using a camera lucida, a prism and set of interchangeable lenses that cast an image on a table so that a draftsman could copy it. His architects produced elevations and floor plans. Hay himself was a gifted artist who produced not only panoramic scenes and drawings of ancient Egyptian monuments, but also exquisite depictions of Islamic architecture and an excellent record of river villages in the 1820s. He eventually returned to England in 1835 with a laden portfolio, but lost interest in ancient Egypt and never published anything, except a sumptuous volume, *Illustrations of Cairo*, in 1840. Thirty-nine volumes of his unpublished drawings reside in the British Museum.

Hay dedicated *Illustrations of Cairo* to one of his Egypt friends, Edward William Lane, who had arrived in Cairo in 1825. Unlike his friends, Lane lived among the Egyptians, on the argument that he wanted to study their literature. He was a loner who spent much of his life in Egypt, returning to England to write, and lived like a hermit. Lane's great work was *An Account of the Manners and Customs of the Modern Egyptians,* published by the London publisher John Murray in 1836.[7] This remarkable work, based as it was on a pioneer form of what anthropologists call "participant observation," remains a classic and established his reputation.

Wilkinson himself left Egypt in 1833. His months in the nobles' tombs at Qurna had taught him much about the lives of ancient Egyptians. A germ of an idea for a book on the subject formed in his mind as he returned to England. His plan fitted well in a popular literary genre of the day, an extension of the travelogue that was more impersonal and a pioneer of later ethnographic studies. *Manners and Customs of the Ancient Egyptians* appeared in three volumes in 1837 under John Murray's imprint, shortly after a more comprehensive volume on Thebes. Wilkinson had written enough material for five volumes, the additional two soon appearing when the book sold well. *Manners and Customs* made Wilkinson a household name, earned him a knighthood, and remained in print throughout the nineteenth century. Unlike the massive, and expensive, *Description*, the moderate price of the book placed it within reach of a rapidly growing number of middle-class readers.

Manners and Customs of the Ancient Egyptians covered more than fifty subjects, everything from daily life itself to chronology and social organization. The format was ideal for a comprehensive journey through ancient Egypt, allowing the author to dwell on such topics as a feast, complete with dissertations on the furniture, music, and food. Wilkinson used his own work and classical sources for his chronology, estimating the date of the first pharaoh, Menes, at about 2320 BC, well after the biblical date of the Creation (4004 BC), which was established theological dogma at the time. Wilkinson brought the ancient inhabitants of the Nile Valley to life in a wealth of detail never possible before, through their sites and particularly from their paintings, papyri, and inscriptions. He emphasized the

FIGURE 12.2 *Persons Coming to Be Registered* and *Brought Before the Scribes,* sketches from Wilkinson's *Manners and Customs of the Ancient Egyptians.*

religion, culture, and daily life of the ancient Egyptians rather than their political history. It was the first study in centuries to look beyond Herodotus and the traditional legends to the Egyptian sources themselves. John Gardner Wilkinson was one of those rare but highly influential scholars with the ability to carry out important basic research while simultaneously possessing the knack of fascinating the general public with more popular accounts of his discoveries.[8]

John Gardner Wilkinson never traveled to Egypt for any more serious research, although he did return in 1841 to carry out research for an Egyptian travel guide for a series of such volumes published by John Murray aimed firmly not at the wealthy but at new generations of middle-class travelers. He traveled in style up the Nile, his baggage requiring a small army of porters. The contents included an iron bedstead, a sword, a velvet waistcoat, and "much more." He lamented the high cost of living. "Egypt's much altered for the worst & has lost much of its oriental character," he wrote to Robert Hay. "The travellers who go up the Nile will I fear soon be like Rhine tourists. & Cheapside will pour out its Legions upon Egypt."[9] These were the very tourists at which his *Handbook for Travellers in Egypt* was aimed. It appeared in 1847; well-thumbed copies journeyed up and down the Nile for many years.

Egypt's heat now bothered Wilkinson, who spent the rest of his life as a gentleman scholar, consulted occasionally by the British Museum about Egyptian acquisitions. He moved out of the mainstream of Egyptology, for his interests were transitory and his working methods more those of a man of letters than an archaeologist. His reputation to the wider world rested almost entirely on *Manners and Customs*, which remained a definitive account of ancient Egypt until superseded by Flinders Petrie's diggings and the University of Chicago's James Breasted's *History of Egypt*, published in 1905, which was based on precise translations of inscriptions and papyri.[10] John Gardner Wilkinson made some of the first accurate copies of Egyptian art, hieroglyphs, and tomb paintings, far superior to anything in the *Description* and in Champollion's work. Sixty years were to pass before new copyists came to the Nile, and these were professionals rather than enthusiastic amateurs. Only in recent years have Egyptologists and a wider audience realized Wilkinson's extraordinary accomplishments. His impact on our understanding of ancient Egypt continues to this day.

: :

Champollion's death, and the departure of John Gardner Wilkinson from Egypt, left somewhat of a vacuum in the study of hieroglyphs. In any case, the days of the amateur investigator were numbered, for museums and universities were becoming the centers of academic inquiry. The next major initiative came from the king of Prussia, who sponsored a huge expedition to Egypt in 1842 with the same lofty goals as that of the Champollion explorations of 1828. Naturalist, cartographer, and artist Alexander von Humboldt was one of the last universal scholars in the natural sciences and the eloquent advocate of the royal expedition. The obvious choice as leader was Karl Richard Lepsius (1810–1884), a thirty-two-year-old lecturer at the University of Berlin. The artist Bonomi and James Wild, an English architect, joined Lepsius and his Prussian staff in an exhaustive survey of the major archaeological sites of the Nile.[11]

The three-year expedition was a great success, largely because Lepsius himself spent a long time in thorough preparation. He visited all the major collections of Egyptian antiquities in Europe, taught himself Champollion's grammar and proved its validity to his satisfaction, and learned lithography and copper engraving before leaving for Egypt. Although the main intention was to survey monuments and collect antiquities, Lepsius did dig at the site of the Labyrinth in the Fayyum and even made accurate drawings of the archaeological layers at the site, a startling innovation for the time. The expedition stayed a long time at Thebes, where Lepsius availed himself of Wilkinson's residence in 'Amechu's tomb.

Lepsius and his colleagues left Egypt with thousands of drawings, as well as 15,000 casts and Egyptian antiquities that formed the nucleus of an Egyptian museum in Berlin. The records from the expedition were invaluable, but Lepsius's collection methods could be brutal. He dynamited a column from Seti I's tomb and carried it off, as well as a section of a tiled wall from Djoser's Step Pyramid at Saqqara, given to the king by Muhammad Ali in exchange for the gift of a fine dinner service.[12]

Karl Lepsius became a professor at Berlin University in 1846, eventually keeper of the Egyptian collections at the museum and keeper of the Royal Library. He devoted the next ten years to publishing the results of the expedition in the twelve-volume set of 894 folio plates, *Denkmäler aus Ägypten und Äthiopien*, probably the largest work on Egyptology ever published. Five further volumes of descriptive text were edited after Lepsius's death in 1884. Together, the subsidized publications of the Lepsius expedition represent a magnificent and valuable source on the monuments of ancient Egypt, still of great use even today.

: :

The Prussian expedition set new standards for the recording of monuments and inscriptions that foreshadowed the more systematic efforts of later scientists, but did not engage in much excavation. By the late 1840s, most of the major monuments of Upper Egypt had been surveyed, at least cursorily, but Lower Egypt and the delta were still archaeologically unknown. Decades of uncontrolled digging had wrought terrible destruction. The few investigators with seemingly more lofty scientific goals were as destructive as tomb robbers. In 1837, Colonel Richard William Howard Vyse, a military gentleman with a strong belief in the Bible, made the first survey of the pyramids of Giza. He had worked with Giovanni Caviglia in 1835, then returned in 1837 for further excavations accompanied by a civil engineer, John Shae Penning. They used gunpowder during their investigations, which caused serious damage to the Great Pyramid but allowed them to enter the burial chamber of the third pyramid of Menkaure. Vyse removed the magnificent granite sarcophagus from the pyramid, then shipped it to England, only to have it lost at sea during the voyage.[13]

Excavation was still largely the domain of the dealer and tomb robber. The resultant destruction was catastrophic and on an immense scale. The volume of protest against wholesale destruction was still muted and hardly loud enough to be heard, for most major European museums and consular officers were busily engaged in searching for new finds. A few solitary voices were raised, among them that of an American, George Robins Gliddon, at one time American vice-consul in Alexandria and later a well-known author and lecturer on ancient Egypt whose travels took him as far west as St. Louis. In 1841 he wrote one of the first appeals to the archaeological conscience, an obscure and little-remembered memoir, *An Appeal to the Antiquaries of Europe on the Destruction of the Monuments of Egypt*, which seems to have been largely ignored.[14]

Gliddon's *Appeal* is a long and turgid documentation of the destruction of the monuments of the Nile since the Napoleonic Wars, damage wrought by both vandals and antiquarians, but more especially by Muhammad Ali and his government. Philae had remained intact only because of the turbulent waters of the First Cataract. The Nilometer had lost its steps, taken to build a palace. Thebes had been decimated ever since Wilkinson's investigations in 1836. Gunpowder could be used on the Karnak temples—for a price. A small bribe could obtain sculptured blocks from the portico. The wooden door on Seti I's tomb, so carefully erected by Belzoni, was removed by Albanian soldiers after Henry Salt's death. A quarter of the temple of Dendera disappeared into the walls of a saltpeter factory in 1835. Only the protests of the French consul, Jean-François Mimaut, stopped its complete destruction. "Strange," wrote Gliddon somberly, "that the Columns erected by a Hadrian to the service of religion, should now uphold a distillery for rum!"[15] Gliddon rightly accused the pasha of deliberate neglect, of exploitation of the temples for building factories that never went into production, and of using *firmans* as political favors for influential visitors.

By the time Gliddon's *Appeal* appeared, public opinion had begun to favor some conservation measures. Champollion had complained in 1829, the French consul Jean François Mimaut, in a new diplomatic departure, in 1839. Lord Algernon Percy, an aristocratic collector, had been moved to comment on the scale of destruction two years earlier.[16] In 1839–1840, the British government cataloged a long list of damage and devastation in a formal report to the pasha. But a public exposé of the situation was delayed in the hope that something would be done by the Egyptian government. The report stemmed from a major study of consular and commercial activities by diplomats in Egypt compiled by Lord Bowring that was highly critical of the antiquities trade. When the report was released in 1842, Lord Palmerston excised those parts that dealt with some of the archaeological activities of consuls, although by the mid-1830s diplomats were too busy on other matters to spend time on archaeology and the pasha's Antiquities Law of 1835 was at least in existence—on paper.

Gliddon's pompous effusion had little apparent effect on the sins of the tourist or treasure hunter, despite his railings against the hammer-wielding chipper of monuments or the "Anglo-Indian gentleman" who cut bas-reliefs off the walls of Amenhotep III's tomb so he could draw them more effectively on board his Nile boat. When the artist had finished, the originals were thrown into the river. Even as Lepsius and his draftsmen were in Upper Egypt, an eccentric French artist and traveler named Émile Prisse D'Avennes stole into the temple of Karnak and removed the magnificent Table of Kings, a series of carved stone blocks recording the portraits and cartouches of many Egyptian pharaohs. D'Avennes had no *firman* and was in open defiance of the antiquities ordinance.[17]

By dint of working at night and in great secrecy, D'Avennes succeeded in packing the stones into eighteen crates before he was denounced to the governor of Esna. The angry official placed his tent under guard. A month later, he bribed the governor and quietly moved the blocks on board a boat after nightfall. On the way downstream he met Lepsius on his way to Karnak and entertained the eminent scholar with coffee as he sat on one of the priceless packing cases. Even the French consul declined to have anything to do with D'Avennes, whose finds were eventually deposited in the Louvre.

The more respectable collectors took refuge behind a familiar nineteenth-century argument, which still circulates today. Surely it was better, they argued, to let scholars and dealers take their precious finds to Europe, where they would be safe from plunder and destruction. As long as there was no museum in Cairo, this position was a defensible one, even more so after the rapid dissolution of the pasha's museum in the Ezbekiya Gardens, its artifacts dispersed as diplomatic gifts. The pressure to copy and record as well as to preserve by export was strong among respectable scientists of the day. This export came at a high price. Dealers and freelance operators threw away, burned, or destroyed thousands of papyri and smaller artifacts in their frantic digging for large antiquities. Every museum in Europe wanted major finds and beautiful papyri. Hardly surprisingly, no one could be bothered to develop systematic techniques for recovery of material from archaeological sites.

: :

Coptic manuscripts were particularly hot properties, especially for museums. Their agents cajoled and flattered remote religious communities out of their libraries, which is why one of early Egyptology's best-known figures, Auguste Mariette (1821–1881), came to the Nile.

Auguste Mariette was born in Boulogne, France, on February 11, 1821. After an uneventful but happy childhood, he went to England at the age of eighteen to teach French at a private school in Stratford-upon-Avon. The job lasted a year, an experimental venture at ribbon designing an even shorter time. So Mariette returned to Boulogne and became a teacher at the local college where he had received his own education. He soon discovered he had a talent for writing and spent his spare time preparing articles on all manner of subjects for newspapers and magazines. Until he was twenty-two, Mariette had no exposure to Egypt or to Egyptology. Then in 1842, the father of a recently deceased artist and explorer, Nestor L'Hôte, who had been a member of Champollion's expedition and died on a later desert journey, was transferred to Boulogne.[18] His son had left an enormous mass of papers and copies that urgently needed organization and publication. L'Hôte's father, a customs officer, was related to the Mariettes. By chance, he asked Auguste to examine the papers. Mariette was fascinated by the new world that opened up in front of him; he became engrossed by the intricacies of hieroglyphs and decipherment.

Soon Mariette spent every moment of his spare time with his new hobby and writing a catalog of the few Egyptian objects in the Boulogne

Museum. On the strength of this piece, he got the city to back his application for official support for an expedition to Egypt, but without success. Mariette impulsively resigned his teaching and editing jobs and moved to Paris. There he pored over the Karnak Table of Kings in the Louvre and wrote a closely reasoned seventy-page paper on the inscriptions that so impressed director and Egyptologist Charles Lenormant at the Collège de France that he obtained a minor job at the Louvre for the energetic young man.[19] Soon Mariette was spending his days cataloging papyri and his evenings reading everything about Egyptology and mastering hieroglyphs to a professional standard.

Lenormant continued to approve. In 1850 he instructed his protégé to collect rare Coptic manuscripts in Egypt. Excitedly, Mariette took ship to Alexandria and contacted the Coptic patriarch in Cairo, only to find him deeply hostile to foreign collectors. Some years before, two Englishmen, Lord Curzen and Henry Tattan, had gotten some monks drunk and made off with an entire library of manuscripts. He was not about to let any other books out of ecclesiastical hands.

Mariette was momentarily at a loss, for it was clearly profitless to look for manuscripts. He turned his thoughts toward excavation, for a supplementary clause in his instructions authorized him to excavate archaeological sites to enrich the museum collections. By the end of October 1850 Mariette had gathered some equipment and was camped in the midst of the Necropolis at Saqqara. He had no *firman* from the pasha, little money, and only the most limited authority from the Louvre. But he was inspired by the head of a sphinx projecting from the sand, similar to other examples from Saqqara that he had seen in Cairo and Alexandria. Mariette's wide reading paid off. He suddenly remembered that the Greek geographer Strabo had referred to a Serapeum at Memphis, in a sandy place where an avenue of sphinxes leading to the tomb of the holy Apis bulls was constantly smothered by drifting sand. Inspired, he gambled everything and gathered thirty workmen at the sphinx to dig for the Serapeum.

Within hours, sphinx after sphinx emerged from the sand. The workers simply followed the avenue from statue to statue. Tombs, seated statues, a phallic god, and two temples of Apis, one Greek and the other Egyptian, soon came to light, the latter containing a magnificent statue.[20] Mariette soon ran out of money, but the French consul, Arnaud Lemoyne, was so captivated by the energy of the young man that he advanced him money to continue while he applied to his superiors in Paris for more funds. Fortunately for Mariette, the Apis finds dazzled the Louvre, which sent an increased subvention.

A few weeks later, Mariette dug up a huge cache of bronze statues of Osiris, Apis, and other Egyptian gods under a temple floor, a discovery that aroused the envy and fascination of Egyptian and foreigner alike. All Cairo was excited, and the dealers jealous. Abbas Pasha, the son of Muhammad Ali, stepped in and tried to confiscate the finds, but the French consul poured diplomatic oil on troubled waters with a token handover of antiquities. The pasha granted Mariette a *firman* on the condition that France renounce all claims to future discoveries, which caused considerable alarm in Paris, since the French government had just voted 30,000 francs to pay for further excavations.

Mariette just went on digging. In November 1851, he finally reached the tomb of Apis, sealed by a magnificent sandstone door. The young archaeologist was soon inside, marveling at the huge granite coffins of the bulls, their lids removed and scattered by tomb robbers centuries earlier. But an enormous amount of material still remained, all of which, under the conditions of the *firman*, was to go to the pasha's museum, where it would probably be given away to distinguished foreign visitors in exchange for political favors. With fiendish cunning, Mariette set up his packing cases at the bottom of a deep pit where a secret trapdoor led to the tombs below. For several months he packed the items from his early excavations ceded to France by day and the contents of the theoretically still-unopened tomb below him by night. The finest relics from the Serapeum duly arrived at the Louvre, while Mariette blandly showed disappointed officials the empty tombs he had just discovered.

Over a period of many months Mariette explored the innermost recesses of the Serapeum. He was lucky enough to find an undisturbed burial of Apis, deposited in the time of Rameses II. Even the footprints of the funeral workmen were preserved in the dust of the tomb, while the sarcophagus contained both the undisturbed mummy and rich jewelry and gold. The Serapeum finds caused a sensation in Paris when they were exhibited at the Louvre. Mariette was promoted to assistant keeper and soon published a series of plates of the Serapeum, titled *Choix de monuments*, that gave a foretaste of what full publication of his excavations might lay before the public.[21]

FIGURE 12.3
A scribe figure from the
Serapeum, found by Mariette.
This illustration comes from his
Choix de monuments (1856).

: :

A perennially restless man like Mariette could never be happy in one place
for long. His contacts among Egyptologists were now wide. A warm and
gregarious man, he had become a close friend of the German Egyptologist
Heinrich Brugsch, an expert on demotic script. Brugsch came on a chance
visit to the Serapeum, and a lifetime of friendship was forged. Both
Brugsch and Mariette were convivial souls, full of bonhomie and fond of
good living. Although Mariette was never especially revealing about his
personal life in Egypt, Brugsch filled in some gaps. He recalled Mariette's
mud house at the Serapeum, which teemed with women, children, mon-
keys, and his laborers. The furniture was spartan at best. Bats flew around
his bedroom. Brugsch tucked his mosquito net under the mattress and
endured the first of many uncomfortable nights.[22]

Mariette also came to the attention of that remarkable diplomat and
visionary Ferdinand-Marie de Lesseps, the genius behind the construction of the Suez Canal. De Lesseps was attracted by Mariette's ambitious
and burning energy, and listened to his proposals for saving the monuments of the Nile. He spoke with Said Pasha, the new ruler of Egypt after

the assassination of Mariette's old adversary, Abbas Pasha, in 1854. Three years later, the pasha invited the French government to send Mariette to Egypt on the occasion of the visit of Prince Napoléon to the Nile. It was only when he arrived that Mariette discovered that he was to dig for fine antiquities to be presented to the royal visitor. He was to proceed upriver, make archaeological finds, then rebury them for the royal visitor to "find." Mariette did not hesitate for a moment. Money and an official steamer were at his disposal. He started digging at Saqqara and was soon at Thebes and Abydos, where Brugsch soon joined him in a happy field reunion. On the west bank near Qurna, Mariette's men unearthed a simple wooden coffin containing a mummy that fell to pieces when exposed to the air. An extraordinary collection of artifacts survived in the bandages, including a gold and bronze dagger, lion amulets, and a cartouche-shaped box inscribed with the name of a king later identified as the pharaoh Kamose, who expelled the Asian Hyksos from Egypt in about 1570 BC. Mariette shrewdly arranged for the pasha to send some nice artifacts to the prince, which ensured him the goodwill of the royal family.

De Lesseps now stepped in and persuaded the pasha to appoint Auguste Mariette *mamar* (director) of ancient monuments in Egypt and curator of a new museum of antiquities to be built in Cairo. Such an appointment was long overdue and was bitterly opposed by dealers and diplomats up to their necks in the antiquities trade. The pasha gave Mariette sweeping powers, ordering him to arrest any peasant who set foot in a temple.

Mariette's position was extremely precarious. He had to depend on the pasha's goodwill for funding. The museum premises consisted of a deserted mosque, small filthy sheds, and a house alive with vermin in which the Mariettes lived. But Mariette was blissfully happy and gathered his family and faithful supervisors around him in an orgy of excavation. Labor was cheap and abundant, for he was able to requisition the entire male population of a village if he wished. His ruthless methods were unpopular, but they certainly produced results. At one point, men were digging under his direction at thirty-seven different locations simultaneously, from the delta to the First Cataract!

Auguste Mariette's discoveries were extraordinary, but excavated with complete abandon. He was mainly concerned with spectacular finds, which he needed to fill his museum and to satisfy the pasha. Dynamite was among his techniques; careful recording and observation mattered nothing—only objects. He emptied more than three hundred tombs at Giza and Saqqara alone. At Edfu he moved the Arab village off the roof of the buried temple onto the plain and exposed this magnificent shrine to full view for the first time in centuries. At Thebes, Mariette's laborers cleared the buried temple of Queen Hatshepsut at Deir el-Bahri, nearly getting in a fight with a British aristocrat, the marquis of Dufferin and Ava, who was quietly removing a large number of carved stone fragments from the mortuary temple of Mentuhotep nearby.[23] The great temple of Hathor, the temple of Amun at Karnak, and many other major sites came under Mariette's attack. He recovered more than 15,000 artifacts from his promiscuous excavations.

Conservation was a new idea, and one that at this point merely implied a cessation of quarrying temples and channeling as many looted and excavated antiquities into official hands as possible. Mariette tried to achieve this by forbidding any excavations in Egypt except his own and making exportation of antiquities a virtual impossibility. He made every effort to get funds for a new museum, but his difficulties were formidable. The pasha had no real interest in archaeology. He had appointed Mariette to appease the powerful de Lesseps and Napoléon III, whom, he felt, would be kept quiet by some gesture toward antiquity. He was likely to cut off funds without warning or give away a choice item in the national collections to a favored visitor. The only way Mariette could keep interest alive was by producing a steady stream of gorgeous finds to titillate the pasha's fancy. This, of course, led to a frantic rush for new discoveries, which corrupted the whole course of archaeology on every official excavation, as other Egyptologists later found out to their cost.

Not that everything flowed into Mariette's hands. In 1855, Anthony Charles Harris, an English merchant and papyrus collector in Alexandria, was offered a collection of papyri found in a tomb behind the temple at Medinet Habu near Thebes. He could not afford to buy them all, but managed to purchase the best, which included the so-called Great Harris Papyrus, a 40.5-meter- (133-foot-) long record of donations to Amun and his priesthood made by pharaoh Rameses III. The others included the famous tomb-robbery trial records between the reigns of Rameses VI and Rameses XI described in Chapter 1. Harris's daughter Selima sold his papyrus collection to the British Museum in 1872, an acquisition that kindled the trustees' thirst for yet more in future years.

FIGURE 12.4
Auguste Mariette in 1861

Early in 1859, Mariette received word in Cairo that his workers had found another royal burial close to that of Kamose unearthed two years earlier. This time the sarcophagus was intact, that of a queen, Ahhotep, a wife of Kamose, accompanied by weapons and a necklace of golden flies, a reward for valor in battle. In Mariette's absence, the local headman at Qena took over the mummy, disposed of the bandages and bones, and shipped off the 2 kilograms (4 pounds) of gold ornaments as a gift to the khedive.[24] Mariette was incensed. He took a steamer upstream with an official order enabling him to stop all vessels on the Nile suspected of carrying antiquities. Passions flowed strongly when the two steamers met. For half an hour the argument raged furiously over the gold, until the Frenchman took the law into his hands and laid about him with his fists in a fury. One man was nearly thrown in the river, another cajoled at gunpoint, until the jewelry was handed over. Mariette rushed to the pasha, presented him with a scarab and a necklace for one of his wives, and averted a tense political situation. The pasha was so delighted with the finds—and, one suspects, the discomfiture of his official—that he ordered a new museum built to house the queen's possessions. A new museum building at Bulaq opened in 1863, filled with Mariette's treasures.

Mariette's long career involved him in diplomacy as well as archaeology. For a while the French government used him on a diplomatic mission to persuade Said Pasha to visit France in connection with a financial loan. Mariette disliked his diplomatic role, but eventually accompanied Said to France, where they visited his hometown of Boulogne and received a tumultuous welcome. Said was so pleased that he gave Mariette the title of bey and a pension. But this friendship was abruptly cut short by the death of Said Pasha six months later.

Bulaq Museum was now a showpiece. Mariette was much in demand to escort foreign dignitaries and maintained academic ties with serious Egyptologists all over Europe. He had even closer links with government officers, dealers, and humble villagers throughout the Nile Valley, contacts that he used to keep an eye on his precious monuments. He worked with an inspired frenzy and was at his desk or out in the field every day at dawn. At lunch or dinner, however, he would relax, for his wife, Eleanore, maintained an open house, which was always crowded with friends and visitors. Work became the only antidote when his devoted wife died of the plague in 1865. Perhaps it was fortunate that he was ordered to Paris for a year to set up the Egyptian exhibit in the International Exhibition of 1867.

Paris was entranced with the splendor of Mariette's exhibits, which purported to reconstruct life in ancient Egypt. He ransacked the collections at Bulaq for their finest pieces. Queen Ahhotep's jewelry formed the centerpiece and sensation of the Paris exhibition. The jewelry excited the cupidity of no less a regal personage than the empress Eugénie herself. She promptly intimated to the khedive that she would be graciously pleased to receive the jewels as a gift. It was a great moment for Egyptian archaeology when the khedive deferred to Mariette. The empress offered him prestigious posts, even a role in writing her husband's biography of Caesar.[25] Neither bribes nor threats could sway Mariette, not even the displeasure of a powerful empress or an indignant khedive. The jewelry returned safely to Egypt.

Preservation was much on Mariette's mind in his later years. "It behooves us to preserve Egypt's monuments with care," he once wrote. "Five hundred years hence Egypt should still be able to show to the scholars who shall visit her the same monuments that we are now describing." Tourists were a thorn in Mariette's side. One American tourist in particular aroused his justifiable ire by touring Upper Egypt in 1870 "with a pot of tar in one hand and a brush in the other, leaving on all the temples the indelible and truly disgraceful record of his passage."[26]

Vandalism was a serious problem, too. The tomb of the Fifth Dynasty official Ti at Saqqara, for example, suffered more damage by the hand of tourists over a decade of Mariette's tenure than it had during the whole of the previous 6,000 years of its existence. Under the circumstances, we can understand why Mariette dug up as much as he could to save Egypt's antiquities for posterity. In all, we are told, Mariette employed more than 2,780 laborers during his career, a number far larger than any one man could supervise at all closely. Workshops for handling the new flood of antiquities were set up at Edfu, Thebes, Abydos, and Memphis, an innovation far ahead of facilities available in other Near Eastern countries. His critics were many, one of them describing him as a "whirlwind" that had descended on the Nile.

Mariette's prodigious energies were not devoted entirely to antiquities. He was deeply involved in the glittering ceremonies that accompanied the opening of the Suez Canal on November 17, 1869. His old adversary, the empress Eugénie, opened the waterway in the French royal yacht *Aigle*. Mariette must have gained some quiet satisfaction in escorting her royal highness up the Nile. The khedive also enlisted Mariette's literary talents for a quite different task, the writing of the libretto for Verdi's *Aïda*, a grand opera with an ancient Egyptian theme composed to commemorate the opening of the canal. Mariette shared this memorable task with C. du Locle, a fellow Frenchman.

The last decade of Mariette's long career was a series of archaeological and personal tragedies. Financial troubles dogged his excavations as the khedive plunged Egypt so deeply into debt that the British and French deposed him in 1879. The year before, the inundation flooded the museum. Much was lost, including many of Mariette's books and priceless notes on the Serapeum. His international reputation grew, and he was honored by the Academy of Inscriptions and Literature in Paris. Back home, Mariette's children died one by one, leaving him with a depleted family and little to live for. A French nobleman left a haunting picture of an elderly and quieter man in 1872: "A man of great stature, broadly built, aged rather than old, an Athlete roughed out of the mass like the colossi over which he watches. His deep-toned face has a dreamy and morose look, yet how many times, sitting on the bank of the Nile, did he speak with feeling of this strange Egypt, its river, its nocturnal skies."[27]

After the British and French takeover in 1872, life became more settled. At least Mariette's salary was paid regularly. But his health was failing, as diabetes weakened his formidable constitution. He struggled back to Cairo from Europe in late 1880 and died peacefully in the house by his beloved museum on January 18, 1881. The Serapeum was still unpublished, but the tide had turned. A permanent museum, filled with the glories of ancient Egypt, had ensured that the course of Egyptology was changed forever and that the rape of the Nile would slow, if never completely cease. A grieving Egypt gave him a state funeral and buried the man it owed so much at the door of his museum.

13 | "In the British Museum He Is Placed Beyond the Reach of All Such Evils"

Luxor is the center of a more or less legitimate traffic in antiquities.

Luxor possesses certain manufactories where statuettes, stelae, and

scarabae are imitated with a dexterity which often deceives even

the most experienced antiquarian.

AUGUSTE MARIETTE,
quoted in Brian Fagan, *The Rape of the Nile*, 1st ed.

Auguste Mariette saw the dawning of an era when tourism changed the face of Egyptology. The steamship and the railroad had started it all—a tourist boom that made travel through the eastern Mediterranean world accessible to a far broader spectrum of European society. Cairo and Alexandria, Giza and Saqqara had long been within the purview of the more adventurous eighteenth-century traveler. Napoléon and Muhammad Ali made Upper Egypt more secure. By 1820, Ali controlled the Nile as far upstream as the Second Cataract, which made it possible for Europeans to travel that far. Soon there were guidebooks. In 1830, Jean Jacques Rifaud's *Tableau de l'Égypte, de la Nubie et des lieux circonvoisons* (Guidebook to Egypt, Nubia, and surrounding attractions) guided travelers up the Nile from Alexandria to the Second Cataract, complete with side trips, an Arabic vocabulary, and essays on geography and local peoples. Rifaud's guide was superficial at best, without maps, and soon superseded by more ambitious works such as John Gardner Wilkinson's handbooks of the 1830s and 1840s.[1]

Egypt was more accessible, but traveling there was still a major undertaking. The passage from southern France to Alexandria could take a month or more under sail until 1837, when the Peninsular and Orient Line (P&O) won government contracts to carry mail by steamship from England to Gibraltar, Malta, and Alexandria. By 1843, P&O steamers took but fifteen days to travel from Southampton to Alexandria. A passenger who went overland to Marseilles could trim four or five days off the journey. Only 275 visitors transited Egypt on their way to and from India in 1844. The number leaped to 3,000 in 1847. By 1858, one could travel from Alexandria to Suez by train. Eleven years later, the Suez Canal opened, so many transit visitors now went straight through to India. Egypt rapidly became a popular tourist destination in its own right.

A rapidly growing tourist infrastructure accommodated the visitor. Wilkinson had recommended a minimum of three months for a journey to the Second Cataract. By 1880, one could dash from London to the same destination and back in six weeks, but most people took much longer. John Murray, Karl Baedeker, and Adolphe Joanne produced objective, comprehensive guides for the average tourist after the 1860s. European-run hotels rose in Cairo, among them the Hôtel de l'Orient, built originally for transitory visitors in 1843, then renamed Shepheard's when an English owner of that name took over. Shepheard's became one of the great Victorian hotels, frequented by the rich and famous and Cook's tourists.[2]

Three modes of transport carried the tourist upstream: the *dahabiyya* (the Nile sailing vessel), the steamer, and the railroad. *Dahabiyya*s were the choice of the leisurely, more affluent traveler and could reach considerable size, with a crew of ten or more. In his *Handbook*, Wilkinson recommended sinking the ship first to rid it of "rats and other noxious inhabitants," and shipping out with a chicken coop and a plentiful supply of biscuits. By 1858, steamers came into use on the Nile, with regular tours from Cairo to Upper Egypt by 1873. The railroad extended as far upstream as Asyut, mainly as a way of exporting sugar cane, but tourists could board steamers at the town, thereby shortening the trip by several days. The lines reached Aswan in 1898, impelled there by Horatio Herbert Kitchener's Sudanese campaign and military needs. Railroad travel cut steamer time by one-half to two-thirds, making the river the choice of the leisured tourist, while *dahabiyya*s faded into history. In 1873, John Murray firmly recommended a sailing boat if time and money permitted. "In a boat of your own you are your own master, and can stop or go on as you feel inclined."³ He pointed out that one might be "amongst a number of people you never saw before," locked into a rigid schedule.

The steamer and the railroad brought mass tourism to Egypt, in the hands of the ubiquitous Thomas Cook (1808–1892), who started his business with morally uplifting railroad excursions in Britain, then in Europe.⁴ His first tour of Egypt came in 1869, when his guests attended the opening ceremonies of the Suez Canal, then followed the Prince of Wales's party upstream in two chartered steamboats. His Nile business boomed, despite naked monks swimming out to his boats, to the horror of the ladies. Thomas Cook had strong evangelical motives. His son John Mason (1834–1899) took over the business and propelled the company into mass tourism. By 1870, Cook ran a steamer and 136 *dahabiyya*s up the river. Twenty years later, the company's tourists packed twenty steamboats. Tourism had come to Egypt to stay. Some people deplored the hordes of visitors, who descended on temple and tomb by the hundred and delighted in inscribing their names there. Others were merely amused: "The nominal suzerain of Egypt is the Sultan; its real suzerain is Lord Cromer. Its nominal Governor is the Khedive; its real governor, for a final touch of comic opera, is Thomas Cook & Son."⁵

Whatever one's view of the tourist, the impact on ancient Egypt was profound and often catastrophic. Auguste Mariette devoted much of his life to watching over the increasing numbers of scholars and tourists who flocked to the Nile. His successor, Gaston Maspero, carried on his work with the Antiquities Service and the museum. And, for the first time, we find a few efforts to make ancient Egypt accessible to native Egyptians.

: :

Auguste Mariette's death in 1881 coincided with a major change in the political scene, sparked both by the khedive's incompetence and by a popular insurrection in Cairo. The British and French governments took an ardent interest in the affairs of Egypt, more so because of the major investments represented by the Suez Canal and other industrial development. At any sign of unrest, allied warships would appear off Alexandria, as if to remind the Turks that others were the masters of the Nile.

A military revolt in September 1881 resulted in the formation of an abortive popular government that lasted but a year. The British demanded the resignation of the new ministry, nominally headed by the khedive Tawfiq, but in fact led by Ahmed Arabi, a young army officer. Public order deteriorated, and Europeans were assaulted in the streets of Alexandria. So the British sent the Mediterranean fleet and an expeditionary force to the Nile. General Sir Garnet Wolseley and his army made short work of the Egyptians. By September 1882, the British had restored order in Egypt, reinforced with all the authority and panoply of Victoria's mighty armies. A British agent and consul general, Sir Evelyn Baring (1841–1917), controlled a puppet khedive. This powerful and righteous man, a model of calm Victorian authority, effectively ruled Egypt for twenty-four years. Although he had no formal authority over the khedive, his word was law and his policies emanated from London.

Baring was an economist with a background in the classics and India who spent his entire career in Egypt placing the debt-ridden country on a firm financial basis through a series of harsh austerity measures that hit all government departments hard, including the Antiquities Service. British civil servants took over the running of defense, police matters, foreign affairs, finance, and public works. But the French remained influential in education, the arts, and archaeology. Rivalry between British and French archaeologists colored Egyptology for much of the late nineteenth century—including arguments over excavation permits, approaches to ancient Egypt, and research methods. The French and Germans were often in violent disagreement, the former preferring a free-flowing approach to Egyptology, the latter obsessed with orderly interpretations and minute details of art and artifacts. Thanks to Gaston Maspero, however, the French effectively controlled archaeology in Egypt from 1881 until as late as 1936.

Gaston Maspero (1846–1916), a young Egyptologist and an expert in hieroglyphs, had become friends with Mariette when a student in Paris in 1867. He was the son of an Italian refugee from Milan, and acquired an interest in Egyptology at an early age. He was soon specializing in hieroglyphs and assumed a prominent role in the Collège de France whilst in his twenties. By any standards, he was a successful scholar, although he did not visit Egypt until he was thirty-four years old.

Maspero used his influential connections to lobby for a French school of archaeology in Cairo, which would perpetuate the strong French presence in Egyptology started by Napoléon and Champollion and fostered by Mariette. He came out to found the school on orders from the French government in 1881, arriving in Cairo just two weeks before the great man succumbed to diabetes. A master of bureaucratic maneuvering, Maspero moved over into the directorship of the Antiquities Service with smooth efficiency, while one of his students took over the school. He completely reorganized the service, worked on the Saqqara pyramids, and became the dominant force behind all archaeology in Egypt for a generation. Maspero was a giant among pioneers of Egyptology, a man whose incredible energy and industry exceeded even that of Mariette. His prodigious talents turned to all aspects of Egyptology from excavation to hieroglyphs, while his popular works on Egyptology and other subjects were widely read in Europe and had much to do with the emergence of more responsible attitudes toward ancient Egypt.[6]

Lord Cromer and Maspero together built up the Antiquities Service from an embryonic organization into a more viable institution with five regional inspectors who regulated all excavations in Egypt. They supervised the reorganization of the huge collections in the Bulaq Museum. Some foreign excavators were now allowed to work under the eye of the inspectorate, although the illegal traffic in antiquities and forgeries continued on the side, encouraged by ambitious foreign museums and unscrupulous private collectors.

∷

The dealers of Luxor always had a ready market for whatever antiquities were for sale. From the 1860s onward the tourist traffic through the area increased steadily.[7] The tomb robbers of Qurna made a comfortable living from the many boats that called at Luxor and Karnak. In 1881, the supply of mummies and other fine antiquities seemed almost inexhaustible, especially those supplied by two known robbers, Ahmed Abd el-Rasul and his brother Mohammed. They smuggled their loot into Thebes in bundles of clothing or baskets of vegetables. Ahmed had accidentally discovered an exceptionally rich cache of mummies and grave furniture at the base of an abandoned shaft into the rocky hillside while looking for a lost goat. For nearly ten years Ahmed and his brother mined the cache for small quantities of fine antiquities that they floated onto the open market a few at a time, to avoid deflating the prices in a rising market.

Greedy American and English tourists soon snapped up the Rasuls' small items of jewelry bearing the royal insignia. Inevitably, news of these exceptional purchases reached Gaston Maspero, who sensed that a spectacular find had been made near the Valley of the Kings. He suspected that some pharaohs' mummies were involved, for many of the Rasuls' pieces were unique and of unquestionable royal association.

Maspero acted with caution, for local officialdom was far from incorruptible in 1881. First, he telegraphed the Luxor police, asking them to keep an eye on local antiquities dealers. Then he dispatched one of his staff to Luxor in the disguise of a rich tourist with money to spend. Maspero's agent quietly bought a few choice pieces to gain the trust of the dealers and soon became one of the obvious targets for the best antiquities. One day a dealer brought him a magnificent funerary statuette from a Twenty-first Dynasty tomb that could have come only from a royal burial. After extended haggling, the agent bought the piece, but not before he had been introduced to Ahmed Abd el-Rasul. Both the police and Maspero's agent suspected both the Rasul family and Mustapha Aga Ayat, a Turk who had succeeded in having himself appointed consular agent for Belgium, Great Britain, and Russia in Luxor, a post that gave him diplomatic immunity and a convenient cover for dealing in antiquities. The Rasul family sold most of their finds to him.

While Aga Ayat was immune from prosecution, the Rasuls were not. The brothers were arrested in April 1881 and sent in chains to the mayor of Qena for examination. The two men pleaded their innocence with eloquence, pointing out that no antiquities had been found in their houses—they were not that stupid—and producing a swarm of witnesses who swore to the high-minded conduct of the Rasul family. Daud Pasha, the mayor, soon released the brothers. Torture and persuasion had produced no firm evidence, and, one suspects, Daud knew the family only too well. Everyone returned home to Qurna apparently satisfied. But a massive family quarrel soon erupted over the sharing of the proceeds of the cache, with Ahmed claiming a larger portion of the loot to compensate for his suffering under torture. Soon the quarrel became common knowledge around Thebes, and the Antiquities Service started fresh inquiries. Mohammed soon realized that his only route to safety was to confess to everything. Three months after the trial he was back in Qena, where he confessed all to Daud Pasha, obtained immunity from punishment, and dictated every detail of the family conspiracy into official court records.

A few days later Mohammed led a small party to the site of the cache. Maspero himself was out of Egypt, so Émile Brugsch (brother of Heinrich) went along as the official representative of the government. Brugsch was understandably nervous as he climbed the steep hillside to the deep shaft where the cache lay, for he feared reprisals from the villagers. Armed to the teeth, he was lowered down the shaft on a long rope with a supply of candles to light the chamber. He had been led to believe that Ahmed's

FIGURE 13.1   Gaston Maspero, Émile Brugsch (bearded, *right*), and Mohammed Abd el-Rasul at the mouth of the Deir el-Bahri cleft (picture from *Century Magazine*, May 1887). "As we ascended from the tomb, I grouped my companions at its mouth, and once again caused the camera to secure a link of history. Professor Maspero reclined on the rocks at the right; Émile Brugsch Bey stood at the palms-log; and Mohammed was posed in front holding the very rope in his hand which had served in hoisting royalty from its long-hidden resting-place."

find was a tomb of wealthy officials, but an extraordinary sight lay before him in the darkness. Maspero quoted from Brugsch's report:

> The Arabs had disinterred a whole vault of Pharaohs. And what Pharaohs! Perhaps the most illustrious in the history of Egypt, Thutmose III and Seti I, Ahmose the Liberator and Ramses II the Conqueror. Monsieur Émile Brugsch, coming so suddenly into such an assemblage, thought that he must be the victim of a dream, and like him, I still wonder if I am not dreaming when I see and touch what were the bodies of so many personages of whom we never expected to know more than the names.[8]

Bronze libation vessels and canopic jars lay on the floor of the chamber. Coffins of eminent queens lay jumbled in heaps.

When he had recovered from his astonishment, Brugsch acted with dispatch. He hired three hundred workmen to work on the clearing and transportation of the precious finds from their hiding place, under the careful supervision of the official party. The government steamer *el-Menshieh* was pressed into service to carry the precious cargo to Cairo. Within forty-eight short hours the first batch of the forty pharaohs and a host of precious antiquities were on board and on their way downstream. As the steamer left Thebes, so Maspero tells us, the women followed the boat wailing and the men fired off their rifles in honor of the ancient monarchs. Other more cynical observers wondered if the locals were bewailing the loss of a highly satisfactory source of income. Later, some of the mummies were unwrapped and archaeologists were able to gaze on the features of the most famous monarchs of ancient Egypt. Seti I was the best preserved, with a "fine kingly head." "A calm and gentle smile still played over his mouth, and the half-open eye lids allowed a glimpse to be seen from under the lashes of an apparently moist and glistening line, the reflection from the white porcelain eyes let into the orbit at the time of burial."[9] Belzoni would have been both fascinated and pleased that the owner of his most spectacular discovery had survived for posterity.

: :

The incident of the pharaohs' mummies caused Maspero to redouble his vigilance. He employed extra guards and instituted new controls to restrict the activities of dealers and the agents of major European museums who were their principal clients. But this did not deter ambitious European or American museums. They certainly infuriated Sir Evelyn Baring, Maspero, and British as well as French officialdom, an impressive enemy list in the changing intellectual climate of the late nineteenth century. Many of them resorted to underhanded dealing to satisfy their backers.

Ernest Alfred Thompson Wallis Budge (1857–1934) was perhaps the most audacious of the breed. He started his long career as assistant keeper of Egyptian and Assyrian antiquities in the British Museum. Budge was a constant visitor to Egypt, the Sudan, and Mesopotamia, where he bought antiquities for the museum. He was also a prolific excavator and writer. His collection methods combined bribery, trickery, and sheer audacity, and were outrageous even by contemporary standards. Budge shrugged off this criticism under the guise of loyalty to the British Museum and its great aims.

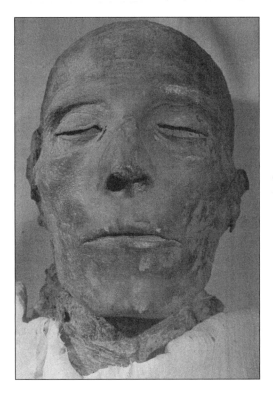

FIGURE 13.2
The mummy of pharaoh Seti I,
Nineteenth Dynasty. Ken
Garrett/National Geographic
Image Collection.

A short, pugnacious man of aggressive and unattractive personality, Budge first visited Egypt on a collecting trip in 1886. He had acquired a working knowledge of Egyptian antiquities and their market value from Samuel Birch, keeper of Oriental antiquities at the British Museum, who had become a famous Egyptologist without ever visiting the Nile.[10] Armed with this knowledge and 250 pounds sterling, Budge arrived to a dusty reception from Sir Evelyn Baring, who had been greatly irritated by the recent activities of British archaeologists and dealers.[11] Budge was undeterred and determined to work by devious means, through the dealers, if necessary. His deviousness infuriated the authorities.

Soon Budge had made useful official and unofficial contacts in Cairo and Luxor. His illegal agents cleared tombs, most of them admittedly already half empty. Some of the fine things from them had "somehow disappeared," but Budge was able to lay his hands on quite a few nice pieces. Senior military officers joined his excursions around Aswan. They mobilized entire companies of royal engineers to help in excavations and to provide tackle for moving large statues. In one instance, Budge collected eight hundred ancient Egyptian skulls for a physical anthropologist at

Cambridge and stacked them at one end of his hut to await packing. The local hyenas were so eager to get at the heads that they broke into the hut and stole several dozen of them. The only way Budge could export the skulls was by declaring them to customs as "bone manure." "When dealing with customs' officials," Budge remarked, "I discovered that, after all, there is a good deal in a name."[12]

The field representative of the Bulaq Museum unwittingly enhanced Budge's reputation by cautioning the locals that the visitor was a wealthy and unscrupulous collector. The dealers promptly offered him all manner of antiquities in the privacy of his hut at night. Such was the reputation of the British Museum that the dealers would even give Budge a valuable piece and tell him to send the money from England later, often funneled through the hands of a cooperative Protestant missionary. Many of his best acquisitions came through the British consul at Thebes, who introduced Budge to the Rasul family. He was regaled with graphic accounts of the tortures used to extract the secret of the Deir el-Bahri cache from them. By the end of the trip he had acquired twenty-four large cases of antiquities that were covertly exported, despite furious objections from Sir Evelyn Baring and the Antiquities Service, simply by placing them under military control. The military, which had little interest in archaeology, was all for excavation and archaeology. Like Budge, it considered the local dealers as reasonable men trying to make a living and the Antiquities Service as a corrupt body whose members sold antiquities for themselves. The trustees of the British Museum passed a special minute in April 1887 commending Budge for his "energy."

Most of Budge's collecting took place in Mesopotamia, but his Egyptian exploits were daring enough. On his next visit to Cairo, the Antiquities Service had him watched by the police, who were instructed to report the names of any dealers who visited him. Budge gaily set off on his buying tour with the police in tow. At Akhmîm, upstream of Asyut, he bought some fine Coptic manuscripts from a French resident, who arranged a large supper for the police while the two collectors transacted their business.

There were further complications at Luxor. Budge was taken in the depths of night to a tomb on the western bank, where an important find of papyri had been made, including one large roll 23.7 meters (78 feet) long, a complete Book of the Dead, written and painted for "Ani, the royal scribe, the registrar of the offerings of all the gods, overseer of the granaries of the lords of Abydos, and scribe of the offerings of the Lords of Thebes." Budge recorded the seal on the rolled papyrus, then carefully un-

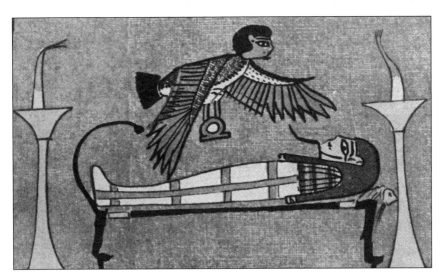

FIGURE 13.3 From Ani's Book of the Dead. The soul of Ani leaves the body in the form of a bird with a human head. In its claws is the symbol of eternity. Bettman/Corbis.

rolled a portion of it. "I was amazed at the beauty and freshness of the colors of the human figures and animals, which in the dim light of the candles and the heated air of the tomb, seemed to be alive."[13] Several other important papyri came from the same location. Budge secured the lot, sealed them in tin containers, and hid them in a safe place.

A few hours later, while drinking coffee with the dealer who had taken him to the papyri, Budge found himself under arrest. The Antiquities Service had placed guards on every dealer's house in Luxor at the order of Eugène Grébaut, Maspero's successor as director.[14] Grébaut's runner, who brought the news of the arrest, revealed that the director's boat was stuck on a sandbank in the Nile 19 kilometers (12 miles) away. It so happened that the captain's daughter was being married that day. Naturally, the boat could not be refloated successfully. Grébaut then tried to ride to Luxor, but no donkeys were available. The villagers had driven them into the fields so that they could not be hired.

Soon news arrived that the steamer had been refloated, that Grébaut was on his way. The chief of police now sealed off all the dealers' houses, including a small house abutting the wall of the Luxor Hotel, where Budge's antiquities lay. At first the dealers tried to get the guards drunk on brandy, but they steadfastly refused to leave their posts. So they commended the guards on their fidelity and resorted to another stratagem. A crew of hefty gardeners entered the hotel garden at sunset, dug a tunnel under the two-foot-thick wall of the hotel that adjoined the house, and entered the basement full of antiquities through a carefully shored-up tunnel. "As I watched the work with the manager it seemed to me that the gardeners were particularly skilled house-breakers, and that they must have had much practice," remarked Budge proudly.

The whole operation unfolded in silence, without alerting the guards on the roof of the house. The manager provided a hearty meal for them while the antiquities vanished through the tunnel. "In this way," boasted Budge, "we saved the papyrus of Ani, and all the rest of my acquisitions from the officials of the Service of Antiquities, and all Luxor rejoiced."[15] One cannot entirely blame Budge for his cynicism. Grébaut's own staff members were selling the antiquities he had collected on the way upstream to local dealers and spiriting them off the steamer while the director ate dinner. Budge was soon in Cairo, where, with a final touch of irony, he managed to arrange for the police, who were watching him, to carry his precious boxes of papyri and tablets into the city. The very same day the papyri were on their way to England in official military baggage.

Budge's activities were perhaps only typical of many European museum officials of the time. He developed a healthy contempt for the Antiquities Service and its servants. Although he got on well with Maspero, and sometimes worked in collaboration with the museum, his relationships with dealers over the years proved far more rewarding. Even the *Egyptian Gazette* disapproved of Budge, describing him as being well known as a somewhat unscrupulous collector of antiquities for his museum. His tactic was to pay fair prices and to spend plenty of money. With his encouragement, dealers duly ransacked Predynastic cemeteries after scientific digs had been completed. Coptic manuscripts, acquired after "much talking and coffee drinking," made the British Museum one of the finest repositories of Coptic materials in Europe.

Despite stricter enforcement of antiquities regulations by an infant service that was now growing into manhood, Budge's expeditions were models of illegal purchase, excavation, and what can only be described as dubious archaeological tactics. His rationale for wholesale removal and purchase of antiquities was simple: he was attempting to prevent the destruction of ancient Egypt. "The principal robbers of tombs and wreckers of mummies have been the Egyptians themselves," he wrote. "The outcry against the archaeologist is foolish, and the accusations made against him are absurd. If one archaeologist won't buy, another will, and if no archaeologist will buy, then the owners of the mummies will break them up and burn them piecemeal." Then, in a splendidly pompous piece of logic, he went on: "Whatever blame may be attached to individual archaeologists for removing mummies from Egypt, every unprejudiced person who knows anything of the subject must admit that when once a mummy has passed into the care of the Trustees, and is lodged in the British Museum, it has a far better chance of being preserved there than it could possibly have in any tomb, royal or otherwise, in Egypt."

After a lengthy description of the dreadful fate that could await a mummy, he continued: "The Egyptian prayed fervently and unceasingly against all these possible, nay probable, evils, as any one can see who takes the trouble to read the charms buried with him. In the British Museum he is placed beyond the reach of all such evils."[16] Furthermore, Budge added, the identity and deeds of the mummy would acquire far more exposure through public but safe display, photographs, guides, and picture post-cards. In enlisting the support of the ancient Egyptians themselves, Budge flattered himself that he had moral right on his side and that looting Egyptian sites was entirely legitimate, provided something was left in the Egyptian collections for the local people to gaze upon and study.

: :

Auguste Mariette had enforced a virtual monopoly on excavation along the Nile, which effectively stopped foreign excavations. As his ban came into effect, the Germans were revolutionizing excavation methods at Olympia in Greece and elsewhere, working with architects and photographers to record rather than just excavate sites for their spectacular contents. Much of Mariette's policing efforts fended off local people who continued to sell antiquities and quarry temples for their stone, burned to produce lime. He is on record as telling a villager in 1880 that he could not quarry the pyramids of Giza for building stone.[17] At the same time, he was stopping the khedive from giving away obelisks that were much coveted by foreign governments to adorn their capitals. Mariette protested that only five remained in Egypt and prevailed on the cabinet to forbid the export of any more "monuments."

Mariette was instrumental in setting up the Bulaq Museum, where he planned to attract not only European visitors but Egyptians as well. Egypt should "love" its monuments. His museum guidebook was translated into Arabic, complete with invocations to the Prophet. By now, there were some books in Arabic on ancient Egypt. Rifaa al-Tahtawi wrote a history, *Anwar tawfiq aljalil fi akhmar Misr wa-tawtihiq Bani Ismail* (Glorious light on the story of Egypt and the authentication of the sons of Ismael), which appeared in 1868. Egypt, said the author, in the time of the pharaohs had been "the mother of all the nations of the world."[18] The pharaohs occupied only one-fifth of al-Tahtawi's long work, but there was now a survey of ancient Egypt available for a local audience.

The khedive Ismail and educational reformer Āli Mubarak wanted to train Egyptians to work in the Antiquities Service and museum.[19] Mariette opposed such a move, fearing for his job. But Mubarak offered Heinrich Brugsch a five-year contract to direct the School of Egyptology, which opened in a dilapidated villa near the museum in 1870. The experiment lasted just those five years before the school closed. Mariette derailed the experiment, banning students from copying inscriptions in the museum and hiring a Swiss inspector, who wrote of the school's deficiencies.

Ahmad Kamal was one of the school's students, and took to Egyptology with enthusiasm.[20] He was forced to become a teacher and translator, until he won the post of secretary-treasurer at the Bulaq Museum soon after Mariette's death. Maspero assigned him to run a small school of Egyptology at the museum. Its only graduates became antiquities inspectors. In 1889, Eugène Grébaut reluctantly appointed him assistant curator, purely to make sure that a British Egyptologist did not get the job. Kamal struggled to establish himself as a serious Egyptologist, despite Maspero's limited support. He was not allowed to excavate, under a policy that forbade non-Egyptologists and those without an official affiliation from digging. Besides, Maspero believed that Egyptians wanted to dig only for treasure and not out of scientific interest. Despite years of hard work, Kamal achieved only limited recognition, retiring in 1914 after lecturing on ancient Egypt at the new Egyptian University in 1880–1889. He also taught Egyptology at the Higher Teacher's School, but the Antiquities Service refused to hire his graduates.

Kamal was alone. He had no obvious Egyptian successor. His son went to Oxford University in 1912 to study Egyptology, but ended up becoming a physician. The ubiquitous Lord Cromer set the tone, when he remarked, "The Egyptians are as yet [not] civilized enough to care about the preservation of their ancient monuments."[21] His assumption became imperial policy until well after World War I.

14 | "A Boating-Trip Interspersed with Ruins"

Here Osiris and his worshipers lived; here Abraham and Moses

walked; here Aristotle came; here, later, Mahomet learnt the best of

his religion and studied Christianity; here, perhaps, our Saviour's

Mother brought her little son to open his eyes to the light.

FLORENCE NIGHTINGALE,
Letters from Egypt: A Journey on the Nile, 1849–1850

By the 1870s, Egypt had become a fashionable place for a winter vacation among both the wealthy and the less affluent. Regular steamship service between Italy and Alexandria, with a schedule that was as regular as clockwork, now made it possible to travel in three and one-half days a distance that had taken the fastest Roman galley six days. Thanks to Thomas Cook and others, a trip up the Nile had become a safe, if slightly exotic, experience.

A half century earlier, European travelers had to grapple with epidemics of bubonic plague. They spent three weeks or more in isolated quarantine on their return home. Fortunately, the slow journey home consumed much of the isolation period. Egypt was the land of the biblical plagues until 1844, when bubonic epidemics mysteriously ceased. In their place came cholera, borne by water and imported from its Indian home in Bengal, transmitted widely through irrigation agriculture along the Nile. Cholera epidemics struck Egypt eleven times between 1831 and

1902. Despite this scourge, a plague-free Egypt became a recommended destination for Europeans with health concerns who suffered during damp European winters. Edward William Lane of *Manners and Customs of the Modern Egyptians* fame had abandoned his career as an engraver and moved to the Nile Valley for health reasons. He was but one of many ailing visitors in later decades who spent months living quietly in hotels along the river. Egypt became a much recommended health resort.

One such émigrée was the formidable Lady Lucie Duff-Gordon, who settled at Luxor in a ramshackle residence known as the French House. Her ruined and spartan dwelling was perched on the roof of a temple near the Nile.[1] From 1863 to 1869 Lucie Duff-Gordon surveyed the local scene, entertained both the great and the lowly, and assimilated herself into local peasant society to an extent that shocked many of her contemporaries. She wrote a steady stream of lively letters to her family, which were published in two widely read volumes that achieved great popularity. They are remarkable reading, unusual for their humility and careful perception of local society. She exposed the outrageous deeds of the khedive's government and the hideous oppression of the common man with tart comment and pitiless detail that heightened public reaction toward the excesses of Egypt's rulers. At the same time, the trivial domestic round of harvest and famine, of dust storm and interesting visitor, came to light in a charming way that captivated her audience.

The Duff-Gordon letters, a revelation to people unfamiliar with the teeming life of the Nile's banks, caused quite a stir. Antiquities were to her as much a part of the landscape as the people. She met an old foreman who had worked for Belzoni and visited Seti I's tomb in the Valley of the Kings. In one letter to her husband, who had thanked her for the gift of a pharaonic lion, she admitted she "stole him for you from a temple, where he served as footstool for people to mount their donkeys. A man has stolen a very nice silver antique ring for me out of the last excavations— don't tell Mariette. My fellah friend said, 'Better thou have it than Mariette sell it to the French and pocket the money; if I didn't steal it, he would'— so I received the stolen property calmly."[2]

Most affluent visitors came to be entertained and informed, taking what the French writer Jean-Jacques-Antoine Ampère epigrammatically called a "donkey-ride and a boating-trip interspersed with ruins."[3] Such tourists almost invariably traveled in a single chartered *dahabiyya*, or sometimes, like Belzoni's friend Lord Belmore half a century before, in a

FIGURE 14.1   A *dahabiyya* at Luxor, by the Victorian artist
David Roberts. "Some are luxuriously fitted up, room even being
found for a piano." From the author's collection.

convoy of hired vessels. Those with time to spare often went as far south
as Abu Simbel and the Second Cataract.

By 1870, three hundred American tourists registered at the consulate in
Cairo in a year.[4] Mark Twain had recently published *Innocents Abroad*, a
widely read and at times entertaining account of his travels. Time was
short, and he managed only the pyramids and the Sphinx before turning
for home. Yet he admired the lushness of Egypt, "the boundless sweep of
level plain, green with luxuriant grain, that gladdens the eye as far as it
can pierce through the soft, rich atmosphere." He described Shepheard's
Hotel as "the worst on earth except the one I stopped at once in a small
town in the United States." One member of his party tried to hammer a
memento off the face of the Sphinx, but Mark Twain was content with ac-
cusing the Egyptians of feeding mummies to their railway engines. Seven-

FIGURE 14.2
Amelia Edwards (1831–1892).

teen years before, the French novelist Gustave Flaubert had enjoyed a bawdy and somewhat riotous voyage up the Nile and had been less polite. He accused the inhabitants of Edfu of using the temple as a public latrine and suffered from the fleas.[5]

Tourists were a nightmare for Mariette and Maspero, but, in the end, they were an important catalyst of public opinion. In November 1873, Shepheard's Hotel welcomed a sunburned visitor, Amelia B. Edwards, a popular novelist, lecturer, and passionate traveler, a tourist whose perception of ancient Egypt was to influence that of thousands of Victorians.

Amelia Edwards (1831–1892) was one of that distinctive Victorian breed of prolific romantic novelists whose literary output more than compensated for the lack of radio and television a century ago. During her sixty-one years, an immense number of articles, lectures, books, reviews, and pamphlets streamed from her facile pen. The daughter of an army officer who served under the duke of Wellington in the Peninsular War, she showed a remarkable talent for writing and drawing in childhood and possessed a fine voice of potentially professional standard. Her first poem was published when she was seven years old.

Ultimately, Amelia Edwards became a journalist, contributing articles on all manner of subjects to popular periodicals such as *Chambers's Journal* and the *Saturday Review*. She wrote eight forgettable but popular novels between 1855 and 1880. Edwards also edited popular books on history and art, most of which sold well and allowed her to live the life of leisured travel and writing that was the right of a successful late-Victorian author.

In 1872, she explored the Dolomites in northern Italy, at a time an out-of-the-way destination even for male travelers. Her first best-selling travel book resulted, issued originally as *Midsummer Ramble in the Dolomites*, and later as *Untrodden Peaks*. During the summer of 1873, she and her travel companion, Lucy Renshawe, planned a walking tour in France. The rain would not stop, so they decided on impulse to travel to Cairo instead. An interest in history and early civilization led Edwards to an extended tour through Syria and Egypt in 1873–1874. The trip changed her life and led to her best-known book, *A Thousand Miles up the Nile*, published three years later. *A Thousand Miles* was a deservedly popular travel book that went through several editions and displays Edwards's lush writing style at its best. She described a typical, fairly luxurious trip to the Second Cataract in two *dahabiyya*s. The party consisted of five English gentlefolk, traveling in company with two English ladies in another craft. They seem to have been typical Nile-goers, young and old, well dressed and ill dressed, learned and unlearned, eager for any new experience, and, like so many Victorians, secure in their own society and conscious of the superiority of its values, religion, and morals over those of "foreigners" and certainly the Egyptians.

Amelia Edwards made full use of her river journey and wrote a book that is delightfully evocative both of the unchanging Nile scene and of the tourist life of a century ago. *A Thousand Miles* is informative, yet bears its knowledge lightly. The facts are accurate, carefully checked by Samuel Birch of the British Museum and by Wallis Budge (who regarded the lady with some distrust). But her own impressions come through strongest. Her feelings in the Hypostele Hall at Karnak cascade in vivid prose, as she compares the columns to a grove of huge redwood trees:

> But the great trees, though they have taken three thousand years to grow, lack the pathos and mystery that comes of human labor. They do not strike their roots through six thousand years of history. They have not been watered with the blood and tears of millions. Their leaves know no

sounds less musical than the singing of birds, or the moaning of the night wind as it sweeps over the highlands of Calaveros. But every breath that wanders down the painted aisles of Karnak seems to echo back the sighs of those who perished in the quarry, at the oar, and under the chariot-wheels of the conqueror.[6]

Edwards was entranced by the temples of Philae:

The approach by water is quite the most beautiful. Seen from the level of a small boat, the island, with its palms, its colonnades, its pylons, seems to rise out of the river like a mirage. Piled rocks frame it on either side, and purple mountains close up the distance. As the boat glides nearer between glistening boulders, those sculptured towers rise higher and even higher against the sky. They show no sign of ruin or of age. . . . All looks solid, stately, perfect. One forgets for the moment that anything has changed. If a sound of antique chanting were to be borne along the quiet air—if a procession of white-robed priests bearing aloft the veiled ark of the God, were to come sweeping round between the palms and the pylons—we should not think it strange.[7]

The party made their way by the now well-known river journey to Abu Simbel and the Second Cataract. An eighteen-day stay at Abu Simbel was broken by a four-day excursion in Belzoni's footsteps to the Second Cataract, where they climbed the rock of Abusir. The summit bore the names of dozens of visitors, including Giovanni Belzoni. Unlike the Italian, Edwards and her companions enjoyed "draughts of ice-cold lemonade" from a goatskin at the summit.

Abu Simbel made the greatest impression. Every morning Edwards rose to greet the sunrise and the miracle of daylight at Abu Simbel. "Every morning I saw those awful brethren pass from death to life, from life to sculptured stone. I brought myself almost to believe at last that there must sooner or later come some one sunrise when the ancient charm would snap asunder, and the giants must arise and speak."[8]

The travelers cleared a small painted shrine with the aid of fifty locals and experienced for themselves the excitement of original discovery, gazing on paintings that had been covered up for centuries. Like Belzoni, more than fifty years before, they had some hectic bargaining with the headman who had to be content with "six pounds for his men, and for

FIGURE 14.3   The landing at Aswan.

himself two pots of jam, two boxes of sardines, a bottle of eau-de-Cologne, a box of pills, and half a sovereign."[9]

By the time of Edwards's visit, Abu Simbel was positively crowded. At one point there were no fewer than three sketching tents pitched at the great temple and a fleet of *dahabiyyas* ranged along the shore. Everywhere along the river there was bustle at the temples and major monuments. At Thebes there were many boats, "gay with English and American colours." American and English tourists were most commonly met with, but Germans, Belgians, and French were also encountered. The dealers of Luxor flocked to each boat as it moored:

> They waylaid and followed us wherever we went; while some of the better sort—grave men in long black robes and ample turbans—installed themselves on our lower deck, and lived there for a fortnight. There we always found them, patient, imperturbable, ready to rise up, and salaam, and produce from some hidden pocket a purseful of scarabs or a bundle of funerary statuettes. Some of these gentlemen were Arabs, some Copts—all polite, plausible, and mendacious.[10]

Earlier Edwards had been shocked by the change in tourist attitudes toward "antikas," including her own. The violated graveyards at Saqqara came as quite a shock, but she wrote:

> [W]e soon became quite hardened to such sights, and learnt to rummage among dusty sepulchers with no more compunction than would have befitted a gang of professional body-snatchers. These are the experiences upon which one looks back afterwards with wonder, and something like remorse; but so infectious is the universal callousness, and so overmastering is the passion for relic-hunting, that I do not doubt we should again do the same things under the same circumstances.[11]

She certainly purchased artifacts for herself. By the end of her life, Edwards had collected more than 3,000 antiquities. She is said to have kept two ancient Egyptian heads in her bedroom closet.

The dealers at Thebes did a roaring trade, not only in genuine antiquities, the best of which were reserved for really wealthy collectors and the agents of foreign museums, but also in forgeries. Everything was grist for the forgers' mill—inscribed tablets, alabaster statuettes, and, of course, scarabs, antiqued by feeding them to turkeys as a bolus, a process from which they "acquire by the simple process of digestion a degree of venerableness that is really charming."[12] A frenetic pace of excavation and forgery led to busy winters in Luxor. The illegal excavators lived in fear of the governor, but carried on their illicit trade as they had done for centuries. They dwelled among the tombs, as they had lived in Belzoni's time, driving donkeys or lifting water during the day and excavating in the tombs at night. Everybody had "antikas" to sell, from the turbaned official on a commercial visit to the "gentlemanly native" encountered at dinner with a scarab in his pocket.

Quite by chance, Edwards and a companion wandered into a forger's workshop while looking for a consulate. They were admitted to a large unfurnished room where three tables were strewn with scarabs, amulets, and funerary statuettes in every stage of completion. The tools of the trade lay around the unfinished objects, together with a large mummy case used for the wood. No one was in the room, but a few minutes later a well-dressed Arab arrived breathlessly and ushered his unwelcome guests out of the house, explaining that the consulate had been moved. "I met that well-dressed Arab a day or two after," wrote Edwards, "and he immediately vanished round the nearest corner."[13]

By this time the Antiquities Service maintained a small gang of official excavators near Qurna, under the supervision of the governor. The mummies they found were forwarded to Bulaq unopened. One day Edwards witnessed the discovery of some burials. Early in the morning the visitors rode out to the Ramesseum, crossing the Nile by boat and then eating their breakfast on donkey back as they rode across the plain. It was a gorgeous morning. The young barley shimmered and rippled for miles in the morning sun. The Colossi of Memnon glistened in the freshness of the new day. Wildflowers were ablaze in the barley. It was a memorable excursion, heightened by the discovery of a carved sarcophagus the moment they arrived at the excavations. The mummy was in almost perfect condition, deposited in a brick-lined vault. The governor himself was supervising the excavations, and invited Edwards to lunch with him in a nearby tomb, now converted into a stable where the mummies were temporarily stored. The lunch consisted of sour milk and a tray of cakes, and it was eaten to the accompaniment of reeking manure.

Edwards seems to have declined refreshment, for the party lunched in the Ramesseum, one of many jolly lunches in the leisured Egypt of the day. Rugs lay among the columns. Waiters flitted to and fro. At a discreet distance the "brown and tattered Arabs" milled, each with a string of forged scarabs, pieces of mummy case, or fake statues to sell. Here, as throughout the voyage, the respectful (and not so respectful) natives paid court to the representatives of civilization vigorously maintaining their rigid social values in the wilderness.

The tourist life of a century ago reverberates solidly through the lush pages of Amelia Edwards's tour de force. We are suitably entranced, educated, enlightened, and shocked through its pages. Once back in England, she plunged into a whirlwind of activity, lecturing to clubs and societies and writing article after article about her experiences on the Nile. She professed horror at the vandalism and destruction of the temples and tombs of ancient Egypt, deplored the lack of sound excavation techniques, and lamented the promiscuous destruction of temples by quarrymen.

Amelia Edwards's pen was a powerful weapon in molding public opinion about ancient Egypt at a time when there was already a devoted interest in things Egyptian among the educated public. Country gentlemen purchased the most learned monographs on Thebes, historical novels featuring the pharaohs sold thousands of copies, and books linking the archaeology of ancient Egypt with the biblical story were popular birthday

FIGURE 14.4   The Victorian tourist at large, "in an Egyptian street." A devout Victorian couple, Scriptures in hand, make their way through Cairo's bazaar.

and Christmas gifts. Interest in all the early classical and prehistoric civilizations was unusually high, thanks to the work of Heinrich Schliemann at Troy and of Austen Henry Layard and others in Mesopotamia, as well as the decipherment of the so-called Flood Tablets from Nineveh in 1872.[14] A classical education was still considered to be an essential attribute of an educated person, as was a thorough knowledge of the Scriptures. Egypt figured prominently in both, and everyone was excited by pyramids, mummies, and the hieroglyphic controversies. Long before Amelia Edwards's time, Egyptology, thanks to Wilkinson, Lepsius, and other scholars, as well as thousands of religious-tract writers, was having an increasing impact on the popular culture of Europe—on architecture, fashion, and, to a lesser extent, on serious literature. Unfortunately, many of these literary efforts were grossly misleading, for it was almost impossible for a middle-class Victorian writer with narrow and well-defined cultural values to understand contemporary Egyptian culture, let alone that of the ancient Egyptians.

Amelia Edwards took up the cudgels on behalf of scientific archaeology in an intense burst of literary productivity that lasted from her return from Egypt until her death in 1892. Three years after her return from the Nile, *A Thousand Miles* was published to popular acclaim. A stream of articles and progress reports on Egyptology appeared in dozens of journals and newspapers under the Edwards name, arguing that the only solution to the orgy of destruction that called itself archaeology was systematic recording of monuments and properly scientific excavations. Amelia Edwards was so concerned that she stopped writing fiction altogether and concentrated on Egyptology to the exclusion of other topics. Her efforts generated polite public interest, but galvanized the somewhat sleepy world of British Egyptology.

Professional Egyptologists in England were, however, deeply concerned about the state of affairs on the Nile. An abortive attempt to found the Society for the Protection of Ancient Buildings in 1880 had come to nothing. In March 1882, Amelia Edwards conceived the idea of the Egypt Exploration Fund designed to carry out scientific excavations in Egypt. She managed to assemble a group of powerful backers, among them Reginald Stuart Poole, a distinguished Orientalist, and Sir Erasmus Wilson, a well-known surgeon who had financed the transportation of the obelisk known as Cleopatra's Needle from Alexandria to London. This enterprise had cost 10,000 pounds, a colossal sum in those days. A prestigious meeting at the British Museum resulted in the foundation of the fund under the presidency of its major benefactor, Wilson. Edwards and Poole became the secretaries. Advertisements were placed in prominent newspapers announcing the formation of the group, appealing for funds, and giving details of sites to be explored. The objectives of the Egypt Exploration Fund were "to organize expeditions in Egypt, with a view to the elucidation of the History and Arts of Ancient Egypt, and the illustration of the Old Testament narrative, so far as it has to do with Egypt and the Egyptians."[15] The Egypt Exploration Fund was among the first organizations to apply for excavation permits with serious research and potential publication as the primary objective, not spectacular finds.

In the 1880s archaeological excavation was still a highly unscientific pastime, a form of licensed—or unlicensed—destruction that concentrated on large and impressive finds rather than the careful examination of a site and its contents. The objective was to find as much as possible in as short a time as practicable. Mariette's field techniques had been horrifying and quite unscientific. So were those of Maspero and many other respected early Egyptologists. Flinders Petrie, a British pioneer of modern excavation methods on the Nile, whom we meet in the next chapter, used to lecture with ghoulish horror about Mariette's digs and techniques. Petrie was a little unfair. Mariette was typical of his age, and he himself was no paragon by modern standards. But change was in the air. The Germans at Samothrace in the Aegean and at Olympia were setting new standards, with architects and photographers on site and the acquisition of information placed before finds. Field archaeology has begun a slow metamorphosis from a treasure hunt into an exact science.

There had been some more careful pioneers in Egypt, too. A quiet Scotsman named Alexander Henry Rhind (1833–1863) had planned to pursue a sedate career at the Scottish bar. But ill health forced him to winter in Egypt in 1855. Rhind spent two seasons at Thebes searching carefully for a complete and undisturbed tomb that he could excavate and record in detail, for he deplored the fact that "attention was given almost exclusively to obtaining possession of the relics without sufficiently careful reference to the circumstances under which they were discovered."[16] The devastation and havoc wrought by Drovetti and Salt at Thebes were such that there seemed to be little chance of locating more than a few undisturbed tombs. Finally, he located an undisturbed sepulcher.

Rhind excavated the site with considerable care. He left a step-by-step description of his dig, the contents of the tomb, and the position of the objects in the grave. He recorded the robbing of the tomb and its reuse and the identity of the last people to be buried there. The papyri found on the bodies gave him the names of the deceased. He described the excavation in his book *Thebes: Its Tombs and Their Tenants*, published in 1862. Unfortunately, Rhind died at the early age of thirty on his way home after a third journey to Egypt. Although Rhind was not the first man to describe an undisturbed Egyptian tomb, there is no doubt that he would have become a great Egyptologist had he lived.

The members of the Egypt Exploration Fund chose a Swiss archaeologist, Édouard-Henri Naville (1844–1926), as their first excavator. Naville, extensively trained in philology, had learned his Egyptology from Karl Lepsius. By the time he was invited to work for the fund, Naville had already acquired a European reputation. His first excavations were at Tell el-Maskhuta in the delta, near the new Cairo-Suez canal. The trustees of the fund had made a deliberate decision not to work in Upper Egypt, but to concentrate on the unknown delta areas where spectacular results might be expected.

Naville's excavations at el-Maskhuta aroused considerable public interest. For years the site had been regarded as one of the two cities built by the Israelites for Rameses II, settlements known as Rameses and Pithom. A link with the Scriptures was definitely an objective of the first season, and one that Naville purported to obtain. He uncovered the remains of a temple, part of a city, fortifications, and a military camp, dating the settlement to between the fifteenth century BC and the fourth century AD. It seemed that Rameses II had built the city, but there was no sign of the Israelites. Naville studied the artifacts from the city and decided that the Egyptians had dedicated it to the god Atum, from which it was an easy step to "Pi Atum" or Pithom. The trustees were delighted; they touted Naville's sensational discoveries in a loud voice, hoping for increased public support and more abundant funds. Although many Egyptologists refused to accept Naville's conclusions, the public was convinced that modern archaeology had strengthened the authenticity of the Scriptures.[17]

Naville was possessed, like so many early Egyptologists, with an extraordinary energy and capacity for hard work. He preferred to excavate large monuments and temples, for his training had been in the rather crude traditions of Mariette and Maspero. But he was a man of formidable intelligence and strong views whose work placed the Egypt Exploration Fund at the forefront of serious research organizations. His excavations at Wadi Tumilat in 1885–1886 and Bubastis in 1886–1889 were the subject of considerable interest.

A broadly built, jolly man, Naville, although trained by the German Lepsius, detested the Teutonic ways of scholarship, with their detailed classifications and card indexes. He continued to work for the fund until 1913, training numerous young archaeologists, among them Howard Carter, the discoverer of Tutankhamun's tomb.[18]

: :

The Germans as well as the British and French made important contributions to Egyptology in the late nineteenth century. Many German Egyptologists owed their early training not only to Karl Richard Lepsius but also to Georg Moritz Ebers (1837–1898), a professor of Egyptology at Leipzig. Ebers, a prolific writer on Egyptian subjects, was also an able teacher. But his great contribution was a series of popular historical novels with ancient

Egyptian themes, the most famous of which, *An Egyptian Princess* (1864), was translated into sixteen languages and sold more than 400,000 copies by 1928. Ebers's Egyptian princess was quite a character, courted by Cambyses, startlingly beautiful and sensitive, regal yet human, the perfect heroine for the suppressed maidens of his time. They could not fail to admire a princess whose "royal purple added to her beauty, the high flashing tiara made her slender, perfect figure seem taller than it really was."[19] Ebers made careful use of the narrative to introduce accurate descriptions of Egyptian artifacts and customs as background color. His florid romances were read by all lovesick young ladies at the turn of the century.

Another German, Adolf Erman (1854–1937), director of Egyptian antiquities in the Berlin Museum, was a man whose influence on Egyptology has been described in *Who Was Who in Egyptology* as "cyclonic and the greatest since Champollion." Erman, predominantly a philologist, altered the grammar and teaching of Egyptian linguistics to the extent that existing ideas on ancient Egyptian were completely revolutionized. He showed the relationship between ancient Egyptian and archaic Semitic languages; divided ancient Egyptian into Old, Middle, and Late versions; and was a pioneer in providing accurate interpretations and translations. Erman was a polymath of Egyptology, for he was interested in archaeology and history as well as languages. One of his most important works was *Life in Ancient Egypt*, a brilliant account of the ancient Egyptians that drew almost entirely on Egyptian sources and is still read today.[20]

Many events conspired to bring archaeology in Egypt to the threshold of a dramatic change for the better. More Egyptologists now worked along the Nile than ever before, many of them engaged in copying and preservation work as much as excavation. Amelia Edwards toured the United States in 1889–1890, speaking about the work of the Egypt Exploration Fund and enlisting American support for the excavations. Her tour was a great success, her lectures well received. She went on to state confidently that there were more ancient Egyptians under the soil of Egypt than there were living people above it. Amelia Edwards lived long enough to witness the dawn of a new era in Egyptian excavation, in large part a direct result of her propaganda. Six years before her death, the Egypt Exploration Fund had engaged a young Englishman to excavate for them in the delta, an association that lasted but three years. The young man, Flinders Petrie, was destined to become one of the seminal figures in archaeological excavation in the Nile Valley.

15 | Science and the Small Artifact

The observation of the small things, universal at present, had never

been attempted. The science of observation, of registration, of

recording, was yet unthought of; nothing has a meaning unless it

was an inscription or a sculpture.

FLINDERS PETRIE,
Seventy Years in Archaeology

"It is really a deplorable thing that we are not better represented in Egypt which is now overrun by German and French students and professors. . . . The Germans push their people and are doing it more than before just because they see we are getting in the saddle." Architect Somers Clarke reflected the feelings of many British Egyptologists of the 1890s. Britain ruled Egypt, but the French exercised almost complete control over the Antiquities Service, first under Auguste Mariette and Gaston Maspero, then under a series of unpopular directors: Eugène Grébaut, who had tangled with Wallis Budge; Victor Loret; and an engineer, Jacques de Morgan. None of these lasted long, so Lord Cromer prevailed on Maspero to return for a second stint, from 1899 to 1916.[1]

After 1882, British military rule ensured a stable financial environment for the next three-quarters of a century and a stable level of funding for the Antiquities Service. Gaston Maspero was a skillful bureaucrat as well as a good Egyptologist, and was well aware of the nationalist tensions over archaeology. He courted the British with charm and sedulous care, ending Mariette's arbitrary monopoly on excavation and encouraging excavators from many countries. The next thirty years were exciting ones for Egyptology, nourished by generous policies for sharing "duplicate" finds and relaxed supervision by Maspero, some of his successors, and then Maspero again. As Nicholas Reeves puts it: "This was to be Egyptology's golden age—the era of Flinders Petrie and Wallis Budge, Theodore Davis, Lord Carnarvon and Howard Carter; a time of tourists and grandees, collectors and forgers, scholars, rogues and some of the greatest discoveries the world has ever seen."[2]

Maspero was especially solicitous of the Egypt Exploration Fund. He told them to excavate for purely scientific goals, without any ambitions for antiquities to take back to London. He in his turn "persuaded" the Egyptian government to give many of the finds to the excavators, despite loud protests in Cairo. Effectively, he gave Édouard-Henri Naville a free hand in Lower Egypt and set a precedent for sympathetic treatment of British researchers that endured, despite occasional controversies, until the discovery of the tomb of Tutankhamun in 1922.[3]

Not that the fund's first excavator was a paragon of archaeological virtue. He had little interest in small finds, preferring large-scale temple clearance to patient dissection of minor sites. But he was light-years ahead of many of his predecessors in terms of his site plans and records, even if they did not match up to modern standards. Naville was well aware of the great excavations at Olympia and elsewhere, where the Germans had renounced all claims to the finds and were digging in quest of information. He urged the fund to do the same, for he was sure that wealthy donors would be glad to pay for research that threw light on the Bible, especially in the delta with its close ties to the eastern Mediterranean world.[4] The biblical associations of Tell el-Maskhuta delighted the fund's supporters, even if Samuel Birch, among others, considered this "emotional archaeology." The Egypt Exploration Fund's expeditions became part of the Egyptian winter scene for decades. The fund also nurtured the career of a giant of Egyptology—Flinders Petrie.

: :

William Matthew Flinders Petrie (1853–1942) was born into a family with a long tradition of travel, casual scientific inquiry, and surveying. His homeschooling was at best casual; the young Petrie picked up an excellent practical knowledge of surveying and geometry from his father. He was soon walking around the English countryside, armed with his father's sextant and a looking glass, plotting prehistoric earthworks. "I used to spend five shillings and sixpence a week on food, and beds cost about double that," he wrote. "I learned the land and the people all over the south of England, usually sleeping in a cottage."[5] All this was invaluable experience for Petrie's later life in the desert, as were his hours of browsing among coins and books in the British Museum.

Both Petrie and his father had long nurtured a strong interest in the pyramids of Egypt, partly from reading the astronomer Charles Piazzi Smyth's *Our Inheritance in the Great Pyramid*, a notorious speculative work on pyramidology that the young Petrie bought by chance at the age of thirteen.[6] Father and son planned an expedition to make a more detailed survey of the Great Pyramid than had ever been attempted before. They cut their teeth with Stonehenge in 1872, producing a plan that was the definitive effort for many years. Then Flinders Petrie left for Egypt in November 1880, embarking on a new life at the age of twenty-seven. To his great regret, his father never joined him on the Nile, preferring a quiet life of research and reflection at home. After a stormy passage, Petrie and his instruments arrived at Alexandria a month later. Within a week, he was comfortably ensconced in a rock tomb at the pyramid of Giza. Permits were no problem, since he had no plans to excavate, and he was thus independent of Mariette and the Egyptian Antiquities Service.

Petrie's two-year pyramid survey was a novel undertaking by Egyptological standards. He spent many weeks setting up accurate survey points and studying the construction of the pyramids. There was ample leisure time to observe the excavation methods of the redoubtable Mariette and his colleagues. He was severe in his denunciations:

> Mariette most rascally blasted to pieces all the fallen parts of the granite temple by a large gang of soldiers, to clear it out instead of lifting the stones and replacing them by means of tackle. Nothing seems to be done with any uniform and regular plan, work is begun and left unfinished; no regard is paid to future requirements of exploration, and no civilized or labor-saving devices are used. It is sickening to see the rate at which everything is being destroyed, and the little regard paid to preservation.[7]

The Englishman's survey work soon attracted attention among more serious archaeologists. Many visitors found their way to his sepulcher home, among them the great general Augustus Henry (Lane-Fox) Pitt-Rivers, a pioneer in meticulous excavations who strongly encouraged Petrie's efforts.[8] Petrie was particularly amused by the pyramid cranks and their measurements; one of them even tried to file down the granite to conform to his specifications. As he measured, Petrie relished the quiet life, walking around barefoot without the constraints of civilized life: "bells, collars, and cuffs." He lived simply. His excavation camps were to become legendary for their austere conditions.

In the intervals between surveying, he collected potsherds and small objects. Maspero told Petrie to take small objects through customs in his pockets, as they would not be searched. Perhaps it was just as well that Maspero was so casual, for Petrie was now convinced that the smaller objects, such as glazed pots, held some of the keys to ancient Egypt. This conviction, and the sickening destruction around him, persuaded Petrie that he should turn his attention from surveying to excavation.

The Pyramids and Temples of Giza appeared in 1883 to favorable reviews. Everyone praised the author's scientific objectivity, for his measurements placed knowledge of the pyramids on a new footing. Influential scholars urged the Egypt Exploration Fund to send Petrie to work in the Nile Delta. Late the same year, the fund's committee dispatched him there. He wrote to Amelia Edwards: "The prospect of excavating in Egypt is a most fascinating one to me, and I hope the results may justify my undertaking such a work. I believe the true line lies as much in the careful noting and comparison of small details, as in more wholesale and offhand clearances."[9]

Egyptian archaeology was in a parlous state. Samuel Birch of the British Museum begged Petrie to bring back at least a box of pottery from each of the "great sites," to use as a means of developing an Egyptian chronology. He was overwhelmed by the scale of the destruction, and felt that he should dig and dig and write everything up when he was sixty years old. Nothing had any meaning to the archaeologists of the day except an inscription or a sculpture. Precision was unknown, looting still commonplace.

Petrie was soon back in Egypt, excavating at Tanis and other Late Period sites, including Naukratis, a site he found by a chance purchase of an archaic Greek statuette, where the whole ground was thick with early Greek pottery and he felt he was committing sacrilege by walking over heaps of potsherds with the fine, lustrous black ware crunching under his boots. Unlike most of his predecessors, Petrie employed his laborers directly and housed them, to prevent blackmail by the headmen who wanted to act as intermediaries and force the men to pay them to let them work. He experienced minimal labor problems as a result. Mariette had used different methods, for the Frenchman had simply requisitioned laborers from local villages, leaving his foremen to collect the levies. So the foremen promptly drafted the richest villagers, who had to bribe them to be exempted. Eventually, the poorest laborers were hired compulsorily and marched off to work. Most local excavations were haphazard affairs. "An Arab's notion of digging is to sink a circular pit, and lay about him with his pick hither and thither, and I have some trouble to make them run straight narrow trenches," wrote Petrie. His own methods, while better, would horrify many modern archaeologists. There were three categories of worker: trenchers, shaft sinkers, and stone cleaners. A small gang of earth carriers supported each group. Petrie's notion was to maintain better supervision of the labor force, although it is difficult to see how he achieved this. He even employed girls as pick workers. "One of them is rather a boisterous damsel, and how she paid out the old man she had to work with! She slanged him unlimitedly, and kept time to her tongue by banging him with her basket."[10]

Work started at 5:30 in the morning and continued until 6:30 PM, except for a rest period during the heat of the day. Petrie would retire to his tent for breakfast and watch the excavations with a telescope. Otherwise, he was always on the site, keeping an eagle eye on the workmen. In contrast, Mariette had visited his dig once every few weeks, ordering the clearing of large areas before his next visit. The foremen had total charge and made huge profits by bribery and levying labor. They were terrified that excavations would be abandoned if they were unproductive. When their digging did not produce enough results, they promptly went to the Cairo dealers and bought sufficient numbers of small antiquities to keep Mariette's interest alive. Important finds were kept back until a psychologically opportune moment, and then produced out of context with a strict profit motive in mind. The Cairo Museum's boast that they obtained everything found from foreign excavations was a joke. Everyone disliked Émile Brugsch, for they suspected him of selling their finds out of the museum collections.

Naukratis was a commercial center mentioned by Herodotus with an effective monopoly on Mediterranean trade after the seventh century BC until it was superseded by Alexandria three centuries later. Petrie's excavations yielded useful results. He cleared part of a temple and great enclosure built by the pharaoh Psusennes I of the Twenty-first Dynasty, and discovered a large quantity of pottery and baskets full of papyri, some of which were later mounted between glass and translated.[11] Many of his finds were exported to England and placed on exhibit in the Royal Archaeological Institute. Petrie spent the passage home writing up the results of his work for prompt publication, thereby setting a tradition that he maintained throughout his career. Amelia Edwards had become a good friend. She was constantly asking for copies of his working journals, from which she wrote attractive articles on Petrie's fieldwork for the London *Times*. It was an auspicious and successful beginning to a lifetime of excavation in Egypt and Palestine.

Flinders Petrie's excavations were much more strictly supervised than those of his predecessors, but his techniques were still rough-and-ready by modern standards. Huge labor forces moved mountains of archaeological deposits. At the 1885 Naukratis excavation, Petrie employed 107 men with only two European supervisors, one of them Francis Griffith, soon to become an eminent academic and eventually professor of Egyptology at Oxford University. So many small objects came to light that small change ran out. Complicated accounts kept track of the *baksheesh* paid to the workmen for their finds. Basically, Petrie was buying the contents of the site in competition with the dealers, as all serious excavators had done before him. He tried to regulate the traffic by paying fixed prices for different categories of objects. If the finder refused Petrie's price, then the object was rejected, a policy that was reasonably successful.

It was at Naukratis that Petrie discovered the critical importance of accurate dating of objects and the strata they came from. After a time, he developed such a good rapport with the workers that accurate dating of many accidental finds was possible. He began to date temples and other structures by correlating the walls with the layers of foundation deposits under the buildings. Many of the objects found in the soil packed into deep foundation trenches were coins or inscribed ornaments that could be precisely dated, once their context in time and space was accurately established. This was a real innovation, never tried in Egypt before.

In 1887 Petrie headed an important archaeological expedition to the Fayyum. By now he had severed his connection with the Egypt Exploration

Fund and was operating as an independent agent. His main objective was the pyramid at Hawara, which Belzoni had admired nearly seventy years before. Working conditions were uncomfortable. Petrie camped in a small tent. "Imagine," he wrote, "being limited to a space six and a half feet long, and about as wide as the length. Besides bed I have nine boxes in it, stores of all kinds, basin, cooking stove and crockery, tripod stand, and some antiques; and in this I have to live, to sleep, to wash, and to receive visitors."[12] Important mummies lay under his bed for safety.

Petrie combined a tunnel into the center of the pyramid with a detailed survey of the monument. Nothing came from the tunnel, for the diggers reached a massive chamber roof that was impenetrable with the time available for excavation. But by this time, Petrie was more interested in the Roman mummies coming from a nearby cemetery, which he dated to AD 100–250. The mummies bore remarkable portraits painted in colored wax on their wooden panels, portraits that had been hung on the wall of a house during life and then bound to the mummy after death. The deceased were kept in family vaults near the home for at least a generation and then moved in batches into pits in a large cemetery near the pyramid.

At the end of the season, Petrie shipped the splendid collection of portraits and sixty crates of other finds to the Cairo Museum. The staff dumped everything outside to rot in the spring rains. Much to Petrie's disgust, the museum kept all the best portraits and most of the fine textiles. But he was able to mount a fascinating exhibition of the exported portraits and mummies in a large room of the Egyptian Hall in Piccadilly, the very same hall used by Giovanni Belzoni for his celebrated exhibition eighty years before. An aged visitor to the exhibition was able to recall the original show and the giant Italian. Petrie's exhibition was a great success and thronged with large crowds. Egyptology had truly become a respectable and widely appreciated science.

The following season saw Petrie back inside the Hawara pyramid. He found a German dealer named Kruger hard at work in the Fayyum with official sanction from Eugène Grébaut, something that Maspero would never have given. He was only out for pillage. Petrie learned that the German had had little success so was turning his eyes toward the sites under the British concession for that season—the el-Lahun pyramid and the Gurab site that Petrie had planned to investigate in a few weeks. He was forced to put two men digging at the el-Lahun pyramid tombs and two more at Gurab in order to stake out a claim. The supervision of these additional sites required a 27-kilometer (17-mile) walk twice a week, exercise that Petrie described as "very unsatisfactory." It took a month to break through the roof of the Hawara burial chamber, which turned out to be fashioned from a solid block of quartzite, 6 meters long by 2.4 meters wide and 1.8 meters deep (20 feet by 8 feet by 6 feet). Two empty sarcophagi lay in the chamber, which was waist-high in water. A cartouche bearing the name of Amenemhet III (1842–1797 BC) on an alabaster vase soon established the ownership of the tomb.

While his workers searched for the entrance to the pyramid, Petrie explored a large Twenty-sixth Dynasty tomb in the nearby cemetery. The family vault of an official named Horuta involved a 7.6-meter (25-foot) descent by rope ladder, a squeeze through a narrow doorway, then a slide down a slope into brackish water. Petrie had to strip off his clothes and slide through the mud-clogged passages, taking measurements on the way. "The candle only just shows you where you collide with floating coffins or some skulls that go bobbing around." A magnificent collection of amulets and hundreds of *shabtis* rewarded his persistence. All the finds were waist-deep in water so salty that even a drop caused the eyes to smart. Petrie removed the *shabtis* from their storage place by lying in the water and using his feet to dig. "I was hauled up looking 'like a buffalo' as the men said," he recalled.[13] The coffin was eventually moved into the light, where Petrie did not have to wade waist-deep amid rotten wood and skulls.

The hectic season of 1888 continued with work at el-Lahun and the nearby workmen's community that Petrie named el-Kahun (or Kahun), built in the Twelfth Dynasty to house the families of those building the pyramid. The compact walled town was virtually untouched since its abandonment. Petrie cleared many houses, finding copper tools, lamp stands, pieces of wooden furniture, and flint sickles as well as other domestic trivia that enabled him to build up a picture of the average worker's life during the Twelfth Dynasty. Previous excavators on the Nile had indulged a preoccupation with large monuments and tombs, at the expense of the archaeology of towns and villages. The finds from the Kahun dig provided much of the basis for Adolph Erman's *Life in Ancient Egypt*, published in 1894.[14]

The finds at Gurab were less spectacular, but the site yielded unexpected chronological riches. He partially cleared the town, especially a large walled enclosure close to the temple that seemed to have been occupied by foreigners. Petrie noticed some foreign pottery on the surface and was soon finding other potsherds of a similar type in houses. It turned out to be Mycenaean ware, of the type found by Heinrich Schliemann at Mycenae in Greece and by others on the Aegean islands, conclusive evidence of contacts between the Nile and the Aegean as early as 1500 BC. Three years later, Petrie was able to visit Mycenae for himself, where he recognized actual Egyptian imports that belonged to approximately the same period—the Eighteenth Dynasty—as the Gurab finds. He declared that the Egyptian imports gave a date for the beginnings of Mycenaean civilization of about 2500 BC, with the later stages of the civilization dating to around 1500–1000 BC. This was one of the first examples of the refined use of the technique of cross-dating, whereby imported objects of historically known age were used to date archaeological sites in countries a long way from the actual point of origin of the imports. This technique is still widely used by European archaeologists.[15]

Mycenaean archaeologists were enthusiastic. Petrie's own pupil Ernest Gardner declared that Petrie had done more in a week than the Germans had done in ten years to date the ancient Aegean. The chronology stood unchallenged for many decades and formed an important basis for Sir Arthur Evans's chronological work at the palace of Minos in Crete. For the first time, an archaeologist had realized that ancient Egyptian civilization had not flourished in isolation, but had enjoyed commercial relations with many other societies, relations that would be reflected in the archaeological record.

Unlike earlier collectors, Flinders Petrie had a broad comparative knowledge of Near Eastern and European archaeology. He moved in a comfortable circle of cultivated and well-versed scholars who were generalists rather than specialists, deeply interested in a wider world than merely that of their own site or the Nile alone. The Schliemanns, Evanses, and Petries of the late nineteenth century enriched one another's academic researches by a constant interchange of visits and informal discussions, as well as by trading artifacts and corresponding with a Victorian alacrity that leaves even the busiest twentieth-century scholars in awe of their work schedules.

Petrie was well aware of the fame that was now coming his way, but he seemed more concerned with loftier goals. "So far as my own credit is concerned," he wrote to a friend at the end of the season, "I look mostly to the production of a series of volumes, each of which shall be incapable of being altogether superceded, and which will remain for decades to come—perhaps centuries—as the sources of facts and references on their subject." This was a contrast to his predecessors who rarely bothered to publish anything or to record the provenience of their finds. He felt that he brought five specific skills to his work, which he set down publicly: First, "The fine art of collecting, of securing all the requisite information, of realizing the importance of everything found and avoiding oversights, of proving and testing hypotheses constantly, as work goes on, of securing everything of interest not only to myself but to others." Second, "The weaving a history out of scattered evidence using all materials of inscriptions, objects, positions, and probabilities."[16] He listed material culture, archaeological surveying, and "weights" as his other specialties. Prompt publication, accurate plans, excavations, records, and precise chronology were the primary goals of all Petrie's work, a striking contrast to Mariette, who took forty years to publish anything other than preliminary notices about the Serapeum.

Meanwhile, Petrie was getting drawn into the political arena in Cairo over the thorny issue of excavation permits and the export of antiquities. Since Mariette's time, French interests had dominated antiquities administration. According to Petrie, the administrative structure was both corrupt and incompetent. Permits were given to dealers and unqualified excavators. The museum was in a shocking state. The staff was uninterested. They left valuable mummies and sculptures in crowded passages and in the open air to rot and decay. Several staff members were covertly in league with Cairo dealers. On one occasion Petrie actually witnessed a transaction between a leading dealer and a keeper at the museum whom a friend had observed with his arms full of packages. He observed that the museum had curious ways of doing business without checks.

By this time, however, there was a rising outcry in England against the destruction of monuments in Egypt, largely as a result of Petrie's exhibitions and Amelia Edwards's eloquent lectures and writings. The Society for the Preservation of Monuments was soon formed, with powerful backers. They proposed the appointment of an independent inspector from England, a proposal that was quashed by the French.

The trouble could be laid to the Antiquities Service, dominated by the French and particularly by Wallis Budge's old adversary, Eugène Grébaut, who was in league with the dealers—or so Petrie alleged. The committee promptly responded to the scheme by introducing new regulations for the export of antiquities that made it quite impossible for any foreign expedition to work in Egypt. Even Petrie was prevented from digging. Intense political pressure ensued, the result of which was stricter but more realistic regulations that defined more closely the specifications regarding exportation, insisted on publication, and made it harder for dealers to make sizable profits.

Petrie's next excavation was at Tell el-Amarna, where he discovered the magnificent painted pavements and frescoes of the heretic pharaoh Akhenaten's palace and the remarkable "Amarna correspondence," which he described in his *Ten Years' Digging in Egypt*, published in 1892. The painted pavements were so important that Petrie arranged for a building to be erected over the palace pavement, which measured about 76 meters (250 feet) square. He erected a walkway over the paintings so that visitors could pass through without damaging the art. Tourists flocked to see the pavements, which were some of the first domestic Egyptian palace art to be exhibited. Unfortunately, the Department of Public Works never built a path to the exhibition shed, and the visitors trampled down valuable crops. An angry peasant hammered the paintings to fragments, and all was lost. Fortunately, Petrie had followed another of his basic precepts and recorded the scenes in color and black-and-white drawings on one-tenth scale.

A peasant woman unearthed the first Amarna tablets, which she sold to a neighbor for ten piastres. A few reached Europe, where they reached, among others, Wallis Budge, who had a working knowledge of cuneiform. He realized their significance and snapped them up. Flinders Petrie identified the spot from which they came and found yet more in a chamber and two pits. Years later, another Egyptologist, J. D. S. Pendlebury, identified the mud-brick building as "The House of Correspondence of Pharaoh, Life! Prosperity! Health!"[17]

The more than three hundred pillow-shaped clay tablets from Amarna bore inscriptions in wedgelike cuneiform, the diplomatic lingua franca of the time. They offered a remarkable window into the eastern Mediterranean world of the day—correspondence about the exchange of gifts, diplomatic marriages, and rivalries between small states to the east. Modern research has shown they were written over about a fifteen- to thirty-year period beginning in about year 30 of pharaoh Amenophis III's reign (ca. 1360 BC) and continuing into Akhenaten's tenure on the throne.

Many young archaeologists learned their craft on a Flinders Petrie excavation, among them Alan Gardiner, a consummate philologist, and a young Howard Carter. Carter had come out to Egypt as a copyist for the Egypt Exploration Fund and shown such ability that he was sent to el-Amarna to learn excavation with Petrie. Nothing prepared him for the austere conditions in the Petrie camp, where he had to build his own mud-brick room, with a board-and-reed roof and a mat door. The interstices between the unplastered bricks provided a wonderful nesting place for beetles and scorpions. Bedding was scorned, but newspapers could be used. He received strict instructions to keep all empty cans for storing small finds. Food came mainly from cans, with everyone foraging from what was open on the table.

At first Petrie had been dubious about Carter, but he soon changed his mind. His technique was to give a newcomer a week to observe the work, then to hand him some trusted workers and part of the site. Carter received the Great Temple of Aten and large portions of the town. The temple was very productive and confusing to a neophyte, but Carter was learning from a master and absorbed his expertise like a sponge. Few better trainings in Egyptian archaeology were available at the time.[18]

: :

Britain's greatest Egyptologist had begun his work with no financial support at all. But in 1892 Amelia Edwards died, leaving her money to endow a professorship of Egyptology at the University of London. Flinders Petrie was the first holder of the chair, an appointment he celebrated with the discovery of Predynastic Egypt.

For years, Egyptologists had puzzled over the apparent lack of ancestors for dynastic civilization on the Nile. It was thought that the first rulers of a unified Egypt had arrived in the Nile Valley from Mesopotamia, bringing their distinctive civilization with them. Then, in 1894, Petrie got wind of a vast cemetery near the town of Naqada in Upper Egypt where numerous skeletons accompanied by pottery and other grave furniture were coming to light. The pots found with these skeletons were quite unlike those associated with Old Kingdom graves, but were skillfully made and the work of a well-established Egyptian culture. At first he thought that the burials were those of Libyan invaders, but he soon realized that the cemetery had been filled in prehistoric times, and set out with his usual gusto to excavate it. In the 1894 season alone, he uncovered nearly 2,000 graves. A few years later, a royal grave found at Naqada itself provided a link between the prehistoric burials and the culture of the earliest dynastic Egyptians. So the roots of ancient Egyptian civilization were now traced back to prehistoric cultures in the Nile Valley, and the migration theories of earlier times fell into disrepute.

As always, Petrie developed his own methods to clear the cemetery. He sent boys to hunt for soft places in the ground; as soon as they had cleared around the edge of a grave pit, he moved them on. Then ordinary workers cleared the burial filling until they located clay vessels lying around the body. Next, expert workers with a delicate touch cleared around the pottery and skeleton, leaving everything in place. Last, his devoted excavator and friend Ali Mohamed es Suefi removed every scrap of earth and left the pits, bones, and beads exposed for recording.

The Naqada cemeteries were undated, with no inscriptions or papyri to provide a chronology. Petrie turned to the hundreds of pots from the graves for enlightenment. He found that there were gradual changes in the shapes of vessels and particularly in the handles on a certain type of jar. These changed from functional designs, obviously for daily use, to more decorative forms, and finally degenerated into a series of painted lines. Similar jars came to light at Diospolis Parva and other Predynastic sites, again associated with characteristic grave furniture.

Eventually, Petrie found so many graves that he was able to build up a series of "stages" of grave-furniture groups, to which he assigned "sequence dates," based on the stylistic changes in the pots. His earliest stage was "ST 30," for he rightly assumed that he had not yet found the earliest Predynastic societies. Fifty stages later he came to "ST 80," which coincided with the beginning of dynastic time and the first pharaoh, Menes. These sequence dates provided the first attempt at a chronology for prehistoric Egypt and were applied by Petrie and others to finds throughout the Nile Valley.[19]

Petrie regarded sequence dating as one of his major contributions to archaeology. "This system enables us to deal with material which is entirely undated otherwise; and the larger the quantity of it the more accurate are the results. There is no reason now why prehistoric ages, from which there are groups of remains, should not be dealt with as surely and clearly as the historic ages with recorded dates." This optimistic statement appeared in Petrie's *Methods and Aims in Archaeology*, published in 1904, where he enumerated his fundamental rules of excavation, honed by many seasons of self-instruction in the Nile Valley.[20] In fact, later research has shown that sequence dating is nothing more than a refined form of ordering undated finds. But, for its time, it was a bold and revolutionary attempt to place Egyptian archaeology on a better chronological footing.

: :

Petrie's zestful researches took him the length and breadth of the Nile Valley. He kept up a running battle with the Antiquities Service, especially with Grébaut and the museum, whose relationships with dealers he strongly distrusted. His autobiography, *Seventy Years in Archaeology*, is replete with stories about the sins of his French colleagues. One Gallic archaeologist worked a royal tomb at Abydos, kept no plans, and boasted that he had burnt First Dynasty woodwork in his camp kitchen. His finds were scattered among his financial partners in Paris and sold by auction. Fortunately, Grébaut resigned in 1892.

Grébaut's successor, Jacques de Morgan, was a more congenial director, an engineer and prospector who came to Cairo with no Egyptian experience whatsoever. He was at work among the pyramids of Dashur two years later, where he unearthed a series of tombs of the Middle Kingdom, including three princesses, two queens, and the pharaoh Hor of the Thirteenth Dynasty (ca. 1760 BC). In a pit near the looted sarcophagus of Princess Sithathor, de Morgan found a wooden box containing her jewels, including pectoral ornaments, rings, and pendants. The following season, he found four intact Twelfth Dynasty burials of Middle Kingdom royalty, among them the undisturbed grave of Queen Khnemet. The *Illustrated London News* depicted a heroic de Morgan displaying the queen's diadem to an admiring audience. For all his flamboyance, de Morgan was a serious excavator who found an early tomb at Naqada that helped define the Predynastic period.

Petrie got on better with de Morgan, who was matter-of-fact about his job, despite a new khedival ruling that placed severe restrictions on the export of antiquities found on foreign excavations. The same could not be said for his successor, Victor Loret, who was more of a scholar and certainly not an archaeologist or an administrator. Matters came to a head when Loret, when told of an example of pillage, casually remarked, "That's impossible! There's a law!"[21]

FIGURE 15.1   The Petrie excavation camp at Abydos. Bettman/Corbis.

Loret was replaced by Gaston Maspero, who was popular with everyone. He allowed Petrie to go to Abydos to clear up the mess in the royal cemetery. He promptly found the tombs of four of the eight kings of the First Dynasty and a queen, identified them, and cleared more than three hundred graves of their servants as well. Even more remarkable was the publication record. The work at Abydos began in November 1899 and was completed in March 1900. By June 22 of the same year Petrie had completed the proofs of the index. The published report was available almost as soon as the finds were ready for display, surely a record for archaeological publication. The First Dynasty finds were duly exhibited in London, and Petrie at last noticed a difference in public attitudes. "A new public feeling appeared; instead of only caring for things of beauty or remarkable appearance, people hang over the tables, fascinated by the fragments of the Ist Dynasty. Some workmen would spend their whole dinner hour in the room."[22]

The tussles with dealers and tomb robbers continued throughout the earlier part of Petrie's long career. Abydos was a bad spot for pillagers. While Petrie was engaged in tracing twelve successive rebuildings of the great temple by examining minute differences in trench-wall colors, the locals had other things on their minds. One man succeeded in removing a statue weighing more than 45 kilograms (100 pounds) from the courtyard of Petrie's house. He was tracked down by the distinctive impressions of his feet in the ground and arrested, but got off by bribing the police. On another occasion, a man loitered outside the Petries' mess hut at night and fired a pistol at Mrs. Petrie from point-blank range. Fortunately, the bullet missed.[23]

Extraordinary precautions were taken during the excavation of a plundered tomb at el-Lahun in 1914. The sarcophagus in the tomb was empty, and Petrie did not expect to find anything dramatic. But a few rings of fine gold tubing came to light at the side of the sarcophagus. Immediately, Petrie dismissed the men and left only a single trusted workman in the trench, joined by Guy Brunton, one of Petrie's students. Together they carefully removed the soil from the gold and began to uncover a spectacular treasure. Brunton lived in the tomb day and night, gently extracting all the objects from the soil without damaging them. Each item was carefully washed and photographed before being packed away. Petrie was so anxious to avoid pillage that he warned all his party not to talk or write about the gold hoard. The collection turned out to be a royal treasure of the Twelfth Dynasty. It was finally bought by the Metropolitan Museum of New York after prolonged but fruitless negotiations with British museums.

The pace and breathtaking scope of Petrie's archaeological life amaze the modern student. Each winter he excavated in Egypt, spending the spring and summer in Europe writing up the previous season's work and exhibiting the finds. At least a book a year flowed from his prolific pen. Dozens of lectures as well as his regular University of London series were delivered every year. In forty-two years Petrie excavated more sites than Mariette and made more major discoveries than any other archaeologist before or after him. Naukratis and Kahun, the el-Amarna discoveries, the tombs of Abydos, and the el-Lahun jewels were only a few of his finds. He resurrected Predynastic Egypt from Naqada and Diospolis Parva. He found the famous Victory Stela of pharaoh Merneptah in the king's mortuary temple at Thebes, which provided the first known Egyptian references to Israel, a find that prompted one of his colleagues to murmur, "Won't the reverends be pleased."[24]

Petrie was an innovator, an Egyptologist who was ahead of his time yet forced to support his excavations by selling his finds to European museums. Unfortunately, he had a somewhat tactless and quarrelsome personality. Distinguished public figures did not impress him, and he was not afraid to describe the aged and authoritative writer Professor John Stuart

Blackie of Edinburgh University as "a genial man who argued on Greek accent all day with all comers, and sang Scotch songs with but small provocation."[25] Petrie's lack of formal education led him in later life to ignore the valuable work of his contemporaries and to insist that he was always right—never an endearing quality in an archaeologist.

Petrie did far more than found an English school of Egyptology and introduce reputable excavation methods into the Nile Valley. He trained a whole generation of new Egyptologists, schooled in hieroglyphs and his excavation methods. Many of them improved on his techniques. Howard Carter (1873–1939) worked with Petrie. Classical archaeologist Ernest Arthur Gardner (1862–1939) learned his excavation at Naukratis and went on to direct the British School of Archaeology in Athens, where he helped Petrie with his work on cross-dating Mycenaean imports from Egypt. Sir Alan Gardiner, one of the greatest British Egyptologists of the twentieth century, was befriended by Petrie and spent a lifetime studying hieratic texts. His *Egyptian Grammar* (1927) is one of the fundamental sourcebooks for all students of ancient Egyptian languages. Guy Brunton, the young assistant who dug up the treasure of el-Lahun, went on to become one of Petrie's most distinguished followers, renowned for his careful excavations of Predynastic tombs and villages. Gertrude Caton Thompson (1888–1985) learned excavation from Petrie. She eschewed ancient Egypt and studied the Stone Age. She excavated the sites of the earliest known Egyptian farmers in the Fayyum Depression in the 1920s and then went on to study the Stone Age hunters of the Kharga oasis. The list of Petrie's former apprentices reads like a who's who of archaeology. Few archaeologists have ever exercised such a profound influence on future generations.

The annual Petrie excavations continued for most years until 1926, when he abruptly transferred his attentions to Palestine. New and stringent regulations to control excavations by anyone except those employed directly by the National Museum or the Antiquities Service effectively prevented Petrie from further digging in the Nile Valley. In part, these regulations came into effect as a result of the discovery of the tomb of Tutankhamun, which focused attention on the liberal conditions under which foreign expeditions were allowed to work in Egypt and to remove most of their finds with them at the expense of the national collections. By this time, Petrie's work was done. Forty years of excavation, training, and publication had improved standards of field archaeology and brought forward a whole new generation of Egyptologists, including some native Egyptian scholars, to man the Antiquities Service. Petrie himself had put more of ancient Egypt on record than any excavator before him. He continued to work every year in what was then called Palestine until the outbreak of World War II. He lived on to the age of eighty-nine as a respected if fiery phenomenon of twentieth-century archaeology. As we shall see, his protégés took over where he left off in a remarkable legacy of discovery and cutting-edge scholarship.

Like so many other Egyptian excavators, even those hungry for plunder and buried treasure, Petrie was at his best in the field. He returned to the quiet and serenity of the desert to escape the batterings of a late-nineteenth- and early-twentieth-century scholarly world where minor quarrels and petty intrigues were all too common. Flinders Petrie believed passionately in the importance of the past: "The man who knows and dwells in history adds a new dimension to his existence. . . . He lives in all time; the ages are his, all live alike to him."[26]

The history of Egyptology is full of men of unusual energy—Denon, Belzoni, Mariette, Petrie, and others—who excavated the length and breadth of the Nile Valley. Each seems to have had a fascination with the desert environment, with its quiet serenity and unchanging sunshine. This tranquil backdrop was the scene of an unparalleled scramble for antiquity that had no rivals in the ferocity and ruthlessness of its aims.

16 | "Wonderful Things"

I still say all the time that you never know what the sand of Egypt

might hold of secrets. And that's why I believe until today we have

discovered only thirty percent of our monuments. Still seventy

percent is buried underneath the ground.

ZAHI HAWASS,
quoted in Nicholas Reeves, *Ancient Egypt: The Great Discoveries*

Flinders Petrie had described the destruction in Egypt in 1880 as akin to a "house on fire." For the next three decades, he bestrode the small world of Egyptology like a colossus. His excavations were a school for an entire generation of young archaeologists, among them Percy Newberry (1869–1949), a botanist and archaeologist who cut his teeth with Petrie at Hawara and Kahun. Newberry was a skilled, if unimaginative, draftsman whose first independent work was in the Middle Kingdom tombs at Beni Hasan, where he worked on behalf of the Archaeological Survey of Egypt in 1890, a scheme concocted by Amelia Edwards and Flinders Petrie to record major sites along the Nile before it was too late. While on a visit to the ancestral home of Lord Amherst the year before, the twenty-two-year-old Newberry admired the work of a young artist who was working on the extensive Amherst collections. The artist's name was Howard Carter.[1]

Howard Carter (1873–1939) was of humble birth. The son of an artist, he showed precocious ability, which came to the attention of Lord Amherst and his daughter, Lady William Cecil. At age eighteen, Carter was employed by the Amherst family to draw items in their collection. Both Lord and Lady Amherst encouraged the young man and introduced him to Newberry, who needed his talents at the British Museum to work up pencil sketches of his Beni Hasan copies. Carter was soon assigned to other tasks, among them copying the minutely detailed drawings made by Robert Hay three-quarters of a century earlier. In 1891, the Egypt Exploration Fund sent him to work with Newberry at Beni Hasan as an assistant draftsman.

He found himself in a small, incestuous world populated by gentleman scholars, in which he and Flinders Petrie stood out for their humble origins and lack of formal education. Carter was confident in his exceptional abilities as a draftsman and watercolorist, which made it easier for him to move in his new social milieu. Beni Hasan's exquisite paintings covered 1,115 square meters (12,000 square feet) and offered a formidable challenge to an artist. Newberry had traced the paintings the year before. It remained for Carter to make color drawings of the details of the murals. He succeeded brilliantly, so much so that he was sent to el-Amarna to work with Flinders Petrie in 1892, on a portion of the site that the latter had "sold" to Amherst. At first Petrie was doubtful about Carter, but his doubts soon turned to admiration, as the young artist took to excavation like a natural.

For the next six years, Carter found himself in demand, at Beni Hasan and also, at Newberry's recommendation, under Édouard-Henri Naville on Queen Hatshepsut's mortuary temple at Deir el-Bahri near Thebes. While Petrie and others violently opposed Naville's appointment to the site on the grounds that he was not careful enough, Carter covered himself with glory during a series of field seasons when he copied wall reliefs, assisted in clearance, and engaged in some architectural restoration. "In those six years, I learnt more of Egyptian art, its serene simplicity, than in any time or place. I had several colleagues to help me; there were tragedies, professional jealousies, and often amusing comedies. But I was lucky."[2] He had achieved a fine reputation as an artist, but he was definitely not considered a gentleman, criticized for his uncouth table manners.

Carter's first break came in 1899, when Gaston Maspero appointed him chief inspector of antiquities for Upper Egypt, one of only two inspectors in the country, as an attempt to internationalize the service. Wrote Maspero: "I find him very active, a very good young man, a little obstinate, but I believe that things will go well when he is persuaded of

FIGURE 16.1   Howard Carter was a consummate painter. In a painting from
1899, pharaoh Tuthmosis I and his mother, Seniseneb, present offerings at the
mortuary temple of Queen Hatshepsut. Courtesy: Egypt Exploration Society.
Photograph by Peter Hayman.

the impossibility of securing all the reforms in one go. The only misfor-
tune is that he doesn't understand French, but he is learning it." Maspero's
"young man" threw himself into a whirlwind of activity. He found himself dealing with tourists, and with the robbing of Amenophis II's sepulcher in the Valley of the Kings. Looters overpowered the tomb guards
and tore bandages off the mummy of the pharaoh.[3] Carter inspected the
ravaged mummy, which had been ripped open by an expert who knew
exactly where to look for jewelry, of which he had found none. Immediate
suspicion fell on the notorious Rasul family, whose footprints were found

in the tomb. While Carter measured them, professional trackers followed the spore to Mohammed Abd el-Rasul's house in Qurna. He was arrested, but the judge would not convict him on the basis of just a footprint.

Much of Carter's work involved conservation in the Valley of the Kings, where he lit some of the tombs with electric light for the first time. His years as inspector brought him in touch with wealthy patrons, among them the New York lawyer Theodore Davis, who received a concession to work in the valley in 1902. Carter supervised the work, under a government agreement that duplicate finds would go to Davis. These researches established Carter as someone with a nose for discovery. He found the tomb of an Eighteenth Dynasty noble named Userhet and that of a Nubian-born child from the royal nursery, which contained a wooden box filled with two exquisitely made leather loincloths. The tomb of pharaoh Tuthmosis IV with a columned burial chamber and quartzite sarcophagus came to light in 1903. Fragments of the original funerary regalia lay scattered over the floor. "Everything had been broken into by those ruthless vandals, who in their thirst for gold had spared nothing."[4] He was able to recover part of the king's chariot and one of his riding gauntlets.

Carter had been a superb inspector in Upper Egypt. In 1904, he was transferred to Lower Egypt. He had never been good with the public, for his stiff and obstinate personality gave him little tolerance for tourists. This side of his personality came to a head in January 1905, when he was involved in a violent altercation with a group of drunk French tourists at Saqqara. The visitors complained, Carter refused to apologize, and he eventually resigned from the inspectorate in disgust. For the next few years, he eked out a living as an artist in Luxor, serving as a guide, painting watercolors for tourists, and painting on commission from excavators such as Theodore Davis. In 1907, his fortunes changed dramatically, when he became associated with a wealthy English aristocrat, Lord Carnarvon.

: :

George Edward Stanhope Molyneux, fifth earl of Carnarvon (1866–1923), was an art collector of cultured tastes and fine judgment, a sportsman, and an ardent fan of motoring in its pioneer days. A serious injury in an automobile accident in Germany caused him to winter regularly in Egypt for his health after 1903. He was soon bored and happened to mention the fact to Lord Cromer, who suggested he take up Egyptology. During his first season, after six weeks "enveloped in dust," he found nothing but a large mummified cat, but caught the excavation bug. Given a permit for a more promising area in the Dra Abu'l Naga area in 1907, he found the tomb of Tetiky, mayor of Thebes during the early Eighteenth Dynasty. Modern houses prevented more than a partial excavation, but he found a few choice objects and uncovered well-preserved wall paintings. Carnarvon also unearthed another tomb containing a writing board bearing a hieratic text recording the pharaoh Kamose's war against the Hyksos of the Nile Delta.[5] By now, he felt a need to enlist the services of a "learned man." Gaston Maspero recommended Howard Carter. The events that led up to the dramatic Valley of the Kings discovery of 1922 were now set in motion.

Carter and Carnarvon became both colleagues and friends, despite the enormous social chasm between them. Carter came under his aristocratic patron's spell, aped his dress, and took to smoking cigarettes with a long holder. Together, they embarked on a five-year project in the Qurna hills, uncovering Middle Kingdom tombs and later sepulchers. They also worked on the Valley Temple of Queen Hatshepsut. Between 1910 and 1914, the two men unearthed rock-cut tombs from the Middle Kingdom, one with so many coffins stacked in it that Carnarvon gave some of them away. In 1912, they published *Five Years' Explorations at Thebes*, which received wide acclaim from Egyptologists. Carter had run a tight ship in the field, setting new standards for investigating previously looted tombs and salvaging as much archaeological information as possible under very harsh conditions. With Carnarvon's assistance, he built himself a fine brick house near Qurna, the bricks for the foundations supplied from his patron's brickworks in England.[6]

By this time, Carter was a prominent member of the small Egyptological coterie at Thebes. He was prickly, sometimes obstinate, occasionally charming, and always forthright, something that did not endear him to some of his colleagues. Arthur Weigall, his eventual successor as Upper Egypt inspector, could not stand Carter. The feeling was reciprocated.[7] He also had an uneasy relationship with the learned and independently wealthy Alan Gardiner. Carter never made close friends, for he was very much a loner, something that was both an asset and a liability when Tutankhamun came along.

In 1915, Theodore Davis relinquished the concession for excavations in the Valley of the Kings, which now passed to Lord Carnarvon, his appetite whetted by his discoveries in the Theban necropolis. World War I and

Carter's war work intervened. When time allowed, he returned to copying, notably reliefs of the Opet ceremony on the walls of Karnak. Not that life was without adventures. In 1916, he heard that some villagers on the west bank had found a tomb in a lonely valley above the Valley of the Kings. Two parties of robbers set out for the site. There was a fight. One band fled, while the others lowered themselves into the narrow defile of the sepulcher. Taking some of his workers with him, Carter climbed more than 550 meters (1,800 feet) over the Qurna hills by moonlight. He arrived at midnight while the looters were hard at work in the tomb. He quickly severed their rope dangling down the cliff and had himself lowered with a rope of his own "into a nest of industrious tomb-robbers . . . a pastime that at least does not lack excitement. There were eight at work, and when I reached the bottom there was an awkward moment or two."[8] He gave the looters the option of leaving via his rope or staying down with no way of escaping. They departed, while Carter remained on watch until dawn. For the next twenty days, he and his workers cleared the grave, which proved to be an unfinished tomb for Queen Hatshepsut. Other burials also came to light in the Theban cliffs during the war, including the sepulcher of three royal women of Tuthmosis III's court.[9] The finds vanished into the Luxor antiquities market before Carter got wind of the discovery. He did all he could to track down the loot, much of which is in the Metropolitan Museum of Fine Art in New York, the Louvre, and the British Museum, through local dealers.

By 1915, Carter was convinced that the burial of the obscure New Kingdom pharaoh Tutankhamun lay undiscovered in the Valley of the Kings. No one knew the valley as well as he. No one had searched more diligently for clues as to the young king's sepulcher. Theodore Davis was convinced there were no more royal tombs, despite finding a cache of sealed pottery jars, some with seals bearing Tutankhamun's name. Davis thought the find unimportant, but Herbert Winlock, an Egyptologist with the Metropolitan Museum, recognized their importance at once. He realized that the vessels were once used during Tutankhamun's funerary ceremonies, then buried and forgotten.[10] Tutankhamun haunted Carter's thoughts. The two excavators began work in 1917 in a long-term search for his tomb that involved digging down to bedrock and removing hundreds of tons of chippings created by ancient Egyptian masons and hasty modern excavators.

The search lasted for six years without success. By 1922, Carnarvon was concerned at the expense, but Carter persuaded him to pay for one last season to investigate a small triangular area near the tomb of Rameses VI,

FIGURE 16.2
Howard Carter opens one
of Tutankhamun's shrines.
Hulton Deutsch
Collection/Corbis.

which they had left on one side so as not to disturb visitors to the sepulcher. Nearby lay some crude workers' huts. What followed is one of the immortal stories of archaeology—some rock-cut steps under the workers' dwellings, then a sealed doorway, a rubble-filled passageway, and another barrier bearing Tutankhamun's seals. At this point Carter waited for Lord Carnarvon to arrive from England. On November 4, 1922, Carter pulled out a few stones from the doorway and shone a flickering candle through the small aperture. "Well, what is it?" asked Carnarvon somewhat impatiently. "There are some marvellous objects there," was Carter's reply, often reported as "wonderful things." The small party entered the antechamber of the tomb in dazed excitement, in what Carter called "the day of days, the most wonderful thing that I have ever lived through, and certainly one whose like I can never hope to see again."[11] That night, Carter, Carnarvon, and Carnarvon's daughter, Lady Evelyn Herbert, returned and cut a small hole into the sealed chamber leading off the antechamber to establish that the pharaoh's sarcophagus did indeed lie there, which it did.

: :

Carnarvon and Carter faced a daunting task—the conservation and recording of an entire pharaoh's tomb with its myriad of objects large and small, everything from items of clothing to funerary beds and prefabricated chariots. The discovery caused an international sensation. While planning the excruciatingly difficult clearance work, Carnarvon found himself fighting off hordes of journalists and mobs of tourists, all anxious to peer into the tomb. Royalty and celebrities clamored to be admitted. Carter called in all the assistance that he could obtain, notably from the Metropolitan Museum of Fine Art in New York, which provided an expert photographer, Harry Burton, and also surveyors and draftsmen. Conservation was in the hands of a government chemist, Alfred Lucas, an expert on ancient Egyptian materials, and A. C. Mace, who also helped Carter write a popular account of the tomb. The conservation laboratory occupied the nearby tomb of Seti II, staffed by what was a unique team of experts for the day.

Carter approached the recording of the tomb in a methodical way, numbering every object, then photographing and cataloging them in place if possible. His artistic expertise produced minute, stunningly accurate drawings of objects large and small. But Carter did not delegate well, and the stress was constant. He erupted in angry tantrums at the slightest provocation, which did not make for smooth relationships either with Carnarvon or with the scientists. When Carnarvon died suddenly from pneumonia and an infected mosquito bite on April 5, 1923, the pressure intensified and continued for the remaining nine years of the clearance. Inevitably, Carnarvon's demise produced talk of the "Curse of the Pharaohs," with a capital *C* and a capital *P*, but the furor over the evil influence of ancient curses was nothing compared with the political ramifications of the discovery, which changed Egyptology profoundly.

The trouble began over press coverage. Neither of the two discoverers were accustomed to dealing with the press. Carnarvon was an aristocrat who disdained the popular press. In late 1922, he forged an exclusive agreement for tomb coverage with the London *Times* over Carter's strenuous objections. Carnarvon had served as a buffer between Carter and journalists, and between his prickly colleague and an increasingly aggressive Antiquities Service, which was concerned that most of the finds would leave Egypt under the generous export laws still on the books. Carter's abrasive and obstinate personality added fuel to the flames. A complex mix of disgruntled journalists, nationalist politicians, and the increasing sensitivity of Egyptians to what appeared to be a foreign archaeological monopoly led to charges and countercharges, as well as studied insults. The director of the Antiquities Service, Pierre Lacau, was insisting that all the Tutankhamun finds remain in Egypt and that the Carnarvon family renounce all rights to the artifacts.[12] Matters came to a head in February 1924 when Carter and his colleagues staged a strike shortly after raising the lid of the king's sarcophagus and exposing the golden mummy inside. Carter posted a notice blaming the work stoppage on the "impossible restrictions and discourtesies" of the Egyptian authorities. The government promptly canceled the Carnarvon concession and locked Carter and his colleagues out of the tomb.

After prolonged negotiations, Carter was permitted to resume work in January 1925 under a new concession. The Carnarvon family renounced all claims to the tomb and its contents and agreed not to take legal action over the cancellation of the earlier permit. In return, the government was prepared to allocate duplicate representatives of the finds to the Carnarvons, provided they did not detract from the scientific value of the tomb as a whole. Visits by outsiders were carefully regulated, most being confined to Tuesdays.

The controversy had provoked strong feelings among Carter's colleagues, many of whom disliked his prickly and often tactless manner. His team of experts was much reduced. He was now left more or less alone to complete his task, which suited him. In 1925, he contented himself with working on the objects already taken from the tomb, including a silver trumpet bearing figures of Amun, Re-Herakhty, and Ptah. Carter told Lady Carnarvon that he had managed to get a good blast out of it. Herbert Winlock praised Carter's delicate touch with the jewelry: "with his fingers of an artist there is no better person to whom this stuff could have been entrusted." The year 1926 saw the delicate task of lifting out the coffin shells from the sarcophagus and the formal examination of the mummy itself on November 11 in the tomb of Seti II. Unlike earlier formal occasions, there were no grandees, just Egyptian government officials, Carter and his colleagues, and members of the Antiquities Service. The mummy was much corroded by the unguents poured over it by the embalmers, but Carter commented that "Tut-ankh-Amen was of a type exceedingly refined and cultured. The face has beautiful and well formed features."[13]

Work on the tomb dragged on for six more years, plagued by visitors and long-drawn-out debates over the question of compensation to the Carnarvon family for the expense of the tomb project. The tortuous politics of Egypt during these years made any form of settlement difficult. The countess of Carnarvon decided, probably with Carter's agreement, not to renew the concession. The actual clearance work was finished, but there remained some important conservation work, especially on the shrines that encased the sarcophagus. Carter now had no formal status as far as the tomb was concerned. He could not even possess a key to the sepulcher, a reflection of changed political times. In 1930, the Carnarvon family accepted £35,867 13/8 in compensation, of which Carter received about one-quarter.[14]

Two years later, in February 1932, Howard Carter completed his enormous task, conducted under appallingly difficult conditions. Much of the time he had worked virtually alone, assisted only by photographer Harry Burton of the Metropolitan Museum and Alfred Lucas, chemist to the Antiquities Service. Tutankhamun had consumed ten years of Carter's life. At the end, he was exhausted. He never wrote the great scientific monograph on the tomb that he had planned, but spent much of his time purchasing fine antiquities for major institutions like the British Museum and the Detroit Institute of Arts. His artifact dealings have been much criticized by today's Egyptologists, but Carter had no formal employment and had to support himself. In this, he was very much an archaeologist of his times. He died in 1939, without honor from his own government, in part because of his humble birth. His proudest accolade was an honorary doctorate from Yale University.

: :

Until World War I, British, French, and German scholars dominated Egyptology. The Americans were late on the scene. All three of America's earliest professional Egyptologists trained in Germany in the 1890s, then began fieldwork along the Nile. Major philanthropists, among them Phoebe Hearst from California, Theodore Davis, and John D. Rockefeller Jr., provided support for major expeditions. Davis we have already met in the Valley of the Kings. Phoebe Hearst supported George Reisner (1867–1942), a rumpled, pipe-smoking scholar who directed the Hearst Egyptian Expedition from 1897 to 1899. With her support, he honed his excavation skills, notably in a Twelfth Dynasty palace at Deir el-Ballas north of Thebes. Appointed to the faculty at Harvard University, Reisner spent the rest of his productive career digging in Egypt and the Sudan. He was a scrupulous excavator whose recording methods and field techniques were far superior to anything seen along the Nile before. He also treated his Egyptian workers exceptionally well, which led to some remarkable finds, including an important medical papyrus. Reisner despised Petrie's rough-and-tumble methods and had little time for Carter and Carnarvon, whom he considered arrogant and colonial. "I have never accepted Mr. Carter or Carnarvon as a scientific colleague nor admitted that either of them came within the categories of persons worthy of receiving excavation permits from the Egypt Government," he wrote privately to Mr. Hawes of the Boston Museum of Fine Arts in 1924.[15] Almost alone among Egyptologists, he did not support Carter in his quarrels with the Egyptian authorities. Unfortunately, Reisner was so slow moving and thorough that many of his excavations still remain unpublished.

Reisner was unusual in that he worked in the Sudan, where he carried out the first systematic survey of Nubian sites. He also dug in the heart of the Nubian kingdom of Kerma south of the Second Cataract in the Sudan, where he excavated a spectacular royal cemetery with burial mounds containing as many as four hundred of the chief's followers who had been buried alive. His careful excavation methods allowed him to describe sacrificial victims with sufficient emotion to allow themselves to be covered with earth: "subsequently little movement was possible and death came quickly. . . . The most unfortunate persons were those, usually young females, who crept under the bed and thus being enclosed in an air-space . . . died much more gradually."[16]

For years, he worked in the Old Kingdom cemeteries near Giza, where he found many papyri and a magnificent seated statue of the pharaoh Menkaure (2532–2504 BC) and his queen. His greatest Giza discovery was the tomb of Queen Hetepheres, wife of King Sneferu and mother of Khufu, builder of the Great Pyramid. The queen lay in a burial chamber so cramped that only two people could work there at a time. Reisner's colleague Dows Dunham dealt with finds so delicate that even a slight vibration caused them to decay. On one occasion he said something funny, Reisner laughed, and a fragment of sheet gold once attached to a piece of wooden furniture slid to the floor. Some 1,700 pages of notes and drawings and 1,057 photographs later, Reisner and his colleagues were able to reconstruct the major finds on modern wood. Unfortunately, her sarcophagus was empty. "Reisner rose from his box and said, 'Gentlemen, I regret Queen Hetepheres is not receiving. . . . Mrs. Reisner will serve refreshments at the camp.'"[17] Reisner was delighted when the gold and silver vessels, a bed complete with a canopy, and other finds momentarily diverted public attention from Tutankhamun.

His contemporary James Henry Breasted (1865–1935) was an early example of an American academic entrepreneur. Like Reisner, he studied in

FIGURE 16.3 Henry Breasted and his family *(center)* at Abu Simbel. Courtesy: Oriental Institute, University of Chicago.

Germany, under Adolf Erman with whom he formed a lifelong friendship. Breasted spent his entire career at the infant University of Chicago, where he soon came in contact with the philanthropist John D. Rockefeller Jr., who funded much of his work. His real expertise was inscriptions, which he published in a magisterial work, *Ancient Records of Egypt,* in five volumes between 1905 and 1909. He became professor of Egyptology at the University of Chicago in 1905, the first in the country, and devoted the rest of his career to fostering Egyptology in the United States. Aggressive, persistent, and constantly on the lookout for new opportunities, Breasted was above all a teacher and administrator who made things happen. With the assistance of Rockefeller, he founded the Oriental Institute at the University of Chicago in 1919, which, with more Rockefeller money, rapidly became the leading institution for Egyptology and Near Eastern studies in the Americas. The ever opportunistic Breasted was on the fringes of the Tutankhamun affair, supported Carter against Lacau, and played a part in the negotiations over the resumption of work in 1925, but he was privately critical. On one occasion he remarked in a letter that "we are familiar with the fact that Carter does not know the meaning of the English language."[18] To Breasted and many other Egyptologists, Carter was a dirt archaeologist and artist, not a scholar or a gentleman.

FIGURE 16.4
Queen Nefertiti from a sculptor's
workshop at el-Amarna, one of the
masterpieces of Egyptian art. Archivo
Iconografico/Corbis.

The Oriental Institute was Breasted's greatest achievement, where he ensured that archaeology, the recording of ancient monuments, and the study of written records went hand in hand. Perhaps his greatest legacies were *A History of Egypt*, which appeared in 1905—one of the best accounts of ancient Egyptian history ever written—and the institute's long-term project of recording inscriptions on standing monuments, begun in 1929 and continued to this day.

Tutankhamun overshadowed many other dramatic finds between 1910 and the outbreak of World War II, among them the 1912 discovery by German archaeologist Ludwig Borchardt of the masterpiece portrait of Queen Nefertiti, found with a unique cache of art objects in a room of the house of the sculptor Thutmose at el-Amarna. In the subsequent division of finds, the head was allocated to the Germans and exhibited publicly two years later. The Egyptian government was outraged and demanded the return of the portrait, but to no avail. Adolf Hitler said, "What the German people have, they keep."[19]

Another remarkable find came in 1923, when Herbert Winlock unearthed a mass grave of early Middle Kingdom soldiers who had died in
combat. The gruesome corpses bore signs of vicious combat—arrow
wounds, head wounds from slingshots, and club blows that finished off
the wounded. They were the bodies of soldiers who had fought for Mentuhotep I (2060–2010 BC), perhaps in Nubia, honored by being interred
close to the pharaoh's mortuary temple.[20] The list of important discoveries goes on and on, as, gradually, science replaced casual excavation and
recording combined with conservation became important priorities.

: :

These discoveries, like Tutankhamun, played out against a backdrop of
rising nationalism.[21] The British made Egypt a protectorate during World
War I, but a revolution in 1919 took them by surprise, forcing them to
concede great autonomy to the Egyptians. A period of semi-indepen-
dence lasted until Colonel Nasser's revolution of 1952, which swept away
the monarchy, the old political parties, and the power of the landlords.

Tutankhamun linked archaeology to the ebb and flow of local politics.
The Egyptians took advantage of their limited independence to overhaul antiquities laws. They introduced far stricter controls on artifact exports, supervised excavation permits more closely, and developed programs to train
Egyptian Egyptologists, despite an obstinate hold on the Antiquities Service
and the museum by Lacau and his successor, Étienne Drioton. Europeans
still headed the Egyptology Department at Cairo University, despite a greater
emphasis on ancient Egypt in local schools. Foreign researchers continued to
work along the Nile, although at a reduced intensity from earlier times, a
product of more rigorously enforced export laws. Increasingly, the emphasis
turned to recording as much as excavation, as Egypt continued to wrestle
with a rapidly expanding tourist industry.

The Egyptians gained full independence and complete control over
their past in the 1950s, after French administration of the Antiquities Service had endured for ninety-four years. In 1952, Egyptian archaeologist
Muhammad Zakaria Gonheim, keeper of the Saqqara necropolis, unearthed a hitherto unknown step pyramid. Two years later, Gonheim removed the masonry blocking the doorway to the underground passages.
Layers of funerary vessels lay on the passage floor, as did a decayed wooden
casket containing a cache of golden armlets, a sheet-gold cosmetic box in

the shape of a shell, and faience (glass) beads. Some mud-sealed vessels bore the name of the pharaoh Sekhemkhet (2649–2643 BC), the successor of Djoser, builder of the well-known Step Pyramid nearby. Unfortunately, Sekhemkhet's translucent alabaster sarcophagus was empty.[22] The Saqqara discovery was a source of great pride to the Egyptian public.

President Nasser made the Aswan High Dam a symbol of the new nation; the UNESCO-sponsored move of the Abu Simbel temples to high ground symbolized a new national pride. An international effort surveyed the area to be flooded by Lake Nasser, resulting in the discovery of thousands of archaeological sites, some of great importance. The Egyptians rewarded major participants with artifacts, even complete temples. The United States was given the temple of Dendur as a reward for its efforts in Nubia. Such is institutional greed that the temple soon became the target of intense competition among the Metropolitan Museum of Art, the Smithsonian Institution, and the Kennedy family, who wished to erect it by the chilly and damp banks of the Potomac beside the Kennedy Center. The Met won, but it had just finished selling off thousands of its smaller Egyptian antiquities—mummies, scarabs, beads, and pottery acquired through large-scale digs in earlier years. The island of Philae, the site of some of Belzoni's adventures, also vanished underwater. The British had partially drowned its exquisite temples when they built the original Aswan Dam amid swirling controversy in 1902. UNESCO now moved them to nearby Agilkia Island, which was landscaped to resemble the original.

Egyptian archaeologists continue to make remarkable discoveries, among them a stela of pharaoh Kamose at Karnak containing details of his struggles with the Hyksos. In May 1954, a young antiquities inspector named Kamal el-Mallakh uncovered the funerary boat pits by the pyramids at Giza, one of which contained a royal boat of the Fourth Dynasty. Today, foreign scholars collaborate closely with Egyptians in research with a common goal, with excavation carefully targeted, with precise goals, to avoid further destruction. Some collaborations have yielded sensational results. Back in 1962, Egyptian archaeologist Kamal Abu el-Saadat persuaded the navy to lift a huge statue of Isis from the waters of Alexandria Harbor. Thirty-two years later, a team of French underwater archaeologists headed by Jean-Yves Empereur began a survey of the seabed that yielded at least forty shipwrecks and what he claimed, controversially, were the remains of the Pharos lighthouse, one of the Seven Wonders of the classical world. Another Frenchman, Frank Goddio, is using controlled diving and satellite imagery to map a submerged palace with marble floors.

Ancient Egypt still grabs international headlines. In 1999, Zahi Hawass of the Supreme Council for Antiquities (successor of the Antiquities Service) announced the discovery of a cemetery with at least 10,000 occupants in the Wadi Bahariya Oasis to the west of the Nile. Most of the excavated dead date to the first and second centuries AD, lying in multichambered tombs on shelves. Much of the importance of the Wadi Bahariya cemetery lies in the information it will reveal about the people themselves—their diet, health, and life expectancy.[23]

The discoveries continue to delight and amaze, but the international climate for archaeology has changed, in a world that is ardently nationalistic and increasingly jealous of its diverse cultural heritages. People are far more aware of archaeology, conscious of the enormous contribution that the discipline can make to the proper study of humankind. The Egyptians know only too well that the wealth of ancient Egypt is spread through the museums of several continents. Mummy after mummy, sarcophagus after sarcophagus, statue after statue, museum storerooms and galleries are filled with the dusty remains of Egyptian antiquity from Moscow to New Zealand, Glasgow to Cape Town. Most of these riches were acquired by private collectors and then donated to the museums, or acquired in massive field seasons, supported by private donations, where often quantity was more important than quality. In 1983, a new antiquities law made all artifacts the property of the state, except for those already in private collections. One cannot blame the Egyptians for being restrictive in their permit granting and nationalistic in their recent attitudes toward ancient Egypt. They understand the importance of the tourist industry to the national economy, of the need to balance conservation with an unrelenting public thirst to enter Tutankhamun's sepulcher and admire Old Kingdom tomb paintings. The authorities face agonizing decisions. Do they admit visitors to royal graves and witness the near-certain deterioration and perhaps disappearance of unique wall paintings from sheer people pressure? Or do they close everything to save it for future generations? The debate on these issues has hardly begun. The dilemma pits the preservation of the priceless and finite archive that is ancient Egypt against the pressing economic needs of a developing country—altruism for future generations against short-term advantages. No one envies the Cairo authorities the decisions that lie ahead in an environment where funds are exiguous and the task of protection and conservation absolutely overwhelming. The rape of the Nile is entering a new phase, where, instead of looting the past, we destroy it with our love, our breath and sweat, and our feet.

In the shadows, the surreptitious treasure hunting continues in an unending war between the government and dealers and villagers with centuries of looting in their bones. As these words are being written, newspaper reports tell of a sting operation by the antiquities authorities at Beni Suef, where some officials were caught with a Greco-Roman mummy in their possession. The lust to collect and to own is a still little-understood human quality, but one that fuels an unending hunger for fine antiquities, for papyri, figurines, and all the riches of ancient Egypt. Much progress has been made in recent years to highlight the evils of the international antiquities trade, but as long as there is demand, there will be people to fill it—quiet expeditions in the dead of night, flashlights glimmering in rock-cut chambers, and carefully wrapped bundles slipped away into hiding in the hours of dawn.

The story of Egyptology is one of heroes and villains, bold deeds and incredible discoveries, of adventure, high-minded research, and down-right skullduggery. In the end, the heroes and the scientists may prevail, but the price we have paid for this victory is enormous. Fortunately, the mystique and mystery of ancient Egypt have survived looters and gunpowder. There is a changelessness about Egypt that captivates the visitor and offers hope for the future. Amun still journeys across the heavens in an endless journey that symbolizes continuity. As Robin Feddon once wrote of the Egyptian winter:

> Rising from the Eastern Desert the sun sips up the heavy winter dews and passes daily across the valley through a cloudless sky. At evening, it sinks behind the Libyan hills, creating, as a magnificent finale, its breath-catching sunsets. Day after day the progress is repeated; day after day the evolution is the same. . . . Ancient Egypt lies there, preserved in the balsam of the sun.[24]

Amun still casts his spell.

Notes and References

I consulted hundreds of articles, books, and reviews in writing this book. These notes make no attempt to cover all the sources that I consulted, but offer the reader an opportunity to delve into a very complex and ever growing literature on the history of Egyptology. Each chapter starts with a Guide to Further Reading, giving some general references, which may also appear in the more detailed entries. (In some cases, the guide covers several chapters, for obvious reasons.) At times, I have attempted a brief identification or summary of a god, an individual, or a site to amplify the narrative.

CHAPTER 1: PLUNDERING THE PHARAOHS

Guide to Further Reading

Ancient Egyptian civilization has been published almost to the degree of eccentricity. General books on the subject abound, so one can offer only a few titles here. Robin Feddon's obscure but wonderfully written *Egypt: Land of the Valley* (London: John Murray, 1977) gives an evocative impression of the land, ancient and modern, like none other I have read. Barry Kemp, *Ancient Egypt: Anatomy of a Civilization* (London: Routledge, 1989), is an analytical work aimed at a more specialized audience. In my view, it is the best analysis of ancient Egyptian civilization in print. Cyril Aldred's classic essay *The Egyptians,* 3d ed. (London and New York: Thames and Hudson, 1998), is an excellent shorter treatment. My own *Egypt of the Pharaohs* (Washington, D.C.: National Geographic Society, 2001) is a superficial history with superb photographs by Ken Garrett. See also Vivian Davis and Renée Friedman, *Egypt Uncovered* (London: Stewart, Tabori, and Chang, 1998), which focuses on recent discoveries. All these sources will guide you to the basic literature.

Three books of more specific focus are worth recommending here. Mark Lehner, *The Complete Pyramids* (London: Thames and Hudson, 1997), describes the history, architecture, and significance of these most striking of Egyptian monuments. Lise Manniche, *City of the Dead: Thebes in Egypt* (London: British Museum, 1987), is more technical but a mine of information on the Theban necropolis. To read hieroglyphs, try Mark Collier and Bill Manley, *How to Read Egyptian Hieroglyphs: A Step-by-Step Guide to Teach Yourself* (Berkeley and Los Angeles: University of California Press, 2003), where numerous references will be found.

1. Howard Carter and A. C. Mace, *The Tomb of Tut-Ank-Amen* (New York: George H. Doran, 1923–1933), 4.

2. For convenience, I have used the term *Thebes* in these pages, only using *Luxor* in a modern context, this being common practice in the literature.

3. T. E. Peet, *The Great Tomb-Robberies of the Twelfth Egyptian Dynasty* (Oxford: Griffith Institute, 1990); quotes in this paragraph and below are from pp. 21, 23. Translations of tomb-robbing records can also be found in Henry Breasted, *Ancient Records of Egypt* (Chicago: University of Chicago Press, 1906).

4. Peet, op. cit. (1990), 17.

5. An incident described at length below, in Chapter 13.

6. Peter A. Clayton, *Chronicle of the Pharaohs* (London and New York: Thames and Hudson, 1994), is an authoritative summary of all that is known about ancient Egyptian rulers, their chronologies and deeds. This book provided the dates used in this book.

7. Pliny quotes in this and the preceding paragraph come from Leslie Greener, *The Discovery of Egypt* (New York: Viking Press, 1966), 1. For convenience, I refer to Muhammad Ali, which complies with the Library of Congress convention. Some authors use Mehmed (or Mehmet), which is the Turkish usage. I am grateful to Professor Donald Reed for his briefing on this arcane point.

CHAPTER 2: THE FIRST TOURISTS

Guide to Further Reading

The colorful history of Egyptology has become a fashionable topic. Peter Clayton, *The Rediscovery of Egypt* (London: Thames and Hudson, 1982), covers early depictions of Egypt by European artists. Nicholas Reeves, *Ancient Egypt: The Great Discoveries* (London: Thames and Hudson, 2000), is a lavishly illustrated chronicle of discovery from 1798 to today, an essential reference for anyone interested in the history of Egyptology. See also Peter France, *The Rape of Egypt* (London: Barry and Jenkins, 1991), which covers much the same ground as the present book. John Marlow, *Spoiling the Egyptians* (London: Andre Deutsch, 1974), is more concerned with the economic, financial, and technological aspects of Egypt in the nineteenth century, but is excellent for the general reader. F. Gladstone Bratton, *A History of Egyptian Archaeology* (London: Hale, 1967), is informative on the early Greek authors and the first tourists. For Roman tourists, see Tony Perrottet's entertaining *Route 66 A.D.: On the Trail of Ancient Roman Tourists*

(New York: Random House, 2002), and Ibrahim Amin Ghali, "Touristes romains en Égypte et Égyptiens à Rome sous le Haut-Empire," *Cahiers d'histoire Égyptienne* 11 (1969): 43–62. Leslie Greener, op. cit. (1966), is a popular work that is good on early visitors. A series of recently published volumes, not available when this book was revised, deal with various aspects of changing attitudes to Egypt and Egyptology, among them David Jeffreys, ed., *Views of Ancient Egypt Since Napoleon Bonaparte* (London: UCL Press, 2003).

1. Allegedly, Pharaoh Amenemhet (1991–1962 BC) wrote these words at the beginning of an instruction to his son Senusret I (1971–1926 BC). He was assassinated in the thirtieth year of his reign. It may be that a royal scribe set these words down on the orders of the new king.

2. Lucie Duff-Gordon, *Letters from Egypt* (London: Macmillan, 1865), 12.

3. Miriam Lichtheim, *Ancient Egyptian Literature, Vol. 2: The New Kingdom* (Berkeley and Los Angeles: University of California Press, 1976), 43–44.

4. David Grene, trans., *The History: Herodotus* (Chicago: University of Chicago Press, 1987), bk. 2.21, p. 139.

5. Ibid., bk. 2.86, p. 166. For mummies and mummification, see Salam Ikram and Aidan Dodson, *The Mummy in Ancient Egypt: Equipping the Dead for Eternity* (London: Thames and Hudson, 1998). A fascinating, if gruesome, account of some of the diseases that afflicted the ancient Egyptians and modern experiments with their mummification techniques can be found in Rosalie David and Rick Archbold, *Conversations with Mummies* (New York, William Morrow, 2000).

6. Manetho (fl. ca. 280 BC) was Egyptian high priest at Heliopolis, whose *Aigypticaka* divided Egyptian history into thirty dynasties that still form the framework for ancient Egyptian chronology.

7. Auguste Mariette in a letter to his friend Desjardins, 1874. Quoted in Greener, op. cit. (1966), 10.

8. Diodorus Siculus, *Library of History*, trans. C. H. Oldfather (Cambridge: Harvard University Press, 1961), 1:67. Percy Bysshe Shelley, *Ozymandias*, a sonnet written in 1818 in friendly competition with another poet, Horace Smith, who wrote a poem on the same subject. The poem is in the Bodleian Library, Oxford, MS Shelley e4, fol. 85r.

9. On Strabo, see H. C. Hamilton and W. Falconer, *The Geography of Strabo* (London: G. Bell, 1906), vol. 3, bk. 17, p. 261.

10. Quotes in this paragraph come from ibid., 262ff.

11. On Rudolph von Suchem, see Greener, op. cit. (1966), 14; and Georges Goyon, *Inscriptions et Graffiti des voyagers sur la grande pyramide* (Cairo: Société Royale de Géographie, 1944).

12. Caius Plinius Cecilius Secundus (AD 23–79), known as Pliny the Elder, was a scholar, naturalist, and encyclopedist. Despite an active and distinguished pub-

lic career, he found time to write at least seventy-five books, of which only one, *Natural History*, published in AD 77, survives. This remarkable work drew on an astonishing range of sources and remained an important reference work right into the Middle Ages. Pliny died during the eruption of Vesuvius in AD 79, which overwhelmed Herculaneum and Pompeii.

13. Grene, op. cit. (1987), bk. 2.168, p. 196.

14. Hypostele halls with their many columns are distinctive features of later Egyptian temples, symbolic depictions of the columns that supported the celestial realm of the sky. Said the pharaoh Amenophis III of Karnak in an inscription there: "Its pillars reach heaven like the four pillars of heaven." The columns also represented the marshland vegetation with its reeds that sprang up around the primeval mound of Egyptian creation.

15. For the Valley of the Kings, see Nicholas Reeves and Richard H. Wilkinson, *The Complete Valley of the Kings* (London: Thames and Hudson, 1996).

16. Quotes in this and the preceding paragraphs come from J. M. Cohen, ed., *The Natural History of C. Plinius Secundus* (London: Centaur, 1962), 440–441.

17. Quoted in Greener, op. cit. (1966), 23.

18. Ibid., 26.

CHAPTER 3: "MUMMY IS BECOME MERCHANDISE"

Guide to Further Reading

John David Wortham, *The Genesis of British Egyptology* (Norman: University of Oklahoma Press, 1971), is a basic source on the period. Leslie Greener, op. cit., is an entertaining account of the early period of Egyptology and later events. Karl A. Dannenfeldt, "Egypt and Egyptian Antiquities in the Renaissance," *Studies in the Renaissance* 6 (1959): 7–27, is a beautifully written study of early Egyptologists. For early decipherment, see Lesley Adkins and Roy Adkins, *The Keys of Egypt* (New York: HarperCollins, 2000).

1. The temple of Horus at Edfu was begun by Ptolemy III in 237 BC and completed 180 years later in 57 BC. Edfu was the traditional location of the mythic battle between the gods Horus and Seth and was sometimes called the "Exaltation of Horus."

2. H. Idris Bell, *Egypt from Alexander to the Arab Conquest* (Oxford: Oxford University Press, 1948), 55.

3. Greener, op. cit. (1966), 27.

4. Ibid., 86.

5. Ibid., 87.

6. Ibid., 26.

7. Ibid., 27–29.

8. Leo Africanus, *History and Description of Africa* (London: Halkuyt Society, 1896), 37.

9. Greener, op. cit. (1966), 40.

10. Ibid., 42.

11. Ibid., 43.

12. Ibid., 86.

13. M. H. Abrams and Stephen Greenblatt, eds., *The Norton Anthology of English Literature* (New York: Norton, 1999), 7:1580; Mark Twain, *The Innocents Abroad* (1869; reprint, New York: Oxford University Press, 1996), 632.

14. Letter from Cairo dated September 18, 1638. Quoted in Greener, op. cit. (1966), 46.

15. James Bruce, *Travels to Discover the Source of the Nile* (Edinburgh: Robinson, 1970), 23.

16. Greener, op. cit. (1966), 61.

17. Benoit de Maillet (1656–1738) made a large collection of Egyptian antiquities, many of which ended up in the royal collections. He later wrote the monumental *Description de l'Égypte* (1735), which Napoléon's savants took to Egypt with them. Quoted in Greener, op. cit. (1966), 66, 67.

18. Ibid., 74.

19. Joan Evans, *A History of the Society of Antiquaries* (Oxford: Oxford University Press, 1956), 233.

20. William George Browne (1768–1813) was an inveterate English traveler who visited Egypt in 1792 and wandered as far as Darfur in the southern Sahara. He was murdered while traveling from England to Tartary in 1813.

CHAPTER 4: NAPOLÉON ON THE NILE

Guide to Further Reading

Christopher Herold's *Bonaparte in Egypt* (New York: Harper and Row, 1962) is definitive. Henry Laurens, *L'Éxpédition d'Égypte* (Paris: A. Collins, 1989), is a standard French history, while Pierre Bret, *L'Éxpedition d'Égypte* (Paris: Technique et Documentation, 1999), commemorates the bicentennial of the expedition. Dominique-Vivant Denon's travels are best read in French, but the English translation, *Travels in Upper and Lower Egypt* (London: Hurst, 1803), is readily available. It is worth going a long way to pore over the *Description de l'Égypte* (Paris: Imprimerie Impériale, 1809–1828). Only those who have admired the plates firsthand can appreciate their true significance. A fair number of English translations and reproductions have appeared in recent years, but their smaller format does not do justice to the original illustrations. Jean Baptiste Prosper Jollois, *Journal d'un Ingénieur attaché a l'Expédition d'Égypte, 1798–1802* (Paris: E.

Leroux, 1904), is informative on Desaix de Veygoux's campaign. Henry Dodwell's *Founder of Modern Egypt* (1931; reprint, Cambridge: Cambridge University Press, 1967) remains the scholarly and definitive account of Muhammad Ali's career. On Henry Salt, see D. Manley and P. Rée, *Henry Salt: Artist, Traveller, Diplomat, Egyptologist* (London: Libri, 2001). See J. J. Halls's typically nineteenth-century hagiography, *The Life and Correspondence of Henry Salt, Esq., F.R.S.* (London: R. Bentley, 1834).

1. The American edition is Frederick Lewis Norden, *The Travels of Frederick Lewis Morgan Through Egypt and Nubia* (New Haven: Sydney's Press, 1814).

2. Ibid., 56, 66. The Battle of Kadesh between the Egyptians and Hittites, fought in 1275 BC, involved 20,000 Egyptian troops and ended in a draw. Both sides, especially Rameses, claimed it as a great victory.

3. A discussion of early theories will be found in Adkins and Adkins, op. cit. (2000), 57ff.

4. Count Constantin-François Chasseboeuf Volney (1757–1820) enjoyed a varied career, spending four years in Egypt and Syria, which resulted in his *Voyage en Égypte et en Syrie*, published in 1787, a book that is said to have strongly influenced Napoléon, although the count was not an avid supporter of the Corsican.

5. The stela was originally thought to be basalt, but recent cleaning has shown it is gray granite with pink veining. Early-nineteenth-century scientists darkened the stone, perhaps with boot polish, to highlight the inscriptions.

6. Quoted in Adkins and Adkins, op. cit. (2000), 35, where an account of the Rosetta stone's discovery will be found.

7. Reeves, op. cit. (2000), 14. Ptolemy V Epiphanes (205–180 BC) ascended Egypt's throne at a young age and was crowned at Memphis during a period of major civil disorder in 196 BC. He allocated land grants and announced tax remissions as part of his coronation, whence the inscription on the Rosetta stone.

8. Quotes in this paragraph come from Denon, op. cit. (1803), 28.

9. Ibid., 66.

10. Greener, op. cit. (1966), 95.

11. Quotes in this and the next paragraphs in ibid., 101–102.

12. Edmé François Jomard (1777–1862) was an engineer, geographer, and antiquarian who was a prominent member of the Scientific Commission. He devoted much of his remaining career to the publication of the *Description* and is also remembered for his opposition to Champollion's decipherment of hieroglyphs.

13. Ronald T. Ridley has done Egyptology a great service with his *Napoleon's Proconsul in Egypt* (London: Rubicon Press, 1998). In particular, he highlights Drovetti's remarkable diplomatic skills and his considerable charm, which served him well in the antiquities business.

Lady Hester Lucy Stanhope (1776–1839) traveled widely in the Near East dressed in male garments before settling in a remodeled, fortified convent among the Druze of Lebanon, who hailed her as a prophetess, a role she embraced with enthusiasm. Quote from ibid., 57.

14. Aksum (AD 100 to 650) is one of the least-known preindustrial states. Centered on the Ethiopian highlands, its rulers traded with both Mediterranean markets and India through their port at Adulis. Their capital boasts of spectacular royal graves adorned with high stelae modeled like multistory buildings. Aksum declined in the face of Islamic expansion during the seventh century.

15. Sir Joseph Banks (1730–1820) exercised a controlling interest over much of British science for the second half of the eighteenth century. A true polymath, he was at heart an expert botanist. William Hamilton (1730–1803), a diplomat and antiquarian, collected antiquities from Pompeii and elsewhere. He served British interests in Naples during the Napoleonic Wars, where his wife, Emma, dallied with Admiral Lord Nelson.

CHAPTER 5: THE PATAGONIAN SAMPSON

Guide to Further Reading for Chapters 5–10

The literature about Giovanni Belzoni is diffuse, and the number of travelers who refer to his work in their travelogues is enormous. In writing this account I have relied very heavily on his own *Narrative of the Operations and Recent Discoveries Within the Pyramids, Temples, Tombs, and Excavations, in Egypt and Nubia* (London: John Murray, 1820). Belzoni's book is long, often self-serving, and stylistically clumsy. But it glows with vivid action and restlessness. There is a gusto about it that led me to regard it as a primary source if critically used. Everyone who writes about Belzoni will rely heavily on Stanley Mayes's definitive and recently reissued biography, *The Great Belzoni* (New York: Palgrave Macmillan, 2003). This is a comprehensive study that involved extensive research into primary sources about Belzoni (a rarity). I found it an invaluable source of background reading and references, and a reliable guide to a complex man. It contains a useful appendix on Belzoni's finds in the British Museum, which helped me through a spellbound afternoon in the Egyptian Galleries. Maurice Willson Disher's *Pharaoh's Fool* (London: Heinemann, 1957) concentrates on Belzoni's theatrical exploits, while Colin Clair's *Strong Man Egyptologist* (London: Oldbourne, 1957) is a small-scale biography.

1. Mayes, op. cit. (2003), 19.

2. Ibid., 42.

3. Quoted in John Thomas Smith, *A Book for a Rainy Day* (1803; reprint, London: Bentley, 1861), 63. See Mayes, op. cit. (2003), 51.

4. *Gentleman's Magazine* (1821); Mayes, op. cit. (2003), 56.

5. Mayes, op. cit. (2003), 70.

6. Youssef Boghos Bey (1768–1844) was of Armenian descent and was Ali's most trusted servant and adviser. He effectively controlled the issuance of *firmans* for excavation throughout Egypt.

7. Louis Maurice Adolphe Linant de Bellefonds (1799–1883) was a French geographer and engineer who began his career as a naval surveyor and then traveled in the Near East. He executed many drawings for the antiquarian William Bankes, whose activities are described below, as well as maps of Egypt. In later life, he was actively involved in the planning of the Suez Canal.

8. Bubonic plague was a regular visitor to Egypt until 1844, when it mysteriously disappeared. Cholera, introduced from India, was troublesome in the late nineteenth century. The only known protection was isolating oneself indoors or, for returning travelers to Europe, quarantine.

9. William Turner (1792–1867) traveled extensively in Egypt and later became a diplomat, serving as British envoy to Columbia. His *Journals of a Tour of the Levant* appeared in three volumes in 1820.

10. The Ibn Tulun mosque was built by the Iraqi Ahmad Ibn Tulun in AD 876–879 and was the short-lived focal point of the city. The mosque is famous for its majestic simplicity and elegant stucco work. For Cairo, see André Raymond, *Cairo* (Cambridge: Harvard University Press, 2002).

11. Quotes in this paragraph come from Belzoni, op. cit. (1820), 7–8. Foreign travelers usually donned Turkish dress for safety when traveling in, and certainly outside, Cairo, as Belzoni subsequently did.

12. Ibid., 22.

CHAPTER 6: THE YOUNG MEMNON

1. Burckhardt letter quoted in Mayes, op. cit. (2003), 142.

2. Belzoni, op. cit. (1820), 26–28. It's interesting to speculate as to exactly how much the strongman knew about ancient Egypt before he undertook his first expedition. Henry Salt's library was at his disposal; he is known to have owned a copy of the *Description* that Belzoni could have consulted. Our hero would certainly have read Denon's book, as well as other early travelers. Undoubtedly, most of his knowledge came as he went along.

3. Ibid., 30.

4. Ibid., 37–38.

5. Ibid., 39.

6. Ibid., 48.

7. Ibid., 47.

8. Ibid., 50.

9. Ibid., 54.

10. Ibid., 62. Kom Ombo boasts of a Ptolemaic temple to the gods Horus and Sobek, a crocodile-headed deity associated with the first pharaoh of Egypt. Ele phantine was revered as the source of the life-giving waters of the Nile.

11. Ibid., 65–66.

12. Ibid., 66.

13. Kalabsha is a late Ptolemaic temple dedicated to the Nubian god Horus-Mandulis, also to Isis and Osiris. The 13,000 sandstone blocks of the temple were moved to higher ground and the temple reassembled just south of the Aswan High Dam in 1962–1963.

14. Ibid., 76.

15. Ibid., 90. Askut was an important Middle Kingdom trading post.

16. Ibid., 100.

17. Ibid., 104.

18. Ibid.

19. For a description of Karnak, see Richard Wilkinson, *The Complete Temples of Ancient Egypt* (London: Thames and Hudson, 2000), 55ff.

20. Medinet Habu was the main temple of Rameses III (1182–1151 BC) of the New Kingdom and contains more than 7,000 square meters (75,350 square feet) of decorated surfaces. The temple was modified continually from New Kingdom to Roman times.

21. Belzoni, op. cit. (1820), 125, 126.

CHAPTER 7: "MUMMIES WERE RATHER UNPLEASANT TO SWALLOW"

1. Giovanni Battista Caviglia (1770–1845) was an energetic Genovese sailor who owned a trading vessel in Malta and dabbled in archaeology. Salt employed him to excavate the Sphinx at Giza, where he discovered the steps leading to the statue and the pavement between its paws. He also explored the pyramids, where he acquired new information about the interior of the Great Pyramid. After working briefly with Colonel Howard-Vyse at Giza in 1835–1836 (see Chapter 12, note 15), he retired in Paris.

Henry William Beechey (?–ca. 1870) was by profession an artist, son of a well-known portrait painter. He served as Salt's secretary from 1815 to 1820, accompanying both Belzoni and Athanasi on their expeditions, as well as drawing Abu Simbel. He and his brother made a successful survey of much of the North African coast in 1821–1822. Beechey emigrated to New Zealand in 1855.

2. Belzoni, op. cit. (1820), 152–153.

3. Ibid., 155.

4. Ibid., 156.

5. Ibid.

6. Quotes in these two paragraphs come from ibid., 156–157.

7. Ibid., 157.

8. Ibid., 181.

9. Charles Leonard Irby (1789–1845) retired as a naval captain on half pay because of ill health in 1815 and traveled widely. James Mangles (1786–1867) also retired from naval service with the same rank in 1815. They published *Travels in Egypt, Nubia, Syria and Asia Minor in 1817 and 1818* in 1821 (privately printed). Mangles was one of the founder fellows of the Royal Geographical Society of London.

10. Giovanni Finati (1787-?1829) entered Muhammad Ali's service after deserting from the French army, converted to Islam, then became a dragoman and interpreter to European travelers, among them Belzoni and William Bankes.

11. Belzoni, op. cit. (1820), 213.

12. Irby and Mangles, op. cit. (1821), 125.

13. Belzoni, op. cit. (1820), 223.

14. Ibid., 227–228. The tomb of Prince Montuherkhepeshef is tomb KV-19, cut into a cliff at the head of the second eastern branch of the Valley of the Kings. Rameses-Mentuherkhepshef was a son of pharaoh Rameses IX (1098–1070 BC) of the Twentieth Dynasty. KV-19 was visited repeatedly after Belzoni's time, but only cleared by American Theodore Davis's excavator Edward Ayrton in 1906. It is the only prince's tomb open to the public in the valley.

15. Rameses I (1293–1291 BC) was a former soldier and vizier who succeeded his confidant Horemheb as pharaoh. His family came from Avaris in the delta. Rameses reigned for but two years. His sepulcher shows many signs of hasty interment, with an unfinished burial chamber that had been planned as an antechamber to a much larger room. Disappointed looters robbed his tomb in antiquity. They smashed small gold-coated statuettes against the plastered walls—to which minute fragments of the foil still adhere. His mummy was sold to the United States in the 1860s and was recently returned to Egypt from Emory University in Atlanta.

16. Neith is the Greek name for the ancient goddess Nit, "Opener of the Ways," patroness of hunting and weaving.

17. Belzoni, op. cit. (1820), 229.

18. The sepulcher of the New Kingdom pharaoh Seti I (1291–1278 BC), known today as tomb KV-7. KV-7 is the longest and deepest of all the royal burial places in the Valley of the Kings. The richly decorated corridors descend more than 100 meters (300 feet) and the same depth underground to reach the burial chamber and feature a false burial room designed (unsuccessfully) to thwart tomb robbers. The actual chamber has an unusual astronomical ceiling, showing the constella-

tions in the northern sky. The sarcophagus is covered with hieroglyphs, once delineated with blue-green paint.

Seti's mummy was moved one step ahead of grave robbers and survived as part of the Deir el-Bahri cache, described in Chapter 13. The king's face is exceptionally well preserved and displays the pharaoh's decisive character.

Son of Rameses I, Seti I had been a vizier and troop commander before ascending to the throne. His thirteen-year reign witnessed an apogee of Egyptian art and culture, as the country entered a prosperous imperial era. Seti led successful military expeditions to Syria on several occasions in the early years of his reign. He also campaigned against the nomadic Libyans. The pharaoh commissioned a magnificently decorated temple in honor of Osiris at Abydos, which shows the pharaoh making offerings in his role as priest. He is shown with his son, later to become Rameses II, standing before long king lists that chronicle Egypt's kings from the earliest times. Seti also began the construction of Karnak's famed Hypostele Hall with its vast columns, a masterpiece completed by his son. Throughout his reign, Seti strove to restore Egypt to its former greatness, after the chaos of the Akhenaten years.

*Shabti*s (sometimes called *shawbti*s or *ubshabti*s) were funerary figures that were called the "answerers." They accompanied the deceased to serve them in the afterworld.

19. Quotes and description of the discovery in Belzoni, op. cit. (1820), 231–248.

20. The second earl of Belmore (1774–1841) came from a landowning family in Northern Ireland. Heavily in debt, Belmore fled abroad in his yacht to live more cheaply. He went on to become a controversial governor of Jamaica in 1828.

Belzoni named the sepulcher the tomb of Apis, later changing it to Psammethis. In the predecipherment era, no one could identify the owner correctly.

21. Edouard de Montulé, *Travels in Egypt During 1818 and 1819* (London: J. Murray, 1823), 26ff.

22. Robert Richardson, *Travels Along the Mediterranean, 1816–1818,* 2 vols. (London: T. Cadell, 1822), 1:307. See also Belzoni, op cit. (1820), 357. Richardson (1779–1847) traveled with the earl of Belmore's party.

CHAPTER 8: "PYRAMIDICAL BRAINS"

1. Sarah Belzoni's journey was a considerable achievement for a woman traveling independently, but she had plenty of experience of journeying in Islamic lands. The male dress was a wise precaution when it was dangerous for women to travel without their husbands.

William John Bankes (1786?–1855) was a traveler, collector, and antiquarian, born of a wealthy family, who owned Kingston Lacy in Dorset, southern England. After serving as an aide-de-camp to the duke of Wellington during the Peninsular War, he traveled widely in the Near East, and especially Egypt. He was violently opposed to Champollion's decipherment of hieroglyphs, but maintained a lifetime interest in the subject. Bankes subsequently became a member of Parliament before being forced to leave England because of his homosexuality. His extensive Egyptian collections are still at Kingston Lacy. A recent biography is Patricia Usick, *Adventures in Egypt and Nubia: The Travels of William Bankes (1786–1855)* (London: British Museum Press, 2002).

2. An exact modern equivalent is virtually impossible to establish, but may have been about US$120, a relatively much larger sum in those days. Egyptian currency was based on the Turkish piastre until Muhammad Ali revalued it and reorganized the monetary system in 1834.

3. Belzoni, op. cit. (1820), 255.

4. Ibid., 266.

5. The pharaoh Khafre (2558–2532 BC) reigned long enough to erect the second Giza pyramid on slightly higher ground than that of his father. This gives the illusion that it is taller than the Great Pyramid, when it is actually shorter, being 136.4 meters (447 and one-half feet) high. The passages from the two entrances join up to lead to the burial chamber. Belzoni left a permanent record of his visit. He wrote his name in lamp black on the south wall of the chamber, where it can be seen to this day.

The Sphinx was part of Khafre's funerary complex, carved from solid limestone as a crouched, human-headed lion representing the sun god, Re-Horakhty, at the moment when the sun rises in the East. Quote is from ibid., 256.

6. Quotes in this and the following paragraphs come from Charles Fitzclarence, *Journal of a Route Across India, Through Egypt to England, 1817–1819* (London: John Murray, 1819), 66ff.

7. Belzoni, op. cit. (1820), 252.

8. Ibid., 294.

9. Ibid., 290.

10. Ibid., 294–295.

11. Frédéric Cailliaud (1787–1869) was a skilled artist, geologist, and mineralogist who produced maps of several Western Desert oases, among them Kharga, which enabled the French savants writing the *Description de l'Égypte* to refine their own researches. Cailliaud also explored the temple of Amun at Jebel Barkal in Nubia and was one of the first antiquarians to describe the city of Meroe on the east bank of the White Nile, some 200 kilometers (124 miles) north of Khartoum in today's Sudan. Meroe prospered off the Red Sea trade from 593 BC to AD 350 and was also an important ironworking center. Cailliaud continued to travel

widely in Egypt and the surrounding deserts until 1822, when he returned to France, never to visit Egypt again. He subsequently published a four-volume work, *Voyage à Méroé et au Fleuve Blanc* (Paris: Imprimerie Royale, 1826–1827). For a biography, see Michel Chauvet, "Les adventures d'un naturaliste en Égypte et au Soudan: 1815–1822," *Toutanhamon Magazine* 8 (1999): 1–6.

12. Belzoni gives a vivid description of the flood in his *Narrative*, op. cit. (1820), 299ff. British irrigation expert William Willcocks, who worked in Egypt during the 1890s, wrote that "the Nile looms very large before every Egyptian and with good reason." He described the frantic efforts made by villagers to divert water from their hamlets and into reservoirs, the backbreaking work of maintaining irrigation works year-round. See William Willcocks, *Sixty Years in the East* (London: Blackwood, 1935), from which the quote also comes (p. 111). Since the average floodplain relief was only about 2 meters (6 feet), the difference between a high and low inundation, between hunger and catastrophic flood, was remarkably small.

13. Berenice owed much of its later prosperity to the discovery of the monsoon winds of the Indian Ocean by an Alexandrine Greek skipper named Hippalus, who was an expert navigator in the first century BC. He sailed direct from Arabia to India on the winds of the southwestern monsoon, and returned on the northeastern one in the course of a single year. Within a remarkably short time, the volume of trade among Rome, Alexandria, and India increased exponentially.

14. The Ababde are a Bedouin group with deep roots in antiquity. Short quotes in the narrative of the Berenice journey are from Belzoni, op. cit. (1820), 316ff.

15. Jean-Baptiste Bourguignon d'Anville (1697–1782) became the most respected cartographer of his time, his maps famous for their accuracy. His African maps, including the Red Sea area, were standard reference works until the great explorations of the nineteenth century.

16. Ras Banas is now a major scuba-diving destination. Quotes from Belzoni, op. cit. (1820), 332.

17. Ibid., 335.

18. Frédéric Cailliaud, *Voyage à l'oasis de Thèbes et dans les deserts et situé à l'orient et à l'occident de la Thébäid*, 2 vols. (English edition, London: Phillips, 1822), 134.

19. Belzoni, op. cit. (1820), 346.

CHAPTER 9: HIGH JINKS AT PHILAE

1. Baron Albert von Sack was a well-known naturalist who traveled extensively in Surinam and Venezuela before coming to Egypt. He was a chamberlain to the king of Prussia.

For William Bankes, see Chapter 8, note 1.

2. Belzoni, op. cit. (1820), 351.

3. Ibid., 349.

4. The Egyptians called obelisks *tekhenu,* objects that were considered sacred to the god Re and to other solar deities. The Philae obelisk is 6.7 meters (22 feet) high and is inscribed in Greek and hieroglyphs with the name of pharaoh Ptolemy VII (116–81 BC), his wife, and sister Cleopatra (no relation to the later queen). Champollion used the inscriptions to identify the hieroglyphic form of the name Ptolemy. The Philae obelisk arrived in England in 1821, but lay in a damaged state on the lawn in front of the house at Kingston Lacy for six years. Bankes persuaded the visiting duke of Wellington to lay the foundation stone for the obelisk in 1827, but it was not raised until 1839. Two years later, Bankes was forced to go abroad and never returned. For a general discussion of these remarkable monuments, see Fekri Hassan, "Imperialist Aspirations of Egyptian Obelisks," in Jeffreys, op. cit. (2003), 19–68.

5. On Edfu, see Chapter 3, note 1.

6. Quotes from Belzoni, op. cit. (1820), 362.

7. Sarah's "Trifling Account" of her travels appears in Belzoni, op. cit. (1820), 441ff. The quote is from p. 471.

8. In retrospect, Belzoni's work on the tomb did incalculable damage—the paintings were much damaged in the copying, the flash flood inundated much of the now open tomb, and hundreds of sweating visitors caused the art to fade.

9. This incident is described in ibid., 365ff, where the quotes in this and the two paragraphs above may be found. Ridley, op. cit. (1998), 85ff, offers a thorough analysis of this incident.

10. Belzoni, op. cit. (1820), 372–373.

11. Herodotus, op. cit. (1987), 241.

12. On William George Browne, see Chapter 3, note 20.

13. Belzoni, op. cit. (1820), 377–378. The Middle Kingdom pharaoh Senwosret II (Khakheperre) (1879–1878 BC) of the Twelfth Dynasty supervised major reclamation works in the Fayyum, converting thousands of hectares of marshland into productive fields. Such reclamation projects were a relic of the famines that struck Egypt at the end of the Old Kingdom, causing economic, social, and political disorder.

14. The Labyrinth (this is the Greek name for the site) was a temple precinct of courts and colonnades erected by Amenemhet III of the Twelfth Dynasty (1844–1797 BC) at Hawara.

Hawara was part of the now largely destroyed mortuary complex of Amenemhet III.

Arsinoe was the capital town of the Arsinoite *nome* and the administrative center of the Fayyum.

15. Ibid., 380–381.

16. Ibid., 381.

17. Two temples adorn this site, the larger two-story structure dating to the Late Period, the smaller temple of Sobek-Re to Roman times.

18. Ibid., 385. The settlement was a small oasis town that flourished in the centuries before Christ.

19. Both quotes in this paragraph come from ibid., 388.

20. Ibid., 390.

21. Ibid., 395–396.

22. Recently made famous in archaeological circles by the discovery of a huge Romano-Egyptian cemetery dating to the first to third centuries AD. See Chapter 16.

23. Quotes in these paragraphs come from ibid., 428ff.

24. Ibid., 437.

CHAPTER 10: "A MULTITUDE OF COLLATERAL CURIOSITIES"

1. Seti I erected the Wadi Mia temple east of Edfu to commemorate the reopening of an ancient desert road, made possible by his well digging.

2. *The Times*, March 31, 1820; Mayes, op. cit. (2003), 249.

3. Belzoni, op. cit. (1820), v.

4. Samuel Smiles, *A Publisher and His Friends: Memoir and Correspondence of John Murray, with an Account of the Origin and Progress of the House, 1768–1843*, condensed by Thomas MacKay (London: John Murray, 1850), 56; *Quarterly Review*, October 1820; Mayes, op. cit. (2003), 256.

5. The Egyptian Hall was developed by a well-known showman of the day, William Bullock (ca. 1770–1849). A naturalist and traveler, Bullock promoted a fashion for Egypt that was prevalent in London academic and artistic circles. His London Museum at 12 Piccadilly Street boasted of two large statues of Isis and Osiris, as well as sphinxes and hieroglyphs. The facade was based on Denon's sketches of the temple of Hathor at Dendera. Inevitably, the museum became known as the Egyptian Hall. After exhibiting Napoléon's carriage, captured at the Battle of Waterloo, Bullock remodeled the interior in an Egyptian style in 1819. By coincidence, one of the first major exhibitions was Belzoni's. See Richard D. Altick, *The Shows of London* (Cambridge, Mass.: Belknap Press, 1978).

6. J. S. Curl, *Egyptomania: The Egyptian Revival* (Manchester: Manchester University Press, 1994).

7. In modern equivalents, this would be many thousands of pounds.

8. Mayes, op. cit. (2003), 289.

9. Both quotes in this paragraph from ibid., 290.

10. In 1805–1806, the Scottish explorer Mungo Park (1771–1806) had pene-trated far up the Niger River, but drowned during his attempt to locate the source.

11. Halls, op. cit. (1834), 157; Mayes, op. cit. (2003), 290.

12. Yanni (Giovanni d') Athanasi (1799–ca. 1850) was the son of a Greek mer-chant in Cairo. He became a servant to Colonel Ernest Missett, the British con-sul, then to Henry Salt. Well known to many Egyptian travelers, he excavated for Salt, then on his own account, accumulating two large collections of Egyptian an-tiquities that were sold at Sotheby's in London.

CHAPTER 11: DECIPHERMENT

Guide to Further Reading

Andrew Robinson, *The Story of Writing* (London and New York: Thames and Hudson, 1995), is an admirable account of decipherment and early scripts. So is Richard Parkinson and others, *Cracking Codes: The Rosetta Stone and Decipher-ment* (Berkeley and Los Angeles: University of California Press, 1999). Lesley Ad-kins and Roy Adkins, op. cit. (2000), place Champollion in a broader Egyptolog-ical context, discuss his rivalry with Thomas Young, and provide an admirable biography. I used this account extensively here. A useful life is Jean Lacouture, *Champollion: Une vie de lumières* (Paris: B. Grasset, 1988).

1. Warren R. Dawson and Eric P. Uphill, *Who Was Who in Egyptology*, 3d ed., revised by M. L. Brierbrier (London: Egypt Exploration Society, 1995).

2. Karl Meyer, *The Plundered Past*, 2d ed. (Baltimore: Pelican Books, 1992), 23.

3. Joseph Ernest Renan (1823–1892) wrote widely admired critical and histor-ical works on the Scriptures. He visited Egypt and was shocked by the destruc-tion. Quote is from François-Marie Luzel, ed., *Correspondance de Renan* (Rennes: Presses Universitaires de Rennes, 1995), 178.

4. Sébastien Louis Saulnier (1790–1835) financed expeditions to Egypt and commissioned Lelorrain to remove the zodiac. He was also interested in roads and railroads.

Jean Baptiste Lelorrain was a French engineer whose only contribution to Egyptology was to steal the zodiac of Dendera.

5. The zodiac (now represented by a copy) lies in the Greco-Roman temple of Hathor.

6. Kircher was also famous for his research on sunspots. Much vilified, he con-tributed a considerable body of knowledge to the understanding of Coptic, much used by later scholars.

Jörgen Zoega (1755–1809) was a highly respected archaeologist and coin ex-pert who worked in Rome and served as Danish consul there.

7. Thomas Young (1773–1829) was a physician and a linguistic genius. At age fourteen, he had some knowledge of eleven languages, including Arabic, Persian, and Ethiopic. He was the first to recognize astigmatism in the eye and published on the undulating theory of light. His hieroglyphic studies began after he was appointed professor of natural philosophy at the Royal Institution, London, in 1801. Young wrote sixteen works on hieroglyphs, including an appendix to the second edition of Belzoni's *Travels*, published in 1821. See Alexander Wood and Frank Oldham, *Thomas Young* (Cambridge: Cambridge University Press, 1954).

The word *cartouche* (cartridge) came from the savants, who remarked on the similarities between such ovals and the cartridges in their guns.

8. Baron Jean-Baptiste-Joseph Fourier (1768–1830) was not only a gifted mathematician but also a skilled administrator who played a leading role in the Egyptian Commission's work. Napoléon subsequently appointed him prefect of the Isère, where he commissioned memorable public works. Fourier was an important mentor of Champollion.

9. Thomas Young, "Egypt," supplement to *Encyclopaedia Britannica*, 1819.

10. Discussion in Adkins and Adkins, op. cit. (2000), pp. 166–167.

11. Jean-Nicholas Huyot (1780–1840) played a key role in decipherment, but his greatest claim to fame is the Arc de Triomphe in Paris. For more detail of how Champollion figured the names, see ibid., 180–181. Quote is on p. 183.

12. Niccolo Francesco Ippolito Baldessare Rosellini (1800–1843) was professor of Oriental languages at the University of Pisa and the founder of Egyptology in Italy. After the Champollion expedition, he published his vast *Monumenti dell'Egito e della Nubia* in three parts (1832–1844), a work still of fundamental importance. Rosellini married the daughter of the well-known composer Cherubini in 1827.

13. Beni Hasan north of Khemenu, "the Eight Towns" (Hermopolis), is modern el-Ashunein. It was the center of power of the fifteenth *nome* and a cult center for the scribe god, Thoth. The tomb paintings seen by Champollion were those of *nomarchs* (provincial governors) of the Eleventh and Twelfth Dynasties (2134–1782 BC).

14. Letter by Champollion to his brother Jacques-Joseph. Quoted in ibid., 254.

15. Rameses IV (1151–1145 BC) reigned for only six years after the death of his illustrious father, Rameses II. His tomb was open in Roman times, but the brightly decorated walls and sarcophagus survive.

16. M. Saulnier, Fils, *Notice sur le voyage de M. Lelorrain en Égypte: Et Observations sur le zodiaque circulaire de Denderah* (Paris: Chez L'Auteur, 1822), 16. Translation by Thompson, op. cit. (1996), 25.

17. Giuseppe Passalacqua (1797–1865) found tomb robbing more profitable than horse trading. He acquired a large collection of Egyptian antiquities, mainly

from Thebes; offered them to the Louvre, which declined; then sold them to Friedrich Wilhelm IV of Prussia for the Berlin Museum for 100,000 francs. He became conservator of the Egyptian collections there as part of the deal, a post he held until the end of his life. There's an interesting sequel to the Mentuhotep discovery. In 1996, a hitherto unknown Seventeenth Dynasty royal funerary diadem came to light in Britain with the death of an English private collector. It was traced back to the early nineteenth century, and to the Qurna region. Perhaps it belonged to Queen Mentuhotep.

A description of the find can be found in Reeves, op. cit. (2000), 27. See also Manniche, op. cit. (1987), for the necropolis generally.

CHAPTER 12: ARTISTS AND ARCHAEOLOGISTS

Guide to Further Reading

Jason Thompson, *Sir Gardner Wilkinson and His Circle* (Austin: University of Texas Press, 1996), is both an admirable biography on one of the leading early (and until now much neglected) Egyptologists and a definitive account of the group of antiquarians and artists who worked in Egypt during the 1820s and 1830s. On Lepsius, see George Ebers, *Richard Lepsius: A Biography,* trans. Zoe Dana (New York: Underhill, 1887). For Mariette and his times, see Elizabeth David, *Mariette Pacha* (Paris: Pygmalion, 1994). I also relied on Edouard Mariette's *Mariette Pacha* (Paris: Payot, 1904) and on Gaston Maspero's *Auguste Mariette, notice biographique et oeuvres diverses* (Paris, 1904). Mariette's own writings, especially *The Monuments of Upper Egypt* (trans. unknown) (Cairo: A. Mourés, 1877), are also informative. R. T. Ridley, "Auguste Mariette: One Hundred Years After," *Abr-Nahrain* 22 (1983-1984): 118–158, offers an excellent appraisal. See also James Baikie, *A Century of Excavations in the Land of the Pharaohs* (London: London Religious Tract Society, 1923).

1. Sir William Gell (1777–1836) achieved fame for his work in the Ionian Islands and Greece. He was intensely interested in hieroglyphs and corresponded with Thomas Young. A brilliant intellectual conversationalist, Gell was a great influence on many scholars from his homes in Naples and Rome, where he entertained numerous travelers surrounded by books, a guitar, and "several dogs." Few scholars of the day exercised a greater influence on early Egyptology. A discussion of this remarkable scholar will be found in Jason Thompson, "'Purveyor-General to the Hieroglyphics': Sir William Gell and the Development of Egyptology," in Jeffreys, op. cit. (2003), 77–85.

2. James Burton (1788–1862) was a traveler and copyist whose drawings and plans in the British Museum are of great value for their details of many now destroyed sites. Many of the artifacts in his collection were purchased by

the British Museum in 1836. In later life, he devoted most of his time to family genealogy.

3. Thompson, op. cit. (1996), 68, where a discussion of Wilkinson at el-Amarna will be found (pp. 67ff).

4. H. R. Hall, "Letters to Sir William Gell from Henry Salt, [Sir] J. G. Wilkinson, and Baron von Bunson," *Journal of Egyptian Archaeology* 2 (1915): 158.

5. 'Amechu was governor of Thebes and grand vizier to the pharaoh Tuthmosis III (1504–1450 BC). Quote from H. R. Hoskins, *Visit to the Great Oasis of the Libyan Desert* (London: Longman, Rees, Orme, Brown, Green, and Longman, 1837), 16.

6. Joseph Bonomi (1796–1878) was of Italian birth, but brought up in England, where he became a highly respected sculptor and artist. He came to Egypt with Hay, worked there for eight years, then worked on a wide variety of commissions. He became curator of Sir John Soane's Museum in London, 1861–1878.

Scottish artist and traveler Frederick Catherwood (1799–1855) visited the Holy Land with Hay, Bonomi, and others. His Egyptian work is less well known than his drawings and paintings resulting from his Central American expeditions with the American traveler John Lloyd Stephens, 1839–1843. Had his Nile work been published, it would have established him as one of the best artists to depict ancient Egypt.

7. Edward William Lane, *An Account of the Manners and Customs of the Modern Egyptians* (London: John Murray, 1836).

8. John Gardner Wilkinson, *Manners and Customs of the Ancient Egyptians* (London: John Murray, 1837). Thompson, op. cit. (1996), chap. 10, offers a superb analysis of the book, to which the interested reader is referred.

9. See Thompson, op. cit. (1996), 169–170. Letter to Hay quoted on p. 170. John Gardner Wilkinson, *Handbook for Travellers in Egypt* (London: John Murray, 1847).

10. James Breasted, *A History of Egypt from the Earliest Times to the Persian Conquest* (New York: Scribners, 1905).

11. Alexander von Humboldt (1769–1859) achieved scientific immortality with his journeys through the Andes and much of South America in 1799–1805. He discovered the Peruvian coastal current that is named after him and was the first person to recognize the value of seabird guano as a natural fertilizer. Guano became a major Peruvian export during the nineteenth century.

James Wild (1814–1892) achieved later fame as decorative architect for the Great Exhibition at the Crystal Palace, London, in 1851. He was curator of the Sir John Soane Museum, 1878–1892.

12. The Step Pyramid at Saqqara was the first such elaborate mortuary complex, built in about 2650 BC by the famed architect Imhotep for the Old Kingdom

pharaoh Djoser (2668–2649 BC). The step design was the forerunner of the perfect pyramid shape achieved by later architects.

13. Menkaure (or Mycerinus) (2532–2504 BC) is said by legend to have been a more benevolent ruler than his predecessors Khufu and Khafre. The king's name is inscribed in red ocher on the ceiling of one of the queen's chambers in the pyramid. The smaller size of his pyramid may have been the result of political and economic strains caused by the huge construction projects of his predecessors.

Richard William Howard-Vyse (1784–1853) enjoyed a successful military career, rising to the rank of major general. His *Operations Carried on at the Pyramids of Gizeh* appeared in three volumes (London: J. Fraser, 1840–1842) and was the standard work on the pyramids until the Flinders Petrie survey of 1880–1882.

14. George Robins Gliddon (1809–1857) was born in England and taken to Egypt at an early age. He succeeded his father as U.S. vice-consul in Alexandria before giving public lectures on Egypt throughout the eastern United States as far west as St. Louis from 1843 onward. He was the first popular writer on ancient Egypt in the United States.

15. G. R. Gliddon, *An Appeal to the Antiquaries of Europe on the Destruction of the Monuments of Egypt* (London: J. Madsen, 1841), 95.

16. Lord Algernon Percy, first baron Prudoe and fourth duke of Northumberland (1792–1865), met Champollion in Egypt in 1859, made extensive Egyptian collections, and became first lord of the Admiralty and a trustee of the British Museum.

17. Achille Constant Théodore Émile Prisse D'Avennes (1807–1879) served as an engineer to the pasha until 1836 before becoming an Egyptologist. He was apparently not an engaging character, so little is known of him.

18. Nestor L'Hôte (1804–1842) accompanied Champollion to Egypt as a draftsman, returning on two later occasions to complete a huge portfolio of drawings that form a valuable archive in the Louvre.

19. Charles Lenormant (1802–1850) also went with Champollion to Egypt and later became professor of Egyptian archaeology at the Collège de France in Paris.

20. The living Apis bull was the manifestation of the god Ptah, creator god of Memphis. All such bulls were black with a white diamond mark on the forehead and other distinguishing characteristics. The bull lived in pampered luxury in Ptah's temple at Memphis, then was mummified after death. Apis was an oracle and prophet, a source of wisdom, so the birth or death of an Apis bull was an important public occasion.

21. Auguste Mariette, *Choix de monuments et de dessins découverts ou executés pendant le déblaiement du Sérapéum de Memphis* (Paris: Gide et J. Baudry, 1856).

22. Heinrich Ferdinand Karl Brugsch (1827–1894) was encouraged in his Egyptian interests by Alexander von Humboldt and developed a knowledge of

demotic at an early age. He is best remembered for his research on hiero-glyphs. Brugsch was director of the pasha's short-lived School of Egyptology, 1870–1879.

Émile Brugsch (1842–1930) was his younger brother. He started as Heinrich's assistant, then worked for Gaston Maspero before becoming conservator at the Cairo museum, a post he held for forty-five years. A somewhat controversial fig-ure, he is said to have sold antiquities through the museum store.

23. The mortuary temple of Queen Hatshepsut (1498–1483 BC) was designed, so the pharaoh tells us in an inscription on the walls, as "a garden for my father Amun." One of the masterpieces of Egyptian architecture, the terraced and rock-cut temple sits against a natural amphitheater of cliffs. Hatshepsut was a strong-willed woman who subverted the position of the child pharaoh Tuthmosis III while serving as his regent. She is mainly remembered for her expedition to the Land of Punt (probably in the southern Red Sea), and may have been assassi-nated by the adult Tuthmosis III.

Mentuhotep I (2060–2010 BC) reigned for fifty years during the Middle King-dom. His mortuary temple at Deir el-Bahri was a stepped podium with square-cut pillars topped with a terrace with a Hypostele hall at the rear below the cliffs.

24. Queen Ahhotep was thought initially to be a wife of the pharaoh Kamose, but the identification has been challenged.

25. Egypt's rulers were now known as khedives, Turkish viceroys who ruled Egypt, at least nominally, from 1847 to 1914. For this incident, see Reid, op. cit. (2002), 128–129.

26. Edouard Mariette, op. cit. (1904), 210.

27. Ibid., 275.

CHAPTER 13: "IN THE BRITISH MUSEUM HE IS PLACED BEYOND THE REACH OF ALL SUCH EVILS"

Guide to Further Reading

Wallis Budge, *By Nile and Tigris* (London: John Murray, 1920), is a boastful chronicle of this British Museum official's often unscrupulous, and, it must be said, ingenious dealings. Donald Malcolm Reid's *Whose Pharaohs?* op. cit. (2002*)*, was an essential source for this chapter.

1. Jean Jacques Rifaud (1786–ca. 1845) was a French sculptor and excavator who worked for Drovetti and spent more than four decades digging (badly) in Egypt.

2. This passage is based on Reid, op. cit. (2002), 73–75.

3. John Murray, *A Handbook for Travellers in Egypt*, 4th ed. (London: John Murray, 1873), xiv. This passage is based on Reid, op. cit. (2002), 84–85.

4. Piers Brendon, *Thomas Cook: 150 Years of Popular Tourism* (London: Secker and Warburg, 1991). Quoted in Reid, op. cit. (2002), 89, who cites John Pudney, *The Thomas Cook Story* (London: Michael Joseph, 1953), 212.

5. The political background is summarized for the general reader by Reid, op. cit. (2002), 153ff. See also Lord Cromer, *Ancient and Modern Imperialism* (New York: Longmans, 1910).

6. Maspero wrote numerous books and hundreds of articles on ancient Egypt, of which *L'Égyptologie* (Paris: Hachette, 1915) is probably the best known.

For a biography, see Elisabeth David, *Gaston Maspero, 1846–1916: Le gentleman Égyptologue* (Paris: Pygmalion/G. Watelet, 1999).

7. From here onward, I use the term *Luxor* to refer to the modern city of that name, a term that came into widespread use during the late nineteenth century. *Thebes* is interchangeable, but tends to refer to the region, both the east and west banks around Luxor.

8. Gaston Maspero with Émile Brugsch, *La Trouvaille de Deir el-Bahari* (Paris: Hachette, 1881), 57.

9. Ibid., 112.

10. Samuel Birch (1813–1885) was responsible for the introduction of the Champollion approach to decipherment to Britain. He spent almost all his career in the British Museum, from where he exercised an enormous influence over Egyptology and Assyriology. Birch never had time to visit the Nile, but compiled the first complete grammar and dictionary of ancient Egyptian.

11. Originally Sir Evelyn Baring, this remarkable statesman and diplomat became Lord Cromer in 1901. Cromer's *Modern Egypt*, 2 vols. (New York: Macmillan, 1908), is a basic source on late-nineteenth-century Egypt.

12. Budge, op. cit. (1920), 95.

13. Ibid., 137.

14. Eugène Grébaut (1846–1915) was more a scholar than an administrator. He was an inept director who offended both Egyptologists and local people, resigning in 1892 to become a lecturer in ancient history at the Sorbonne in Paris.

15. Quotes in these two paragraphs are from ibid., 143–144.

16. The extended quotes in these three paragraphs are from ibid., 145ff.

17. Reid, op. cit. (2002), 101.

18. An admirable analysis appears in ibid., 109–112.

19. Āli Mubarak was a cabinet minister, educational reformer, and engineer who planned modern Cairo. He wrote a classic geographical encyclopedia, *Al-Khitat al-tawfiqiyya al-jadida* (1886–1887).

20. Reid, op. cit. (2002), 201–203 and other pages, offers an analysis of this important figure.

21. Quoted in ibid., 201.

CHAPTER 14: "A BOATING-TRIP INTERSPERSED WITH RUINS"

Guide to Further Reading

The travel literature of the period is rich and often repetitive. No one should miss Lucie Duff-Gordon's *Letters from Egypt,* op. cit. (1865). John A. Wilson, *Signs and Wonders upon Pharaoh* (Chicago: University of Chicago Press, 1964), discusses American tourists of the day, while David Reid, op. cit. (2002), is an admirable guide to the literature on early tourism and its wider context. Joan Rees, *Amelia Edwards: Traveler, Novelist, and Egyptologist* (London: Rubicon Books, 1998), offers a short biography of this all-important tourist. Amelia Edwards, *A Thousand Miles up the Nile* (New York: Scribners, 1877), is a classic of Egyptological literature.

1. Authoress Lucie Duff-Gordon (1821–1869) was the wife of Sir Alexander Duff-Gordon and a prominent literary figure in London. She settled at the Cape of Good Hope from 1860 to 1863, then moved to Luxor. Her *Letters from Egypt* are perceptive, at times pithy, and often deeply moving.

2. Duff-Gordon, op. cit. (1865), 110.

3. Jean-Jacques-Antoine Ampère, *Voyage en Égypte et en Nubie* (Paris: Michel Lévy, 1868), 3.

4. Discussion in Wilson, op. cit. (1964), chap. 5.

5. Twain, op. cit. (1996), 628. See Gustave Flaubert, *Flaubert in Egypt: Sensibility on Tour* (London: Bodley Head, 1972).

6. Edwards, op. cit. (1877), 224.

7. Ibid., 307.

8. Ibid., 415.

9. Ibid., 487.

10. Ibid., 600–601.

11. Ibid., 76.

12. Ibid., 601.

13. Ibid., 604–605.

14. The decipherment of the so-called Flood Tablets from Nineveh in 1872 was one of the great popular sensations of the day. Bank engraver-turned-epigrapher George Smith found the fragmentary tablets in the royal library of the Assyrian king Assurbanipal (668–627 BC). They bore a tale of a seer named Hasisadra and a great flood that bore a remarkable resemblance to Noah's flood in Genesis. Smith subsequently discovered the missing portions of the tablets in Austen Henry Layard's spoil heaps at Nineveh. The devout hailed the Flood Tablets as proof of the historical truth of the Old Testament, but even Smith realized that he was reading late copies of an ancient legend. For the story, see Brian Fagan, *The Return to Babylon* (Boston: Little, Brown, 1979).

15. The Egypt Exploration Fund still flourishes and commemorated its centenary with a history: T. G. H. James, ed., *Excavating in Egypt: The Egypt Exploration Society, 1882–1982* (London: British Museum Publications, 1982). Quote from p. 23.

16. Alexander Henry Rhind, *Thebes: Its Tombs and Their Tenants, Including a Record of Excavations in the Necropolis* (London: Longman, Green, Longman, and Roberts, 1862), 110. Rhind also wrote an obscure handbook on Egypt as a winter resort six years earlier.

17. Wadi Tumiliat was a fertile depression in the eastern delta that served as a route to the Red Sea. The ancient Egyptians called it "Sweet Water." Bubastis, north of Cairo, was a cult center for the cat goddess, Bastet, and a center for major religious festivals. The Ramessid pharaohs built a huge temple there in her honor. A great catacomb contains numerous mummified cats.

18. On Howard Carter's early career, see T. G. H. James, *Howard Carter: The Path to Tutankhamun* (London: Kegan Paul, 1992), which offers a comprehensive analysis. See also Nicholas Reeves and John H. Taylor, *Howard Carter Before Tutankhamun* (London: British Museum, 1992).

19. George Moritz Ebers, *An Egyptian Princess* (New York: A. L. Burt, 1868), 17.

20. Erman's names were Johann Peter Adolph, but he was universally known as Adolf. Adolph Erman, *Life in Ancient Egypt* (London: Macmillan, 1894). For *Who Was Who* quote, see Dawson and Uphill, op. cit. (1995), 99.

Chapter 15: Science and the Small Artifact

Guide to Further Reading

Late-nineteenth-century Egyptologists have become a fashionable subject for biography in recent years. As a result, this chapter is based on far more sources than those available a quarter century ago. Julie Hankey, *A Passion for Egypt: Arthur Weigall, Tutankhamun, and the "Curse of the Pharaohs"* (London: I. B. Tauris, 2001), treats of relatively minor player, but provides rich perspective on the small world of Egyptology in the 1880s and 1890s. So does Nicholas Reeves and John H. Taylor's *Before Tutankhamun*, op. cit. (1992). Flinders Petrie is the subject of a definitive biography by Margaret D. Drower, *Flinders Petrie: A Life in Archaeology* (London: Victor Gallancz, 1985), which was a major source for this chapter, as was T. G. H. James, op. cit. (1992). I also drew on Flinders Petrie's own writings, notably *Seventy Years in Archaeology* (London: Low, Marston, 1931) and *Ten Years Digging in Egypt, 1881–1891* (London: Religious Tract Society, 1931), as well as consulting many of his technical reports. Margaret Drower, ed. *Letters from the Desert: The Correspondence of Flinders and Hilda Petrie* (London: Aris and Phillips, 2004) is a fascinating window into the Petries' life in Egypt.

1. Somers Clarke (1841–1926) was an expert on cathedrals and served as surveyor of the fabric at St. Paul's Cathedral in London, then as architect to Chich-

ester Cathedral. He retired to Egypt, carried out some restoration work, and brought much higher standards to the study of ancient Egyptian buildings. Quote from a letter from Clarke to Egyptologist Francis Griffith (1899) cited by Hankey, op. cit. (2001), 47.

Victor Loret (1859–1946) was a distinguished Egyptologist who did much good work during his tenure as director. He was, however, totally unsuited for any form of administrative post and alienated virtually every archaeologist working along the Nile, including Naville, Newberry, and Petrie. He later founded a school of Egyptology in Lyons and became a successful teacher.

Jacques Jean Marie de Morgan (1857–1924) was an engineer by training who worked as a prospector in many parts of the world before serving as director of antiquities in Egypt, 1892–1897. He made remarkable discoveries at the pyramids of Dashur and worked on the Predynastic, as did Petrie. He later worked at Susa in Persia, where he made important discoveries.

2. Reeves, op. cit. (2000), 62.

3. Margaret Drower, "Gaston Maspero and the Birth of the Egypt Exploration Fund (1881–3)," *Journal of Egyptian Archaeology* 68 (1982): 300. See also James, op. cit. (1982).

4. Naville also set another Egypt Exploration Fund precedent, that of prompt publication. His *Store-City of Pithom and the Route of the Exodus* (London: Trübner and the Egypt Exploration Fund) appeared in 1888.

5. Petrie, op. cit. (1931), 14.

6. Charles Piazzi Smyth (1819–1900) was a distinguished astronomer who became astronomer royal of Scotland and professor of astronomy at Edinburgh University. Smyth surveyed the Great Pyramid at Giza in 1865 and proposed fantastic theories that became fashionable with fringe pyramidologists. He is the only scientist ever to have resigned from the Royal Society of London, which refused to publish one of his papers on Giza.

7. Ibid., 26–27.

8. General Augustus Henry (Lane-Fox) Pitt-Rivers (1827–1900) was an expert on firearms, ancient and modern, as well as the evolution of artifacts of all kinds. He inherited the huge Cranborne Chase estates in southern England in 1880, and spent the rest of his life excavating sites on his land. His excavation methods were rigorous, far more so than the Germans' at Olympia, paying special attention to surveying, stratified layers, records, and even the smallest finds. An expert surveyor, Pitt-Rivers exercised a strong influence on Petrie. His archaeological methods form the foundation of modern digging techniques.

9. Ibid., 38.

10. Ibid., 47, 48.

11. Little is known of the reign of pharaoh Psusennes I (1039–991 BC). His undisturbed stone-built tomb was discovered by French Egyptologist Pierre Montet at nearby Tanis in 1939–1940.

12. Ibid., 87.

13. Ibid., 103.

14. The el-Lahun pyramid complex includes one erected by Senusret II (1897–1878 BC), the sides held in place by stone and faced with limestone. The tombs of the royal family of that period lie at the north end of the necropolis.

Kahun was one of Petrie's classic excavations. A superb modern-day analysis of the community can be found in Kemp, op. cit. (1989), 149–157.

15. Schliemann had found the spectacular Shaft Graves at Mycenae in 1876, the first evidence of a widespread Bronze Age civilization in mainland Greece. Petrie himself called Gurab a "historical plum."

16. Discussion in Petrie, op. cit. (1931), 112–113.

17. John Devitt Stringfellow Pendlebury (1904–1941) worked mainly in Crete after his Amarna work, and served as curator of the Palace of Minos at Knossos and British vice-consul. He was shot by the Germans in 1941 when he refused to disclose information about British military positions.

There is a huge literature on the Amarna tablets. One good source and starting point is William L. Moran, *The Amarna Letters* (Baltimore: Johns Hopkins University Press, 1992).

18. Reeves and Taylor, op. cit. (1992), 33–43, describes Carter's apprenticeship with extracts from his writings.

19. Petrie described sequence dating in a famous paper: W. M. F Petrie, "Sequences in Prehistoric Remains," *Journal of the Royal Anthropological Institute* 29 (1889): 295–301. The same basic principles of artifact ordering are still in use today, often called "seriation."

20. Flinders Petrie, *Methods and Aims in Archaeology* (London: Macmillan, 1904), is, in many respects a startlingly modern essay on archaeology, with remarks on basic ethics that many modern scholars have forgotten. The book is worth a close perusal. Quote from pp. 129–130.

21. Petrie, op. cit. (1931), 180.

22. Ibid., 193.

23. Flinders Petrie married Hilda Urlin (1871–1956) in 1896. She proved an ideal companion, and the marriage was a very happy one. Hilda administered their field projects, raised money, and acted as secretary of the British School of Archaeology in Cairo.

24. Merneptah (1212–1202 BC) was Rameses II's second son and well into his sixties when he ascended the throne. He provided grain to the drought-plagued Hittites and moved aggressively to preserve Egypt's frontiers. The twenty-eight-line Victory Stela found by Petrie in 1896 refers to Merneptah's military campaigns against Libyans and Syrians: "Libyans, slain, whose uncircumcised phalli were carried off 6359." See Clayton, op. cit. (1994), 186–188.

25. Petrie, op. cit. (1931), 140. Professor John Stuart Blackie (1809–1895) was the much beloved professor of Greek at Edinburgh University. A charismatic teacher, Blackie traveled widely in Mediterranean lands and fought hard to establish a chair of Celtic studies at Edinburgh. The day of his funeral was a national day of mourning in Scotland.

26. Petrie, op. cit. (1904), 193.

CHAPTER 16: "WONDERFUL THINGS"

Guide to Further Reading

Nicholas Reeves, op. cit. (2000), is the best source for discoveries after 1900. Timothy Champion, "Egypt and the Diffusion of Culture," in Jeffreys, op. cit. (2003), 127–146, describes some of the extravagant theories surrounding the diffusion of civilization from Egypt that were popular in the early twentieth century. Reeves's *Tutankhamun* volume, op. cit. (1992), is the comprehensive source on that remarkable discovery. For a general account of American Egyptology, see N. Thomas, *The American Discovery of Ancient Egypt* (Los Angeles: Los Angeles County Museum of Art, 1998). For recent history, see also Reid, op. cit. (2002), and, for tourism, O. El Daly, "What Do Tourists Learn of Egypt?" in *Consuming Ancient Egypt,* ed. S. MacDonald and M. Rice (London: UCL Press, 2003), 139–150.

1. Newberry later superintended excavations for several wealthy patrons and became professor of Egyptology at Liverpool University, 1906–1919.

William Amherst Tyssen-Amherst (1835–1909) was a celebrated patron of excavations in Egypt. An early supporter of the Egypt Exploration Fund, he supported excavations by Petrie, Carter, and others, and used Egyptologists such as Newberry to purchase choice items for his collection, which included notable papyri, including the so-called Amherst papyrus that describes tomb robbing in the Theban necropolis around 1100 BC.

2. Quoted in Reeves and Taylor, op. cit. (1992), 51, 54.

3. Maspero quoted in ibid., 56. Victor Loret had opened up several tombs in the Valley of the Kings in 1898, among them that of King Amenophis II. Thirteen royal mummies came to light, which Loret removed despite government opposition. In 1900, Carter placed Amenophis II's mummy back in its sarcophagus, where it was robbed a year later. Carter opened the tomb to an enthusiastic public shortly afterward.

4. Quoted in ibid., 75.

5. Pharaoh Kamose (1573–1570 BC) reigned from Thebes for a short three years, but marched in a surprise attack against the Hyksos in victories recorded on what is known as the Carnarvon Tablet, now in the British Museum. His suc-

cessor, Ahmose I (1570–1546 BC), resumed the attacks in about 1558, conquered the Hyksos, and pursued them into what are now Israel and Syria, ushering in the New Kingdom.

6. Lord Carnarvon and Howard Carter, *Five Years' Explorations at Thebes: A Record of Work Done* (Oxford: Oxford University Press, 1912).

7. Arthur Weigall (1880–1934) served as Petrie's assistant and was inspector of antiquities for Upper Egypt, 1905–1914. He was responsible for much conservation work and closely associated with wealthy excavators like Sir Robert Mond and Theodore Davis. Weigall could be arrogant toward his colleagues and was not always popular, especially with Howard Carter, whom he disliked. He moved out of Egyptology in later life, having written a series of popular books on ancient Egypt, and made a sporadic living as a writer about theater and a journalist, in which capacity he covered the Tutankhamun discovery. He was recently the subject of a biography by Julie Hankey, op. cit. (2001).

8. Quotes in this paragraph come from Reeves and Taylor, op. cit. (1992), 130. The Opet ceremony was held annually in the second month of the inundation. A procession of images of the Theban deities moved between Karnak and Luxor either on land or by boat, each god or goddess having his or her own conveyance. Dancers, musicians, priests, and soldiers accompanied the parade, a time when the public could present pleas to the gods and before colossal statues of the pharaoh. The walls of the temples commemorate the procession.

9. Menhet, Merti, and Menwi were interred with rich grave furniture, including golden sandals, canopic jars, and much jewelry.

10. Davis found the funerary cache in 1907 in a small tomb known as KV-54. He thought it was Tutankhamun's sepulcher, but both Winlock and Carter disagreed. They believed that he was interred nearby. The cache may have been placed originally in the entrance of the young king's tomb, then removed and reburied when ancient looters entered the newly sealed sepulcher.

Herbert Winlock (1884–1950) was a distinguished Egyptologist and an excellent field-worker who later became director of the Metropolitan Museum of Fine Art in New York.

11. There are numerous accounts of the "day of days." See Reeves and Taylor, op. cit. (1992), 138ff; and Carter and Mace, op. cit. (1923–1933).

12. Pierre Lacau (1873–1963) was a protégé of Gaston Maspero and his successor as director of the Antiquities Service. He returned to France in 1936 and became professor of Egyptology at the Sorbonne.

13. Details of the agreement can be found in an admirable description and analysis by James, op. cit. (2001), chaps. 12–14. I drew on these chapters here. Winlock quote is from p. 403. Carter quote is from his diary; James, op. cit. (2001), 405.

14. Quoted in James, op. cit. (2001), 434–435. The modern dollar equivalent is about $60,000, but, of course, it was a relatively much larger sum in the early 1930s.

15. Quoted in Reeves and Taylor, op. cit. (1992), 161.

16. A lengthy extract from Reisner's report on Kerma's royal cemetery can be found in Brian Fagan, ed., *Eyewitness to Discovery* (New York: Oxford University Press, 1996), 116ff.

Kerma was the kingdom of powerful African chiefs in Middle Kingdom times who became wealthy off a lucrative trade in gold, ivory, and other tropical products with the pharaohs to the north. Their capital, Kerma itself, was a small town with palaces and temples, fortified with elaborate defenses and four gates.

17. Comment by artist Lindon Smith, quoted in Reeves, op. cit. (2000), 171.

18. Letter quoted in Reeves and Taylor, op. cit. (1992), 162. More on Breasted and Reisner can be found in John A. Wilson, op. cit. (1964).

19. Quoted in Reeves, op. cit. (2000), 136, where a full discussion of the find appears. Anyone interested in archaeological discoveries during the twentieth century will find comprehensive coverage in this fine, lavishly illustrated book.

20. Herbert Winlock, *The Slain Soldiers of Neb-hep-et-Re, Mentuhotpe* (New York: Metropolitan Museum of Art, 1945).

21. This discussion is based on Reid, op. cit. (2002), 292ff, where a much more comprehensive analysis will be found.

22. Muhammad Zakaria Gonheim (1911–1959) had a distinguished career with the Antiquities Service, serving as chief inspector of Upper Egypt, then keeper of the Saqqara necropolis. He was appointed director of the Cairo Museum in 1958, but died before he could take up the appointment.

23. Zahi Hawass, *Valley of the Golden Mummies* (New York: H. Abrams, 2000), contains a general description of this remarkable find.

24. Feddon, op. cit. (1977), 28.

Index

About the Author

Brian Fagan was born in England and studied archaeology and anthropology at Pembroke College, Cambridge. After seven years working on ancient agricultural societies in East and southern Africa, he came to the United States, where he taught at the University of California for thirty-six years. He is now emeritus professor of anthropology.

For more than three decades, Brian Fagan has focused on communicating archaeology to general audiences, and is now regarded as one of the leading archaeological writers in the world. His many books include seven college texts; *The Rape of the Nile*, first published in 1975; *The Adventure of Archaeology*; and *The Long Summer*, an account of the impact of climatic change on human society over the past 15,000 years. He lives in Santa Barbara, California, with his wife and daughter, four cats, and, at last count, seven rabbits. His other interests include bicycling, kayaking, sailing, and civilized dinner parties.